A Life on the Fiddle

MAX JAFFA

A Life on the Fiddle

Hodder & Stoughton
LONDON SYDNEY AUCKLAND TORONTO

British Library Cataloguing in Publication Data
Jaffa, Max
  A life on the fiddle.
  1. Violin playing. Biographies
  I. Title
  787.2092

ISBN 0-340-42381-1

First published in Great Britain 1991

Published by Hodder and Stoughton,
a division of Hodder and Stoughton Ltd,
Mill Road, Dunton Green, Sevenoaks, Kent TN13 2YA
Editorial Office: 47 Bedford Square, London WC1B 3DP

Photoset by Litho Link Limited,
Welshpool, Powys

Printed in Great Britain by
St. Edmundsbury Press,
Bury St. Edmunds, Suffolk

With much love I dedicate this book to Jean –
a wife, mother and cook in a million, or two, or
three, or four.

Contents

Illustration Acknowledgments

Acknowledgments

I acknowledge with grateful thanks the help given to me by:

Valerie Albu
Martin Beaver, AB Consultants
Jill Byfield
Ruth Denton, EMI
Ros Drinkwater, BBC
The Guildhall School of Music and Drama
Lisa Hawkins, Blue Star Line
Gladys Kilbey
Maggie Livingstone, BBC
Priscilla Newman
Valerie Smith, BBC
Brian Underwood, for his photographs of Sascha Lasserson
Yvonne Walker, J. Lyons and Co. Ltd.
Phyllis Weil, for photographs of Ciro's Club.
Natalie Wheen

Also – and particularly – my thanks to my daughters Naomi and Lisa – without whose constant badgering, and enormous help, this book might not have been completed. For which, dear reader, I hope you too will be thankful.

Thanks also to my daughter Jenny, for her support from afar, and to Jane Osborn for her editorial patience and help.

Prelude

It was a grand farewell, the last night of all my last nights on the Spa at Scarborough. It was the end of an era for me, twenty-seven seasons following a long tradition of music at the seaside. I felt part of the English heritage!

In front of me stretched a sea of enthusiastic faces. Everyone was enjoying themselves and the concert was going well. I had been dreading it because the last night of a season always brings nostalgia—the summer's over, it's goodbye till next year. But after this year, I wasn't coming back. I was very nervous. There were too many memories to crowd in and upset the show. With Yorkshire Television there to record every moment, I didn't want to let the audience down.

The Grand Hall on the Spa seats two thousand three hundred when full, but it was more than full—it was bursting at the seams. So many people wanted tickets that I'd heard rumours they'd come to blows over them. Scarborians had to compete with summer visitors who'd returned after their usual holidays; there were cricket friends, racing friends, professional colleagues and fans who'd come for the occasion from the remotest corners of the country. Some had even travelled from Australia.

That night I realised they were all there for me. This was my party. I was very moved, even choked. It hadn't occurred to me that my music had meant so much to so many people. The announcement that this was to be my last season had caused considerable fuss—I thought it was simply because everyone had grown 'accustomed to my face'! But they were writing to the papers, there was heated debate in the bar after concerts and people constantly came up to me to say: 'What are we going to do next summer when you're not going

13

The audience at my last night on the Spa

to be here?' and: 'We're going to cancel our annual booking, we certainly won't come if you're not going to play.' I didn't know how to respond. I hoped that there would always be music on the Spa for them to enjoy. Surely the long tradition was going to continue and they would come for the music, whoever was making it?

I promised everyone that we would carry on with the last night as usual—a miniature Last Night of the Proms, with the same splash and drama and the musical build-up through the evening to the rousing finale of the Sea Songs, 'Rule Britannia' and 'Jerusalem', and all the razzmatazz that goes with it.

For those of us on stage, it had always been like an end-of-term party. The orchestra had played hard during the season with their two concerts a day, and the younger players had learnt a great deal by playing live. By now everyone deserved a holiday. It was fun, an occasion, and everyone was there to have a good time.

But as that last concert went on, emotions were running high on stage. I had to concentrate very hard indeed to make sure that everyone in the hall felt they were part of it, that the music was going

14

smoothly. It would have been all too easy to build up to a climax too soon.

So I wasn't really paying much attention to the orchestra, and by the middle of the second half I left them to their own devices—after all, they knew very well what was required of them. As the time drew closer for the speeches, the thank-yous, the farewells, I could only face out front, swallowing hard, breathing deeply. There were some powerful feelings swirling about inside me.

Behind my back, I could hear shuffling—more than there ought to have been. I remember thinking: the players are restless—is my speech really that bad? But I thought, it's my last night, I'm going to indulge myself. After all, once we'd done the final medley of the evening they wouldn't have to put up with me any more!

But, when I turned around, I couldn't believe my eyes. The stage was filled with musicians. The regular orchestra had been joined by dozens of players from the past: some who had been with us quite recently, others who had long since grown up and away from the little Scarborough orchestra. They had come from all over the country, taking time off work, just to play again in that Grand Finale.

It was a conspiracy of friends, co-ordinated by my wife Jean and Eric Mills, my leader, who had spirited them into Scarborough during the day while I was busy with other things. In the evening, there had been more tactical planning to get them into the Grand Hall so I wouldn't see them. They'd hidden themselves about the building, in the audience, in the gallery—all over the place. During the second half, they all quietly made their way round the back to gather in the band room, with their instruments, their own music stands and extra copies of music provided by Jean.

I didn't know what to do! Afterwards, of course, there were hugs and thankyous and we had a great reunion, but at the time, all I could manage was to give the downbeat for the finale. And what a sound we all made. We played our hearts out, Jean sang her heart out. That was what it was all about: the sense of occasion that's so important to musicians when we're playing to an audience, the sense of making a special event for the people who come to listen.

We gave concerts every morning and night, seven days a week in a seventeen-week season, for twenty-seven years without missing a day. We played and people listened; there was that thread of communication joining us that has always been important to me, whatever the technology—from the early days of radio, through records to television and beyond.

I find it astonishing sometimes that I've been playing my kind of music—the evergreen tunes, the classics of 'light music'—for over sixty years now. We've added new tunes, while others have faded into the distance—but it's music that people go on loving. Old friends in the audience have stayed with us, and brought their children and their grandchildren too.

Nevertheless, my world of music had changed faster than I would have dreamed possible when I started playing, in the days of the silent cinema. I now record for compact disc and watch sport and my favourite horse-racing on satellite TV. There are only one or two of us still alive and working from this venerable vintage—but I think we must have been the most adaptable musicians ever. The worlds we lived and worked in vanished almost as soon as they began; our rate of evolution will surely never be matched again.

But some traditions—or should I say, institutions—change and survive in all kinds of climates. The day the Beatles played at Scarborough, I said to Jack Byfield, my friend and pianist for the Spa Orchestra: 'Well, we might as well stay at home tonight. No one will want to hear our kind of music.' But we were wrong. That evening, we broke the box-office records for the season—the Spa Grand Hall was full to overflowing!

It's very interesting to discover how different people see me. I've always thought of myself as a musician, someone who plays the violin, who has done nothing really except play the violin—for better or for worse. But I discover, these days, that I seem to have become an institution in my own right. There was a time when I was a household name, which I always felt put me in the same bracket as Harpic or some other useful domestic product. Being an institution is rather more monumental, as I read in the paper in that final Scarborough season: 'Max Jaffa is to be dislodged at the age of 78 from his plinth on the open-air stage of the Scarborough Spa after 30 years.'

Since I was seventy-four, didn't play on a plinth, and the Grand Hall stage was certainly protected from the elements—and I had been playing there for only twenty-seven years—it just goes to show that you should never believe all you read.

It made me laugh at the time, but I wondered why people should talk about me like that. If only they knew, I often think, how my playing life has really been: a matter of chance encounters and lucky choices. Looking back on those seventy-odd years of making music, I'm struck by the strange series of turnings I took to get me where I am now.

There's a famous musicians' story of the young boy who gets lost in New York on his way to a concert. 'Please,' he asks the grand-looking man in the street, who happens to be a famous conductor, 'how do I get to Carnegie Hall?' I'm sure everyone knows the reply: 'Practise, practise, practise . . .' That's probably why I didn't make it to Carnegie Hall. But I have other marvellous places, exciting times and wonderful people to remember—and I can't think of many people who have had my good fortune and have enjoyed their lives more.

I have always been diverted from the straight and narrow by what I could see out of the corner of my eye. However, I've invariably been lucky enough to find the more entertaining way to the next stop. And it's been rather marvellous, retracing my steps to remember how it was that I ever managed to get anywhere . . .

CHAPTER ONE

A Young Fiddler

My sixth birthday, the first birthday that I can remember, was a terrible disappointment. My father woke me up as he came into my bedroom, wishing me a happy birthday and saying as he handed me a long box: 'You're going to be a violinist!' And there in the box was a little fiddle. I never had any choice in the matter. I would have much preferred to have been given a toy but instead there was this musical instrument.

I knew nothing about music, nothing about violins, I'd never heard any music being played and had never been to a concert. My father was certainly no musician either, though he loved the singing in our local synagogue, so it's difficult to know why he had decided I should play the violin. Father always 'decided' what we were going to do, and no argument was tolerated.

However, he hadn't come to this decision by himself. Everyone in his group of friends decided at the same time that their sons, if they had them, should start to learn the violin and they very seriously and thoroughly went about buying instruments and finding a teacher. It's only now, since I've committed myself to writing about me, that I have begun to understand what this extraordinary decision was all about.

Father's friends were a close group of about eight young men who had all travelled to London from Estonia, Latvia and Lithuania. Those three states on the Baltic coast had been occupied by Russia for many years and technically were part of Tsarist Russia—and yet they were proudly independent people, with a history and culture which had nothing to do with Russia.

My father and his friends always took an interest in what their fellow countrymen were doing; and at the end of October 1917 there was an item in the papers which might have been just as exciting to them as news of the start of the Russian Revolution. There were reports from New York of a brilliant young violinist who had set the whole town buzzing after his magnificent debut at Carnegie Hall. He was only sixteen, and had just arrived in America from Lithuania — his name was Jascha Heifetz.

Just two months later, my fate had been decided for me. After all, there was, and is, a strong tradition of Jewish boys being very good at playing the violin and being very good musicians in general. It was worth the investment in a few lessons to see whether I had any of the talent.

The group of friends found a man called Emanuel Kempinski who specialised in teaching beginners. They clubbed together to rent a room in Charlotte Street which they turned into a studio so that he could give all of us our lessons in one place. We trooped along one after another to scrape our way through the scales and bowing exercises, and occasionally we got together to give a little recital to the fathers who'd all sit around, arguing about which of their sons was the best player.

I realise now of course that Kempinski probably wasn't a very good teacher; he was someone who liked music himself, but he couldn't inspire his pupils. There was nothing to interest us beyond the mechanics of playing, and these are really very dull in the early days. He was good enough to get us started in the right direction as he'd obviously done with his own three children, Emanuel, Zara and Isidore Kempinski, who had become a very well-known professional piano trio. However, he had been brought out of retirement to teach us. I wonder now whether he knew his own limitations.

I don't know if anyone could have said that I was going to be good at the instrument at that early stage. I certainly wasn't very interested in it. I had lessons from Kempinski until I was about eight and I suppose I must have learnt something. But then, I'd had enough. I didn't want to play the violin any more and gave it up completely.

Practising the violin was a chore in itself, but it was made much worse because I was absolutely forbidden to do anything I really liked when playing with my friends at school. I wasn't allowed to play any games or to join in the fun in the playground, and there was to be no football or cricket in case I injured my hands. I certainly wasn't allowed to box, which I loved, and even swimming was banned for some unaccountable reason.

When I told Father that I didn't want to learn the violin any more, he was—for once—very sensible and calm about it, which was the best way to treat an eight-year-old who'd had enough. There was no fuss and the fiddle was quietly put away. No one ever mentioned it. This was very clever, because one day, after I hadn't touched the instrument for almost a year, I suddenly realised that I badly wanted to play again. I wanted to get the violin out and start to practise. I'm certain that it was the magic of Jascha Heifetz that changed my mind. He was the only player my father knew about, or rather, Heifetz was the only player who actually moved Father to buy tickets for a concert. And he took me with him.

Heifetz's career was legendary: as a teenager he was no longer a child prodigy but he played so beautifully and musically that he was already famous throughout the world. He was reckoned to be head and shoulders above the crowd of concert violinists. So when it was announced that he was to make his London debut at the Queen's Hall—our neighbourhood concert hall—the buzz really went round the fathers of our little fiddle school.

It was just a recital: Heifetz playing with a piano accompaniment. I don't remember what pieces he played; but the sounds he made with that violin completely turned my head. I knew immediately I wanted to be able to play like that. Of course I had no idea what it took to achieve such beauty of sound, the technique, the phrasing, the perfect intonation. I probably didn't even know what all those things were—but I certainly knew that *this* was the only way that I wanted to play the violin.

I obviously showed the family that I was very serious about wanting to return to playing the fiddle. So I wasn't sent back to the Kempinski regime. Instead, they found Wilhelm Sachse, who had a studio above a violin dealer and repairer called Gustave Meinal in Hallam Street. This was nearer home and so it was convenient.

More important, Sachse had some proper credentials: he claimed to have studied with Joachim, the great nineteenth-century violinist who was a friend of Brahms. That impressed me greatly—so I'd obviously started to take an interest in the history of violin playing. I certainly knew the names of some of the great players of the past and Joachim's was one of the most famous.

One of the hallmarks of a good teacher is that the student wants to make progress; Sachse really made me interested in playing. He was a strict disciplinarian when it came to what I now know are all the fundamental principles that make a good fiddle player. It's very important to start with learning the right way to hold the instrument and the bow, so you don't tie yourself up in knots physically as you try to play. The more natural it feels to hold the instrument, the easier it is to play. Many players have pads and special devices on their instrument to help them hold it under the chin, but I've never done that. Sachse taught me to hold it quite naturally on my shoulder, without any kind of artificial support.

He was also very practical. One day I came for a lesson immediately after school was over, took my fiddle out of the case and started to play. But he banged his bow across my fingers on the fiddle: 'You haven't washed your hands,' he said. 'And you can't make music with dirty hands!' So I was sent off to wash them, and it's a rule I have followed ever since. I just can't play unless I've washed my hands; they don't feel right.

Even though he was very strict, I liked Sachse, I respected him and really looked forward to my lessons. The only time I didn't was when I felt I hadn't practised enough—which is the story of my student life if I'm honest! There was always too much to do and sometimes practising went by the board. However, Sachse introduced me to the right kind of studies and technical exercises which gave me a strong foundation for my playing, and the pieces he taught me soon built up into a respectable collection.

Studies are the backbone of every musician's technique, making the fingers work to become separate and independent and of course to move easily around the violin. I still practise the same pieces— studies by Rode, Ševčík, Kreutzer and that famous set, Dont. That set I always keep on my music stand, with the title facing me. When I look at it and think of practising—all it says is Dont. But it reminds me that in fiddle playing there are so many things that one 'don't' ought to do!

It's strange what one remembers from those very early years: the first concerto I played, Concerto for Violin by Accolai, I have never ever heard or seen since, yet I remember it well. I can still see the cover of the score in my mind's eye—but can only recall about two bars of the music itself. I've played them to a number of violinists, but no one else seems to have been given this particular piece and I haven't met anyone yet who knows anything about it.

I gave my first public concert when I was nine. I was to play at

Dressed for my first concert, aged nine

the Palace Pier Theatre in Brighton for a Sunday concert during the season. I'm certain that Sachse arranged the engagement because Father wouldn't have known anything about that sort of thing. So I must have made fairly rapid progress because I had hardly been with Sachse a full year. There was great excitement about it at home and tremendous bustle to have a special velvet concert suit made for me. They were all very proud and I was taken along to the photographers to pose for a portrait of The Young Artist. I think I looked exactly like Little Lord Fauntleroy.

When we actually set off for the concert, it was treated as a very ordinary affair. My father took me on the train while Mother stayed at home. The music was strictly his business although he didn't know much about it. However, this concert must have given them the first evidence that I had potential as a musician—moreover, there was a fee involved, which would have interested Father.

I was to get ten shillings for playing and the organisers would pay for a third-class return rail ticket from London. Ten shillings was untold riches to me, as I was used to pocket money in pennies. However, I'm not sure that I ever saw more than pennies from it; Father pocketed the rest as the first dividend on his investment.

The Palace Pier was grand enough to give me my own dressing room. But as I walked in I was completely overwhelmed by the experience—or rather by the smell of it. These Sunday concerts were booked into theatres during the summer season to entertain the holiday-makers when the regular show took their night off. And from the atmosphere in it, my dressing room must have been occupied by the chorus girls during the week. It reeked strongly and unpleasantly of greasepaint (there is a world of difference between the smell of modern make-up and old-fashioned greasepaint) and I was promptly and violently sick. That seemed a most unpromising start to my concert career.

Nothing would make me go back into that room. I simply couldn't do it—and I'm still affected by the smell today. However, I wasn't sick with nerves; I don't think children and young players have any nerves, they just get on with what they have to do. The most extraordinary example of this phenomenon which I witnessed myself was when Yehudi Menuhin made his London debut. The Albert Hall was packed with violinists who had flocked to hear this famous young player and he came out alone on stage to play the great Bach Chaconne, for unaccompanied violin. This starts with a series of chords, and the third one is played with an open 'E' string in it. As soon as he played the chord we could all hear that the string was out of tune—but Menuhin didn't turn a hair. He stopped playing, didn't say a word to the audience but just walked across to the piano, struck the 'A', tuned up his fiddle and came back to the centre of the stage to start all over again. You can't do something like that if you're nervous. Menuhin was completely unperturbed.

My new velvet suit was much more important to me than what actually happened when I was on stage. I don't remember what I played or who played the piano for me. I know there was an audience listening because they applauded and I would have bowed nicely. By this time, I'd already been taken to several concerts and so I knew what was expected. People were also kind to me because I was by far the youngest artist on the programme and Father was simply bursting with pride at being the parent of such a young talent.

I'm certain that I was far more interested in everyone else who was performing that afternoon—concerts like these were always shared between a group of artists. There was a ballet dancer named Marianne Pola who took me under her wing and showed me how the backstage part of a theatre worked. Never having been backstage or even in a theatre before, I would have had no idea how to get from the dressing rooms into the wings and ready to go out on stage for my turn. She must have been about eighteen, a fully fledged professional who had already done a number of these Sunday concerts, so it must have amused her to be able to show me the ropes. Her brother Eddie Pola was also with her, and I know I was very impressed by him because he worked as an announcer for the wireless and played records on the young British Broadcasting Company. If I could find someone with a crystal set, I could go home and listen to him.

Once it was all over, that was that: there was no more fuss to be made, no more talk about the occasion. The next morning, it was back to the normal household routine and I became a schoolboy again, doing my lessons during the day and practising hard after school.

It would have been unthinkable to invite friends from school back to our house, and I was never invited to theirs. Within the family, we kept ourselves to ourselves and it was demanded of me that I work hard and improve myself. I would come back from school, eat tea as quickly as I could, do my homework and then off I'd go to the special room which was given over for my practice. We didn't have a piano, but there was a coal fire and a music stand, and I was expected to continue for three hours, sometimes even four. After that it was bedtime, perhaps with a hot drink or a cup of soup. There wasn't much time for anything else.

But this concentrated practising produced good results in the five years or so that I went for lessons with Sachse. When I was thirteen, he said I was ready for the kind of teaching one could get at the Guildhall School of Music. This was a conservatoire run by the City of London, which promised a good musical education from the best of teachers. It was an alternative to that offered by the Royal Academy and the Royal College. The Guildhall was supported by funds from City institutions so it cost less and took in pupils from all kinds of social backgrounds, while the College and Academy gave themselves airs about the social standing of their students.

It was certainly Sachse's influence that sent me to the Guildhall. Logically I should have gone to the Royal Academy of Music since the building was a short walk away in Marylebone Road. Or I could have gone to Trinity College which was just off Wigmore Street. However, most teachers have their personal connections and Sachse must have had associations with the Guildhall and with their senior violin professor, Max Mossel, whom he wanted as my next teacher.

The Guildhall's philosophy had always been to help all kinds of people to make music. You paid two shillings and sixpence for the audition; the fees—if you were accepted—were six pounds a term, for twelve lessons. My father calculated that he could afford it and took me down to John Carpenter Street in the City of London where I played to the Registrar, Saxe Wyndham.

I think that was the only audition I've ever given in my entire career and the school accepted me on the strength of it. Furthermore, I was assigned to the senior violin teacher, Professor Max Mossel— which is why I'm sure that Sachse had put in a good word before my audition. Father was pleased at what he knew was good value for money—we could never have afforded Mossel's fees for private lessons. It was only later on that I realised I'd been given a very special privilege; senior professors are always extremely particular about whom they choose to teach.

In fact, Father was so pleased that he even went to Gustave Meinal's shop and spent fifteen pounds on a full-sized violin. He realised that if I was going to be a serious violinist I should have a proper instrument with a decent bow and a case in which to carry it across London. After all, it was quite a journey to make each week, from Oxford Street to Blackfriars.

We didn't know it at the time, but it was going to be a symbolic journey too—the start of leaving home.

CHAPTER TWO

The Family at Langham Street

It's always said that Odessa, in the Ukraine, was a good breeding ground for musicians, piano players as well as violinists. That rather pleases me because my mother's family came from Odessa—I like to think I might be part of that tradition. My father, Israel, came from Latvia, on the Baltic coast right at the other end of Russia. He used to tell us that he was the eldest of seventeen children, most of whom were sent away to make their fortunes, to South Africa, America and Canada. He arrived in London when he was fourteen or so, to stay with his uncle and eventually found a trade as a tailor's presser. He never went back to Russia and never saw his own family again, even though his father lived till he was over ninety. (We're a long-lived family—my father was ninety-six when he died in 1972.)

Mother—who was always known as Milly, although her name was actually Imogen—was born in London. Why she was called Imogen is a complete mystery as it's such an English name and neither of her parents would have spoken much English at that time. But then it's equally strange that she was known as Milly!

Her father, Grandfather Makoff, was also in the tailoring business—which must have been how my parents met each other. Actually Grandfather was more than just a tailor. He was known as the 'Great Master Tailor' who did all the various parts of tailoring himself, cutting the material, fitting, stitching, buttonholes, cuffs—everything. He was spoken of in hushed tones because he really was most unusual. There weren't many others who did all the work on every garment. Generally, a tailor worked his way up in a workshop, learning the various tasks which would make him a master tailor. Once he was a master, he would pass on the separate tasks to other workers.

Each tailor had a special skill. One might concentrate on jackets or overcoats, another would be known as a waistcoat-maker, another a trouser-maker and so on. Lower down the scale were tasks like buttonhole making, which were usually done by the women. Finally, when the whole suit was ready, it was finished by the presser. This was my father's job. Heavy irons were heated in gas fires using specially made slotted iron containers. All the creases, pleats, lapels and cuffs were carefully pressed following instructions from the tailor in overall charge of the garment. It's still known as 'pressing' today—not ironing.

Of course, there were tailors and tailors, but even in those days there was very little tailoring done in those famous Savile Row premises. These were simply showrooms for a customer to choose the cloth and be measured by a salesman and the cutter, and to discuss the details of how the shoulders should be padded or the lapels shaped and so on. The cloth would be cut in Savile Row and that gave the suit the special Savile Row look, but then the measurements, the cloth and all the instructions would be passed on to tailors like my father, who worked outside in their own workrooms.

But Grandfather worked for no one. He never took in Savile Row jobs and I suppose today he would be described as self-employed. We never knew how he managed to make any kind of living because he hardly appeared to work at all. It must have been slow and laborious without anyone to help him, so even if he did charge Savile Row prices for the quality of his work, the money would have to be eked out over a long period of time until the suit was finished. His one great customer was the family doctor, who lived in Fitzroy Square and always dressed in a grey morning coat with a top hat and, of course, carried his Gladstone bag.

However, there wasn't much money in tailoring. Our family was very poor—even though my father and a few of his cronies had their own private customers, such as they were, to top up the money they earned from the Savile Row jobs. On the other hand, we all felt that Mother's sister had done well for herself by marrying a butcher. That was considered a highly profitable line of work and everyone thought that the Raznick family was very well off. My cousins each got two shillings a week pocket money. I was lucky if I got tuppence for the whole week. Later on that was supposed to go up to a penny a day, but more often than not Father would say: 'No, I haven't got anything for you, you can't have it this week.'

I instinctively knew that money was scarce and I learnt the value of it very young. Mother was careful about what she spent and we never had any outstanding bills. It was pay as you go and we never ran anything up 'on account'.

Strangely enough, our house was really rather large considering our circumstances. It was in Langham Street, right in the middle of London's West End, just north of Oxford Circus. Of course we didn't own it, we rented by the week as everyone else did. We lived in a tight community where most people worked in the rag trade. It's still a centre of the rag trade today, but now it's the fashion end of the business and filled with showrooms of dress manufacturers. I doubt if there are many tailors of the old-fashioned sort still around.

Life in that community also taught us self-sufficiency; it was a hive of industry everywhere you looked and there were always people who wanted an errand run. If you were quick at fetching and carrying, there would be extra pennies and halfpennies. It was like a Jewish village where everyone knew each other and everyone helped each other. I'm sure that many people, like my father, had only recently left one of those tightly closed little enclaves which fought for survival in so many European cities. Re-creating the 'village' gave them a sense of security.

It was also scrupulously fair. When they didn't have a lot of money, people remembered a good turn that had been done to them and honoured it in kind when they could. I was given my first suit with long trousers because of this code of conduct. The tailor owed my father a favour and they agreed he'd repay it by making a suit for me. It was all very neighbourly; I had only to go round the corner from our house to his workshop in Great Titchfield Street to be measured up and to have fittings. When it was finally delivered, I remember quite clearly noticing that the total cost of this hand-made suit — including the cloth — came to four pounds and fifteen shillings!

I was born on December 28th 1911. That year, two and a half thousand children had died in a heatwave during the summer. In the winter that followed, the cold was so intense and unprecedented that it killed off even more. There was an astonishing difference in the standard of living between the rich classes and the workers. Today, everything has changed so much that it's difficult to imagine what conditions were like. I certainly find it impossible to understand now how the five of us could have lived without a bathroom in the house.

My first photograph, aged three: the apple of Mother's eye

The country was torn apart by strikes and industrial trouble well before the First World War. It was felt that it was about time things changed, that people should be paid a fair wage and be given decent conditions in which to live and work. I can't remember the strikes; I was far too young. Nor can I remember much about the war itself. There was the day when a Zeppelin was spotted in the sky and because they were known to carry bombs, all the children were hustled away to safety. We went down the road to Regent Street to the air-raid shelter in the basement of the Polytechnic. In 1917, when the German planes started bombing London, the whole neighbourhood would go there for safety. On the first day that the planes flew over London, people were so amazed that they stood rooted to the spot, watching the bombing. As a result many of them were hurt.

Of course the war was responsible for fundamental changes in British society. History books talk of everything being in a ferment and of attitudes changing rapidly. Perhaps there was something in the air, a mood or a feeling which affected us profoundly. However, in my narrow world, it was the birth of my sister Anne which changed my life; she was born when I was four, and my brother David when I was ten. With their arrival, I was expected to get on with my life and look after myself.

However, I don't remember turning to friends for company; at least, when I look back to those days before I was ten or eleven, I always see events in terms of a very personal and singular experience. No one else of my own age seems to have been very much part of my life. If anyone was at the centre of things, it was Mother. I felt I was her special boy, the apple of her eye, and some of my earliest memories are of when she and I would go off on outings together.

She particularly loved films and our nearest cinema was on the corner of Poland Street and Oxford Street (it later became the marvellous Academy, now sadly and recently closed). She would go there regularly each week to see the new episode of the current cliff-hanger. I wouldn't always be with her, but seeing Pearl White—who was called the 'Queen of the silent serials'—being strapped to a railway line as the train rushes on towards her is one of the abiding images of my childhood.

Charlie Chaplin was my favourite. I can't have been more than about six when we went to see *Shoulder Arms*, that wonderful film where Chaplin escapes from German soldiers by hiding in a hollow tree and then moving away a few steps when they're looking in the opposite direction. That was also the film where Chaplin captures a German trench single-handed and without firing a shot, simply by throwing away a ripe old cheese he'd been sent in his food parcel. Everyone ran away from the smell of it. I was most impressed and for weeks I wondered how I could find a cheese that would be as effective.

That cheese and similar details were much more memorable than the music that was played to go with the pictures. For silent films, every cinema in London's West End had its little group of musicians or just a piano to set the mood for the film. These days people think there was only a pianist playing away, but in the smarter places there'd often be a small orchestra. Nevertheless, subconsciously I must have registered the musicians and the idea that there were jobs to be had playing in the cinema. It was certainly the first place I went to look when I had to earn some money.

That time, however, was still a long way off. Outings with Mother also meant afternoons together in the park—Regent's Park was a five-minute walk from home, or we would take the bus up to Cricklewood, six miles away in north London, for a whole day's excursion. Cricklewood then was still in the country, there were open fields and the feeling of being out of the city. They had started to build houses at the edge of these open spaces, but still we could go out for the day in the summer, take a picnic and get away from the hot and close environment of Langham Street.

It's extraordinary to think that until quite recently, the country wasn't that far away from central London; there were farms in St John's Wood and market gardens close to the city. Even in our home neighbourhood, the local dairy in Clipstone Street kept a couple of cows in the backyard. They were the first cows I ever saw, and Mother made a point of taking me there to look at these rather special animals and then to have a glass of 'fresh milk, straight from the cow' as they advertised in the dairy. I think our milk was 'fresh from the cow' anyway—the milkman came round with the churns and a tin ladle, and I would be sent out with a jug or bowl to be filled, and to pay for it there and then.

Strangely enough, I have no visual memories of the inside of the house in Langham Street; I remember only certain details. As I've mentioned, there was no bathroom in the house, although there was an inside lavatory and another one out in the backyard. Once a week we were all taken to the public baths, usually to Marshall Street, just across Oxford Street. Sometimes Mother used to vary the visits by going to the baths at the corner of Marylebone Road and Seymour Place, now the Marylebone Magistrates' Court. That was both a bath house and a swimming pool, which is where I learnt to swim. I have a certificate to prove that I could swim ten yards. And looking at it, I still feel the pang of disappointment when Father stopped me from swimming any more!

The house was heated with open coal fires, one in every room. If I concentrate hard, I can still bring back the smell of that coal—and in my mind's eye, I can see that small boy practising night after night in front of the fire. When there was the great miners' strike throughout the winter of 1920, they cut off the electric power regularly because of coal rationing. Then the fire gave the only light in the room. The strike didn't end until the following summer, so I suppose my parents must have also thought my playing was worth it to have a fire lit even when coal was so scarce.

For a long time, the evenings were lit by that soft glow from gas mantles and when we changed from gas to electricity, it seemed as though we'd moved into another, brighter world. Of course it meant a complete change of job for the man who once worked the gas. In an Orthodox Jewish neighbourhood, such as ours, there was work for him to do every Friday evening going all round the houses and lighting the gas lamps. Our man kept up his business by learning to be an electrician.

The Sabbath starts after dusk on Friday, and no good Jew would break the Law by doing any kind of work. That included striking a match—or even turning the oven on or off. You couldn't carry money on the Sabbath, and at one point I heard a ruling that you shouldn't even put yourself to the strain of carrying a handkerchief. That, I thought, was really too much, and besides, it was a pretty filthy idea not to have a handkerchief at all!

Our local area was possibly even more Jewish than the East End of London—and it did have some strange notions, now that I think about it. People who lived on the north side of Oxford Street thought themselves a cut above those who lived on the south side, in Berwick Street, Poland Street or down in Brewer Street. 'You know Old Joe?' they used to say. 'He lives on the other side . . .' and there was no more to be said, everyone knew what was meant by 'the other side'. It was exactly the same difference in social degree for Londoners as was meant by living on the north side of Hyde Park, rather than the fashionable south side. Of course this division between north and south London still exists today.

There were other snobberies and rivalries too. For example, Russian Jews and Polish Jews were always feuding. The Russians looked down upon the Poles who they thought were inferior— mainly because they spoke neither Russian nor German, but the colloquial language which was Yiddish. What's more, to Russian ears, the Poles spoke a heavily accented Yiddish. This made it easy to say that they were uneducated or uncultured. The actual language wasn't different, it was simply a matter of pronunciation.

As for the East End community, they were completely separate from us; the West End community knew nothing about them at all. Even now, when I know so many people from the East End and I have chaired a committee for charity which has many Jewish people on it, I feel like a stranger when they start reminiscing about their childhood there and talking about great events in East End history like the Sidney Street Siege. I have no idea what they're talking about; we could have been living in different countries, our way of life was so separate.

Once or twice when I was a child, we went down to the East End on Sunday as a special outing; but I only really began to explore that part of town much later on when I was about seventeen. The Sunday market at Petticoat Lane was such a contrast to Great Titchfield Street market; with street after street of shops and market stalls, you could buy anything you wanted in Petticoat Lane.

I was deeply impressed by all the tradesmen, selling live chickens, eggs and vegetables fresh from the country. Then there were the bakers' shops—which is where I first found out about bagels, that special hard flour bun which you can have flavoured with egg or onion. (These days the Americans even put raisins in them.)

Then I discovered the famous Bloom's Kosher Restaurant. When I first got to know it, Grandfather Bloom had opened this restaurant just as a sideline to his butcher's shop, and it only sold sandwiches. Everyone sat around a large scrubbed table where they were served the famous hot salt beef sandwiches. There were also Vienna sausages and pickled cucumber if you wanted a change, but the hot salt beef always won with me. I've remained good friends with the Bloom family since those first visits. I think they saw at once that I was a stranger, but when I came back for a second visit and then a third and so on, they always made me very welcome. I would sit at the table, wide-eyed, listening to the colourful stories people were telling. It was noisy and exuberant and it felt like being in a foreign country.

I always went alone. On Sundays, my day off from studies, I liked to wander off and explore London. It's a habit that's stayed with me; even now I enjoy walking alone. I like to stroll at a reasonable pace and see what's going on, window shopping and looking at the passers-by.

However, I did take Jean to Bloom's, much later on, when the restaurant business had become so successful that they'd given up the butcher's shop and moved around the corner to Whitechapel Road. Bloom's is so famous these days that you can never get in on a

Sunday—there's always a long queue which is kept happy by a waiter who comes out at regular intervals with a huge tray of sliced sausage so that people don't faint with hunger while they're waiting for a table. Of course, it also whets their appetites for the meal to come.

A second and third generation of Blooms now run the business and they are very kind to us. One day we were spotted at the back of the queue and Mrs Bloom called out: 'Mr and Mrs Jaffa, your table is ready for you!' We felt very privileged as no one is ever allowed to book a table at Bloom's! When Naomi and then the twins were born, they sent Jean great bouquets of flowers, a lovely gesture for her: as for the hungry father, waiting around for the happy event, I'm not sure that I wouldn't have preferred a salt beef sandwich!

My grandparents were traditional, old-fashioned Jews, and to me they were very special people. It was at their house, almost next door to ours, that we invariably gathered for the Friday night supper: all of us children clean and tidy and on our best behaviour. I can still see Grandmother lighting and blessing the candles and cutting the Chollah bread to start the Sabbath. There would be a certain amount of praying followed by good eating and a lot of talking among the adults.

When the whole family was together, it was a very tight fit indeed in the little rooms in Middleton Buildings. There were three daughters—my mother, Bessie who married the butcher, Katie who married a tailor—their brother Isadore and all the grandchildren.

Passover was a very special occasion, and my grandparents would always go through the proper Orthodox rituals. It's a wonderful ceremony and I'm sure every Jewish child has memories of those Seders—the first two nights of Passover, great feasts accompanied by prayers and a reminder of the Jewish history. 'Why is this night different from all the other nights?' is the first of the four questions to be asked by the youngest person present at the table and which starts the evening.

The prayers that follow then tell about the bad times—when everyone stops to eat bitter herbs—and the good times—when you drink a sip of wine, never emptying your glass, which is constantly kept topped up. A large glass of wine is left full in the centre of the table, because at a certain point in the evening, the door to the room is opened and kept open for Elijah to come in and drink the wine. He never arrived, which was a terrible disappointment to me as a child.

When the praying is over, everyone settles down to eat and

drink, and several courses of food are served in a traditional sequence. Part of the ritual was to change all the cutlery, plates, pots and pans completely; a special set of everything was kept separately for Passover. It is astonishing to think a household as poor as ours could afford such extra expense.

Passover was also the time when it was important to eat truly Kosher food, properly supervised by the official board of rabbis. At least everyone believed it had been properly supervised. I remember the milkman delivering the milk to Mother as usual, but because it was Passover, he handed her some labels to stick on the bottles. The idea was that good Jewish housewives could 'prove' that everything was according to the rules. It all seemed farcical to me; and I just added it to the many other reasons why I could never take the traditions as seriously as the rest of the family.

Grandfather was extremely devout and very Orthodox. On winter Fridays he hardly ever did any work because most of the morning was spent cleaning the workroom in preparation for dusk and the start of the Sabbath. He would put dustsheets over the work table and all the machines, and tidy up the room methodically. Then he would pare his nails, taking care to keep the parings safe; they were all put into a little sack which was to be buried with him.

He would spend Friday evenings, the eve of the Sabbath, in the synagogue, and the next morning would go to the full service, three or four hours long—and then go again in the evening for the service which marked the end of the Sabbath. Then on Sundays, the Christian Sabbath, rather than go back to work he stayed at home quietly out of respect for his neighbours.

Despite this religious obsession, Grandfather was a person I could talk to. In fact he was fascinating about the religion and I learnt a great deal from him. He may have been devout and God-fearing, doing everything according to the law, but he wasn't a bigot, nor was he forbidding and patriarchal. He seemed a gentle, kindly man who looked exactly like King George V—he had the same shape to his beard. There were a few exceptions of course; he didn't approve of children playing in the street, or making a noise in the house when they shouldn't.

I used to go with him to the synagogue practically every Saturday morning; my father would occasionally come too, but Grandfather was one of the elders and very much respected by the community. However, on Saturday afternoons I would often go off to Regent's Park, to play either football or cricket. This was dangerous stuff, because Grandfather was in the habit of taking a walk in the park on Saturday afternoons and it wouldn't do for me to be caught breaking the Sabbath, given his standing in the community. Everyone in the team knew that he might walk past our game, so they had to keep a watch out for the old man and be ready to hide me away. This was only ever necessary once, but that anxiety of expectation was part of the excitement of Saturday afternoons.

Grandmother was the sort of woman you couldn't help but love, a dear woman, sweet and gentle. She knew exactly how to make a young boy like me feel important and as though I had something to say. We all called her 'Boh-bah' which was our affectionate form of the Russian name for Granny, 'Babushka'. I would go round to see her when I had time to spare, and the old lady would be in the kitchen, cooking or preparing food. That's where I learnt a great deal about Jewish food and especially how to prepare it.

She was very particular about the ingredients she needed and would often send me off to the grocer's shop at the corner of Riding House Street and Great Titchfield Street to buy 'a quarter of a quarter of dried mushrooms'. If it was a special occasion I would be told to get two ounces of smoked salmon. If smoked salmon sounds extravagant, in those days it probably cost the huge sum of threepence. Nevertheless, it should be said that a good Jewish household, however poor, will always have enough food and know in some extraordinary way how to make the best of what is available. My grandparents certainly lived a hand-to-mouth existence, but Grandmother knew how to make a little go a long way.

Funnily enough, one of the strongest memories I have of Mother is seeing her cooking and preparing food. It's through her and Grandmother that food has become one of the delights of my life. We never ate large quantities but what there was, was beautifully prepared. It was in the Jewish style of course, where everything is cooked right through—you never find a crisp vegetable or a good red steak. My tastes have long since changed but at the time I thought this was perfect.

My grandparents belonged to a world that had vanished with the First World War and the Russian Revolution. But they kept the old customs going and still spoke Russian and Yiddish between themselves and with their friends. They certainly never managed to learn more than a very simple kind of English.

Mother, however, didn't speak Russian; she was brought up and went to school in London, and therefore spoke English. In our house she spoke English to the children and Yiddish with my father who never learnt to speak English properly in spite of arriving in London as a fourteen-year-old. There was no real reason for him to bother because most of his friends were Latvian, all about the same age and from similar backgrounds. Not one of them spoke English without an accent.

Looking back, I have a strong feeling that my grandparents' house was a refuge that allowed me to escape from home. At times, our house must have been very difficult to live in because Father had a dreadful temper and could be violent. He was opinionated but also very ignorant, having had no education whatsoever.

Arguments were always bitter. If he made up his mind that a black coat was white, then it was white, and if his friends didn't agree with him then they could clear off. He'd even kick them out while they were still drinking their tea.

Tea drinking was another great custom of course, although we didn't actually have a samovar. I'm sorry about that because it would have been rather a nice detail to look back upon and be able to boast: 'My family were so Russian that they always had a samovar on the go.' But tea was always served in the Russian style: this is just ordinary tea with lemon, but you drink it in a special way, taking a cube of sugar, biting into it and then sucking the tea through this cube. That is Russian tea, and that's the way the Russians drink it. At least, so I was told when I was a boy.

For a while, my life was like any other small boy's, divided between home and school, which was run by the local church, All Souls Langham Place, in a building close to the Middlesex Hospital. It was a Church of England school and it was difficult to mix the strictures of my home life with the English values which prevailed in the classroom. It wasn't that I didn't want to ask my friends from school to come home with me, I wasn't allowed to, and certainly playing with them in the street was considered almost a crime. Behaviour like that was not expected from any son of my father. Looking back, I realise now that my strict upbringing made me a loner at a very early age.

So I lived a double life and on the way back from school I was tempted—as all the children were—by the wonderful market in Great Titchfield Street; the whole street was filled with stalls selling everything you could imagine. Everyone's favourite was the ice-cream man, an Italian, who seemed foreign and exotic. He sold beautiful ice-cream, the best I've ever tasted.

There was a special way to eat it, making the taste even better because it was so elegant. You could buy your ice-cream slotted between two wafer biscuits at a penny each or piled into a halfpenny cornet, but if you had the time to stand right by his stall, the Italian would give you a 'penn'orth', a penny's worth of ice-cream, dished up in a glass and you ate it with a spoon. I can still see the glass, which was thick and heavy and didn't hold as much ice-cream as you thought you were going to get, given the size of it! But I used to feel very grand standing there—it was quite different from eating whilst walking down the street. Of course it tasted much better.

One day, my father caught me there and dragged me away, slapping down the hand which held the spoon. 'How dare you!' he shouted. 'Eating in the street!' It was absolutely ridiculous of him, but he was the arch Patriarch and what he said was Law. It was only as I grew older, and became more independent and could contribute to the family coffers, that he began to mellow a little. But he was a very harsh man and I was frequently beaten, unmercifully at times, and usually for the most trivial of reasons.

It wasn't because I didn't behave properly at school, or didn't work hard enough. Punishment came when I failed to conform to his code of behaviour, a code which was very difficult for me to identify with or to believe in. What alienated me most from my father was being punished when he considered I had been rude or unappreciative towards my mother.

Mother was his great love. He was always very attentive to her, and in later years when we moved out to north London, he would telephone her from work at least twice every day to make sure that she was all right. It actually became a bit of a joke between us children; the phone used to ring at the house and we'd say: 'Mum, it's for you. It's your lover calling you again.' We were always right.

But I'd have to watch what I said or did because it was so easy for Mother to say something off-hand or trivial which would result in Father completely losing control of himself. There was a terrible evening when Mother casually reported: 'Well, that boy Max, you know, he gave me terrible trouble today and didn't want to eat what I'd cooked for him,' and I could see that there was going to be a huge row. I didn't want to be beaten and ran out of the house, trying to hide in the outside lavatory down in the backyard basement. But Father had gone berserk and was searching the house, shouting my name, coming to get me. It didn't matter that I'd locked myself into the lavatory; he tore the door off its hinges and dragged me out and beat me just the same.

After that, there was punishment after punishment—the humiliation as I had to kneel, kiss my mother's hand and beg her forgiveness. It sounds terrible these days, absolutely horrifying—but I have to remember that my father came from a completely different culture. To him, it was only right and proper that I should obey him according to his rule-book.

We never knew when Father was going to explode, how his temper would manifest itself. There was a very embarrassing occasion when I must have been about seven years old. On Sundays, if the weather was good, he would like us to take a picnic tea to Hyde Park. We'd walk down Great Portland Street to Oxford Street and then straight along to Marble Arch and into the big open field of Hyde Park.

Oxford Street had street vendors all along it just as it does today, but then the fruit sellers pushed their barrows along the street instead of staying in one place. Their barrows were flat trolleys with two long handles and all the fruit was piled high on top. On this particular day, we were passing a barrow opposite Selfridges when my sister decided that she wanted a banana. (Then about three years old, she was being pushed along in some kind of chair.) She wouldn't have the banana that Mother had already packed for the picnic, but wanted a fresh new banana from the barrow.

Leaving us on the Selfridges side of the street, Mother crossed over to the fruit seller. There seemed to be some problem as she was buying the bananas, apparently she wanted only two and the barrow man said she'd have to buy a whole bunch or nothing. Father was across the street as soon as he realised there was trouble, and we could see that he didn't like what he heard when he got there. I can remember holding my breath, knowing he was going to do something awful.

He put his foot underneath one of the handles, tipped the whole barrow over and the fruit rolled all across Oxford Street. He then walloped the barrow man hard, sat him down on the ground, on top of all the fruit—and told me to go and fetch a policeman. I was rooted to the spot in horror and couldn't move. But then Mother came back to us, gathered us all together and took us off to the park as quickly as possible. Father followed along behind muttering: 'That'll teach him to be anti-Semitic.'

Anti-Semitism was very common in those times as many refugees had recently come to Britain, hounded out of Europe and Russia, and had grouped together in communities with very different customs from those of the British. People feared newcomers; after the First World War, there were industrial problems of all kinds, with many workers out of a job and others striking for a better wage and shorter working week. In 1919 the railways went on strike and the country returned to food rationing. It was easy to accuse the newcomers of eating all the food, taking all the jobs.

I can't blame Father for being touchy about it. Clearly he'd been sent to London to escape some dreadful persecution in Latvia, and it must have been very hard to leave his family at the age of fourteen to be sent off to an uncle he could have hardly known. I never heard him talking about brothers or sisters, or what his mother and father did back in Latvia. All I know is that his father, like my mother's father, was a very religious and Orthodox man who spent much of his time in the synagogue, probably more time than he spent with his family. That kind of early life explains a great deal about Father's behaviour even though it was hard to understand it—or as a child to forgive it.

CHAPTER THREE

Scholarship Boy

The strict routine and discipline also paid off with my schoolwork. I'd moved on from the All Souls school to Caplan Street Central, where they certainly did everything they could to further our education. At the age of twelve, I was awarded what was known as a Junior County Scholarship which took me to the famous Marylebone Grammar School. Housed in a proud, red-brick building on the corner of Lisson Grove and Marylebone Road, this was a London landmark. Sadly the school was closed some time ago and the building has now been turned into offices. It was a fine school and always at the top of the league in producing good exam results. In those days, becoming a grammar school boy really put you on the road to success.

I didn't stay at the school very long and my eventual destination wasn't quite what they would have expected of a scholarship boy. However, I had time to learn one vital lesson, much more important than facts and dates and any other rigid notions of what going to school is all about. At Marylebone Grammar they believed that learning could never be confined to the classroom; you could learn and benefit from any experience — and the more interest you showed the better.

When I first went there, I was completely in awe of the teachers, in awe of authority and the heavy burden of 'learning', the need to fill my head with 'knowledge'. The Headmaster, Mr Burbridge, was responsible for changing all that. He believed that learning could be, and should be, fun. After my parents' ideas, this was a revelation.

Burbridge was a mathematician and a very good one, but he would invariably hold the class's attention by showing us astonishing party tricks with numbers and then asking us to work out how he reached the result. I remember that the class favourite was the great adding-up game; it wasn't actually a trick, but it proved that the human mind can be trained to work efficiently. On the blackboard Burbridge would write up twelve rows of five-digit numbers which we would call out from the class. Any old numbers and in any sequence. Then, taking a long ruler, he would sweep it down the rows of numbers in a single, unstopping movement (which was actually quite fast), adding them all up as he went along. We thought it was wonderful and practised mental arithmetic like mad.

Since the school believed you could learn from any situation, we were regularly sent out on visits and expeditions. When they put on the British Empire Exhibition at Wembley in 1924, we all went to see it, class by class. Like most schoolboys, we were excited at the prospect of a day out of the classroom and what impressed me most was the great funfair, or side-show, run by Canadian Pacific Railways who also gave us name tags to identify which school we came from. Our group was supposed to go round the various pavilions, to see what the French did or what was on display in the Indian stand, but three of us drifted away from the main party, drawn like magnets towards the switchback and the dodgems where we spent the rest of the afternoon.

My father would have had a fit if he'd found out. A year or two earlier the family had spent an evening at Luna Park, a great open-air site at the corner of Tottenham Court Road and Oxford Street— where the Dominion Theatre now stands. Luna Park was sheer magic to me with the bearded lady, coconut shies, helter-skelters, the rifle range and exotic side-shows. At every turn there was some new amazement, a promise of excitement or a demonstration of dare-devil skills—like the man who climbed up to the top of giant scaffolding, set himself alight and dived off into the tiniest tank of water. How we all held our breath in case he broke his neck.

Father wasn't worried about my neck so much as damage to my hands or fingers. Alas, the switchback, the roller-coaster and the dodgems, which beckoned the most at Luna Park, were not for me. I had to watch the others from the ground.

The easiest rule to break was his insistence that I wasn't to mix with other boys in the neighbourhood. He'd forbidden me to play in the street, but Regent's Park was just up the road and once through the formal gardens, there were acres of open fields to kick footballs in or play cricket. There were always groups of boys out there, some from school, some from home, and we could enjoy ourselves without nosy neighbours to spy on us.

I became very keen on sport, and often went to watch it with a group of friends from Regent's Park. We knew our sporting world very well indeed. Tottenham Hotspur has been my football team ever since they beat Wolves in the Cup Final in 1921. Going to watch them play meant another journey across London from Oxford Circus; but in the summer I would be off to Surrey's ground at the Oval, south of the river, to support my great cricketing hero Jack Hobbs who was the opening batsman for the English Test side. How we sat on the edge of our seats when Hobbs was building up to his hundredth century! A couple of years later there was even more excitement when he outscored W. G. Grace. He really seemed to be the greatest batsman ever. But the whole Surrey team were pretty wonderful to me—it was a much more interesting side than Middlesex, which was my local team. I can still remember most of the players: Sandham, Duckett—and the captain was P. G. H. Fender who sported a huge moustache. The most marvellous wicket-keeper of all was Strudwick; he was almost as much of a hero to me as Hobbs.

I used to save up my pennies and go and watch Surrey play as often as I could. My father was certainly happier knowing that I was watching the game rather than playing it, as his greatest fear was that I would hurt a finger or break my wrist.

Since most outdoor activities were forbidden, I turned to books and became a voracious reader, picking up anything I could lay my hands on—and if I have any knowledge at all, it's come from reading, not from school. I certainly read a newspaper every day, and there were books to be borrowed from the lending library. This wasn't the public library; it charged a small weekly fee and stocked the kind of books that the local council library wouldn't have—or certainly wouldn't let youngsters look at. I prided myself on having advanced tastes for my age.

It was having scarlet fever in 1924 that converted me to reading. This was considered a serious illness and I was sent to an isolation ward in a hospital in Hampstead. After that I went to convalesce in a nursing home in Dartford, Kent. It was wonderful to be out in what was proper countryside compared to Langham Street, and I felt very grown-up. I was away from the family and having to look after myself.

Here I fell in love for the very first time. Nurse Braithwaite was the perfect vision to fill any young man's dreams. There was no doubt about it as far as I was concerned; it was a matter of destiny that I should be sent to this place and find this miraculous creature waiting to care for me there.

It was September, and we would go blackberrying together—a new experience for me. I used to wait for her to come on duty, watching the minutes tick by on the clock with my heart pounding. Then I would follow and talk to her as she did her rounds of the other patients. I must have been the most terrible nuisance.

Night shifts of course were the best of all. I would keep awake to have Nurse Braithwaite all to myself, when we would whisper and giggle together while everyone else was asleep. I thought she was deeply in love with me too—but I soon learnt about heartbreak as well as falling in love. Only a few weeks after I came home I was devastated to get a letter from her inviting me to her wedding. My dreams were shattered!

You didn't need much money to enjoy yourselves in those days. I grew up with the music hall by going to Saturday afternoon matinees at the Coliseum and Alhambra (now the Odeon Cinema in Leicester Square). I started very young, and must have been about ten when my 'rich' cousins, Manny and Fay Raznick, asked me if I would like to come out with them. There was consternation at home at the very idea of going to the theatre on the Sabbath, but I think Father agreed to it as a form of keeping up with the Joneses. If the Raznicks thought it was all right for the children to go to the theatre, then it was all right for a Jaffa.

Going to the theatre was really magical; I would drink in that feeling of excitement and expectation among the audience, waiting to marvel at the stage and the show. It seemed to me that the performers were out of this world and I'm sure we have nobody to match their talents today. Of course, that's the way it always seems when you look back!

The shows we saw would alternate between the two theatres, one week at the Coliseum and then on to the Alhambra. They were glorious, three-hour-long entertainments with a wide variety of acts. I first saw the Diaghilev Ballet at the Coliseum, but also George Robey, Billy Bennett, and Vesta Tilley. This was where I first became interested in snooker when I watched Joe Davis doing trick shots on stage, which we all saw through a huge mirror fixed at an angle

45

above the billiard table.

Those matinees were tremendous value for money in every sense. A seat in the gods (in the topmost gallery) cost ninepence, but children under fourteen could go half-price. Fourpence halfpenny for three hours of entertainment which could include the Diaghilev Ballet! Then afterwards we used to go a few doors along the road in St Martin's Lane, to a J. Lyons and Company teashop. There we would treat ourselves to some great ice-cream concoction, a whole dishful of ice-cream which might set us back sixpence. That was really pushing the boat out!

We felt very grand on these outings. Most of the other children sitting in the gods were accompanied by their parents, while we were allowed to go by ourselves. My two cousins were about the same age as me and became my closest friends through these music-hall adventures. They lived near Fitzroy Square and part of our fun was to walk down St Martin's Lane, looking at all the people and the shops. Of course I had to walk; if we'd gone by bus I'd have had less money to spend and I was determined to pay my way. As I knew my cousins would have a couple of shillings to spend each week, I had to plan very carefully for these outings and try to run as many errands as I could to save up the necessary sum of tenpence halfpenny for the theatre and ice-cream tea.

Sadly, as we grew up we drifted apart. There wasn't any quarrel, but neither Manny nor Fay was really interested in music and I suddenly realised that we hadn't seen each other for ages. The next news was that Manny had died, still a very young man, only a year or so after he'd got married. Once I was married, I started to see Fay again—we even lived in the same block of flats for a while. Then the war came along and that changed everything.

However, music also had to fight quite hard to keep me interested, because Marylebone Grammar opened the doors to so many distractions. I was absolutely fascinated when we learnt in science classes how to make a wireless set with cat's-whisker and crystal. Of course, like everyone else, I wanted to build one to take home and show the family what I'd done. I remember all that business of winding the wire around a cylindrical piece of cardboard and then attaching some piece of apparatus which moved across the whole affair to tune in to various frequencies. And somewhere in the midst of all this you played around with that cat's-whisker on the crystal— which sounds very primitive in these days of high technology. I actually made two attempts to build a radio; the first was a failure and I had to start all over again. But we also had three or four sets of headphones which we discovered would make something of a loudspeaker if we put them all into a large saucepan. Then everyone could listen together. We didn't mind what it was, we'd listen to anything that we found through the hiss and crackle.

Later on, when the family bought a proper set, I discovered a station somewhere around the 550-metre band which was my absolute favourite. Every night from about ten o'clock onwards I would tune in to Radio Budapest and listen to this extraordinary gypsy band broadcasting from one of the restaurants or cafés in Budapest. They were fantastic players, completely natural gypsy fiddlers who'd probably never had lessons in their lives, playing away with such virtuosity and passion, all with such wonderful rhythm. I just listened in awe.

Eventually I saved up and bought a record of Imré Magyar, a famous Hungarian gypsy fiddler, and listened hard to understand what this kind of playing was all about. I think I learnt a great deal from those players, because I've always loved gypsy music (or rather those pieces that are written in a gypsy style like Monti's *Czardas*). The very first record I made was playing gypsy violin with a Romanian cimbalom player.

However, Father was definitely growing uneasy with all these enthusiasms, these passions, ideas which threatened to interfere with the great plan that I should become a violin player. He had a very clear idea of what he wanted me to do, and a very clear idea of the goal I should achieve.

Technically speaking, Father didn't know very much about music, but he certainly had a feeling for it and enjoyed listening to the few records we had for our wind-up gramophone. His particular favourite was the wonderful singing of a famous Hebrew cantor from America. Indeed, many of his quarrels with his friends sprang from heated debates on the merits of the different cantors at the synagogues in the neighbourhood.

In the United Synagogues, the very Orthodox synagogue, the tradition was to have a rabbi to intone prayers and blessings while the cantor (who was also a rabbi) sang set pieces during the services for Sabbaths and holy days. A cantor had to have a beautiful voice, though it wasn't necessarily trained, and naturally enough each congregation took an immense pride in their own cantor.

It grew into quite a competition: 'Our cantor—you must come and hear him,' people would say, and it became part of the social round, going to each other's synagogues comparing the quality. I always felt that cantors were more intent on showing off their vocal prowess than on bringing out the beauty of the Hebrew texts they were singing.

Father must have known something about the concert world— after all he had taken me to the Queen's Hall to hear Heifetz. But he was a practical man, and probably thought that aiming for that kind of career was beyond my talents. On another occasion he took me specially to hear a violinist who he thought would make a much better model. We went off to have a cup of tea at the Lyons Corner House in Coventry Street where there was a band playing, led by Albert Sandler. 'There, that's what I want to see you doing,' he said. 'That's where I want your playing to take you. You know, he's earning twenty pounds a week!'

There's a famous story fiddle players tell each other along these lines: a father takes his young son to the Albert Hall to hear Fritz Kreisler (another of my favourite violinists) and while everyone is listening hard to the music, marvelling at the artistry, the sensitivity and the elegance of the performer, the father turns to the son and says: 'You see that man, he's earning hundreds of pounds and he's just standing there playing the violin! Now will you practise?' I've no idea how my father knew the sum of money that Albert Sandler was earning at Coventry Street, but it was typical of him that the financial reward was far more important than the musical side of playing the fiddle. But they were prophetic words indeed, because this attitude set the seal on the kind of violinist I would eventually become.

I was once offered the chance to concentrate on becoming a concert violinist. It was a very serious occasion, organised by my Guildhall professor, Max Mossel. He could see that too many distractions were threatening my concentration and my development into a responsible concert artist—though I think his views on what might stop me were quite different from my father's.

I was asked to go and play for a group of people who were said to be very interested in hearing me. I remember being dressed up in my best suit, with Mother fussing over me. Father and I went off together and found ourselves in a room filled with earnest-looking men, concentrating intently on my playing. They were polite and formal, and it was all very unnerving as I had absolutely no idea of the reason why I was playing to them.

They were in fact members of a philanthropic organisation created to help young talent, but their philanthropy was balanced by an awareness of the potential for a financial return on their investment which could be used to support other up-and-coming players. After I had shown them that I could play they offered to support me—with certain conditions.

While I continued studying the instrument, they would take over all the expenses. They'd pay for lessons, a good violin and bow, all the music I needed, pocket money, concert suits, in fact everything that was necessary to allow me to concentrate totally on learning the violin. Then, once I was launched on my career, I'd pay them back with a percentage out of my earnings. Father, however, failed to grasp the long-term benefits of such an arrangement. Apparently he understood only that when I started to make a career for myself, I wouldn't be earning my full fees—and he decided that he'd prefer to keep the business within the family. That shut the door on my becoming a solo concert violinist. You need financial support to help you concentrate single-mindedly on all that practising day after day to learn the technique and the repertoire. We didn't have that kind of money. So that was that.

However, Father took in one part of the gentlemen's argument. If I was a good enough player for them to consider supporting me, then I should be allowed to get on with playing the fiddle without any other kind of interference. So he decided that going to school was an unnecessary burden on the music, and removed me from Marylebone Grammar—without any warning or explanation to anyone. I was just told that from now on there wasn't going to be any more school. I'd hardly been there a year—and I wasn't yet fourteen.

The authorities were furious and the Headmaster sent a note to my father, demanding to know where I was. The two of them met to consider the issue and from what Father repeated of the confrontation, he for once had to do the listening, as they threatened to take him to court. Patriarch that he thought he was, he suddenly realised that other people had strong principles too. The London County Council took a dim view of Father's decision as they reasoned, quite justifiably, that he'd taken an opportunity away from somebody else who would have been longing for the chance to work through the whole curriculum of the grammar school and might well have gone on to university and the professions.

As for me, I am, unfortunately, almost completely uneducated, because I never opened another schoolbook. However, I was very pleased and proud that Marylebone still thought of me as an Old Boy of the school when they wrote me a charming letter on my receiving the OBE.

My limited education was of no importance to Father, who had tunnel vision once his mind was made up. I was going to be a violinist and that was that. He couldn't see the need to go to two schools at once, Marylebone and the Guildhall School of Music; one was enough. After all, he had started work when he was fourteen and a Jewish boy traditionally becomes a man at thirteen, when we have the Bar Mitzvah. I'd done all that, I should be allowed to go on my way. If I was going to play the fiddle for my living, that's what I should be studying.

CHAPTER FOUR

The Guildhall School

Travelling to John Carpenter Street in Blackfriars was a regular pilgrimage for six and a half years and I'm sure that having to go so far was an important step for me. If I'd gone to one of the local colleges, the Royal Academy or Trinity, I would have grown up within the neighbourhood, staying part of the Langham Street community. The Guildhall turned out to be rather more than another school of music; there was an atmosphere and an attitude in the place which couldn't have been better for the kind of player I was going to be. And just as my mind had been opened by Marylebone Grammar, so the Guildhall was to make it impossible for me to see that tight little community in Langham Street in the same way ever again. I felt really different, I was expected to think for myself and in my music I had found something I could do that left them all behind. It gave me confidence to break out in all kinds of ways.

The Guildhall is the youngest of London's music colleges and has always been supported by the business community of the City of London. They wanted the school to have a different emphasis from the 'royal' institutions of Marylebone and Kensington Gore, which were keen on producing well-drilled performers who could play their instruments to the highest standards. To keep the numbers up, just as any school will do today, they also took in lesser talents, which in those days were usually rich young society ladies.

The Guildhall's amateurs were of a quite different kind. It welcomed City workers who would come in after office hours for classes in musical appreciation or elocution, piano lessons or singing lessons. It was hoped these classes would give some respite to the daily grind at City ledgers. At one point, up to three thousand students were coming through the door for enlightenment.

The Guildhall School of Music and Drama in John Carpenter Street

Sir Landon Ronald

Nevertheless, there was a small core of serious students, many of them supported by scholarships endowed by the City livery companies and generous private patrons. The elocution side fast turned into a very successful dramatic training ground and many students went on to find work in professional companies.

Looking back over the history of the Guildhall, it's clear that Sir Landon Ronald, the Principal at the time I was there, was responsible for filling the place with fresh and practical ideas for music students, which really challenged the other institutions. He'd been trained at the Royal College and had quickly built a successful career as an accompanist, conductor and also a composer of well-loved songs like the famous 'Down in the Forest'. When he came to the Guildhall in 1910—as quite a young man of thirty-eight (and going places)—he brought with him a personal knowledge of what it meant to be a practical musician.

He set out to make sure that the school would become, as he said to everyone, 'absolutely modern and progressive'. He separated the amateur and professional sides to ensure that each got the best kind of teaching for their needs. The amateurs still came in for their lessons after work and all kinds of tuition were offered to them. However, the students who wanted to make a career of music were put through their paces in the most rigorous and professional way.

As he was a music-maker rather than an academic, Landon Ronald was electrifying. We all knew that he conducted regularly all over the country and abroad. He had even conducted the Berlin Philharmonic Orchestra, who considered themselves the greatest in the world and were very particular about the artists with whom they would work. Landon Ronald also knew the most famous musicians. One of his first professional jobs was to accompany the Australian soprano Nellie Melba and he went on to conduct her orchestra on a tour of America. He used his musical contacts ruthlessly to convince people to come and teach at the school. Nellie Melba was soon persuaded to found a singing scholarship, but she was so nervous at making the speech the first time it was awarded that she had to bow out gracefully and allow Sir Landon to read her paper for her!

Sir Landon laid down standards which became the backbone of the school; he was interested in every aspect of being a musician and he knew perfectly well that being able to play an instrument well, or having a beautiful voice, was only the beginning. For him, musicians needed personal manners, a good presence, and if possible brains, as well as good looks. Training musicians was not simply about teaching students to play their instruments, it was also a matter of giving them a practical sense of how to earn their living—and especially how to earn their living in changing times.

He'd been interested in the gramophone industry from its very early days; in fact the Gramophone Company had asked him to use his musical connections to persuade people to make records for this new business. He knew the value of silent cinema as well and he even conducted his orchestra, the New Symphony Orchestra, to accompany a film of the life of Wagner. As for broadcasting, he was in with the BBC right from the beginning. They started to relay student concerts from the Guildhall as early as 1923.

Guildhall professors definitely had to know the music business from personal experience, and I couldn't have had better luck than to be studying with Max Mossel. He was a Dutchman, a good concert violinist as well as the most rigorous of technicians and he commuted between London and Holland where he ran his own concert series. He was very grand and came from a different world from the one I knew. He was almost a hunchback but always immaculately dressed and very sophisticated. His clothes came from a top Savile Row tailor—I could see that from my knowledge of cloth and cut—and his boots were an absolute marvel, handmade by Lobbs. There were never boots like that in Langham Street. He lived at a very elegant address, Bank Chambers in Jermyn Street, and he was always driven to the Guildhall in a Rolls-Royce. In my mind I have this picture of him getting out of the car wearing a long coat with a fur collar and a black top-hat—while I was just a young lad in awe of him, with absolutely nothing to say for myself.

Perhaps that was why he took a personal interest in me: Max Mossel and Sir Landon Ronald both really became my godfathers in the profession. They gave the long-term education, the values and the knowledge which stick with you for the rest of your life. You could say that they rescued me from the narrow and limited outlook of my father.

There was a crisis almost as soon as I got to the Guildhall (while I was still at Marylebone Grammar School). Of course I was far too young to know anything more than that I had been taken there to play some pieces and I had then been accepted as a student on the everyday basis of nearly all the students at the school. It was a very simple arrangement; the school provided premises at John Carpenter

Street and a selection of the best teachers, and each student paid for the tuition they wanted. One of Britain's best singers, Carrie Tubb, remembered working in a laundry to be able to afford a single lesson a week. When I got to the Guildhall, it was six pounds a term for twelve lessons.

The money must have run out unexpectedly, because I don't think even my father could have imagined that one term of lessons would transform me into a professional musician. I was told that I had to inform Max Mossel that I wouldn't be coming back for any more lessons the next term. I must have known what that would mean as far as my playing went, but we all knew how to be careful with money and I had long learnt not to argue with my father.

The effect on Max Mossel was electrifying. He asked me to repeat what I'd said, then he asked me why—which of course I couldn't answer. 'Wait here,' he said, and hurried out of the room, rushing back in again a few moments later to take me by the hand, down the stairs and into the Principal's room. I didn't even have time to think about being frightened, or about being in front of the great man himself or even that I was being ordered to play something to him. Max Mossel was very agitated: 'You see, you see,' I remember him saying, 'we can't possibly let it happen. He must stay on. You must give him a scholarship!'

Max Mossel was very difficult to refuse and somewhere Sir Landon Ronald found the money. I became the holder of the John Saunders Scholarship which was worth fifty-two pounds a year and would pay for all my lessons at the Guildhall School. I kept that scholarship right the way through my time there and it paid for violin lessons and then chamber music, orchestral rehearsals, score reading and conducting classes. By the end of my days at the school I was fully trained in all the things you need to know to be an accomplished musician.

The education and the support went on in other ways too. My fifteen-pound fiddle from Meinal's was just not helping me to progress as quickly as I should have done, so Max Mossel lent me one. Like many violinists and many teachers he had a collection of good instruments and bows which he would lend to students who needed help. I found myself playing a violin made by Carlo Bergonzi, who came from a well-known family of makers who had learnt their craft from Stradivarius. At the time, I just thought it was a rather better fiddle than my own: I know now that it was worth a lot of money.

It was a very sad day when I had to give it back to him. They told us at the Guildhall that he had suddenly become very ill; in fact I think we all knew he was dying. So I did the proper thing and went to visit him in Bank Chambers, taking the instrument with me. I knew that he wanted me to have it, but he was past caring about who owned it, and he was too ill to be able to give it to me formally.

I was desolate when I left: I walked away from his flat knowing that I had lost a friend and a true mentor, who had taught me everything I knew about being a musician. We weren't close, as friends might be close; but I looked forward to my lesson with him every week. We discussed so much about music; we would go to concerts together when Sir Landon was conducting at the Queen's Hall and he would point out the important details—good and bad—of the music being played. Even though he would never have broken the convention that kept the professors aloof from their students, he took enough trouble over my education for me to understand somehow that he sympathised with my situation. It wasn't exactly a friendship but he cared that I always seemed to be struggling with the burden of a father who so clearly didn't understand anything about his responsibilities.

Father may have thought that it would be a short time before I was earning my living playing the violin, but there was a great deal to learn before I could seriously think of anything beyond just practising. Max Mossel, like any good teacher, believed that you could only play properly when you were absolutely certain how everything was going to work. It's no good going on stage thinking: 'Oh, there's a difficult bit coming up, I hope I get the octaves in tune,' or 'There's this tricky fingering on the next passage,' or 'I really feel uncomfortable with this bowing I've decided on.' All that should have been sorted out and become second nature well before the performance.

Max Mossel's teachers had included the great Spaniard Sarasate who was both a brilliant virtuoso player, technically able to play anything on the violin, and a very sensitive musician who knew all about playing the serious classic pieces. Several composers wrote music specially for him—Lalo's *Symphonie espagnole*, Max Bruch's *Scottish Fantasy*—and he was reputed to have perfect intonation and an enchanting tone to his playing. Those were the demands that Max Mossel made of me. I had to learn not only to play the violin, but how to make music, to make a good sound, to use my imagination so that I could bow a piece of music to make it 'speak' and express different things. There was so much to learn because playing an instrument seriously is a very different matter from playing it as a hobby. The fingers have to be trained to work in ways that they're not really intended to by nature and you have to practise that every day.

So I was put to learning scales up and down the instrument, in single notes, in thirds, sixths, octaves and played with all different kinds of bowing. Then there were studies, which concentrated on certain aspects of playing, to help the fingers move in ways that were actually quite difficult. You can't get that sort of thing right by just working at it for a couple of hours. These are exercises which you need to do every day—I still do some of them even now.

In a strange way, the better I became at the instrument, the more time I had to devote to practising it. That was why it had been difficult to find enough time to manage both the practising and the growing amount of schoolwork I was getting at Marylebone Grammar. But as soon as my father made me concentrate on the music it took over almost all of my time. In the 1920s, the Guildhall started to offer full-time courses of study, so as well as my hour-long lesson with Max Mossel, I found myself playing in the Friday orchestra rehearsals and being involved in chamber music classes, playing sonatas, string quartets or piano trios and learning about that side of the repertoire.

Sir Landon Ronald was adamant that to be a good musician you needed a breadth of study and experience. As soon as I was old enough, I was put into the new conducting class, taken by Aylmer Buesst, and learnt the valuable skill of reading an orchestral score of twelve or more lines of music at once. That was certainly an important lesson in understanding what orchestral music was all about, and I think I became quite a decent conductor. At least, that's what some players said, years later, when we invited the Royal Liverpool Philharmonic Orchestra to come over and join the Spa Orchestra at Scarborough for a celebration, and I conducted them. I must say, the idea made me quite nervous beforehand, but once I got up in front of what seemed an immense group of musicians, it all seemed to work well.

I would certainly have picked up good orchestral habits from playing in the Friday orchestral rehearsals which were taken by Sir Landon himself. This was the most marvellous institution; all through the week we'd work at the music in our separate sections—the first and second violins, violas, cellos, the woodwinds and brass. Then on Friday mornings we'd all meet together in the concert hall for a full rehearsal, when the students would be joined by the principal woodwind and brass players from the London orchestras. They were first-rate professionals like the horn player Aubrey Brain, Archie Camden on the bassoon, the flute player Alec Whittaker and one of the Goossens sisters—was it Marie, playing the harp? It was a wonderful way to learn all the major pieces.

Sir Landon knew exactly how to make us all work at the music and listen to each other. He would say: 'If you can't hear the tune, you're playing too loud,' and he would work us hard to balance our playing to get the right sound. You have to take it on trust sometimes though; in a piece like Elgar's Enigma Variations, there's often so much going on right down at the bottom of the orchestra that you can't possibly hear it if your part takes you right up to the top of the violin.

However, even though he was rigorous about discipline and standards, Sir Landon was not a pompous man and there are two stories about him which show his generosity. He couldn't by any means have been described as handsome, though he certainly had a memorable face. Meeting him for the first time, people were always struck by the size of his nose, which was more than prominent. And one story goes that when he was taking an orchestral rehearsal, a fly settled on the end of his nose which he didn't seem to notice and it was bothering the leader of the orchestra. Eventually he leant forward and told Sir Landon about it. 'Oh well,' came the reply, 'you knock it off then, you're nearer to it than I!' It was the sort of story that endeared him to us students.

When I first played at the Trocadero Grill Room, Sir Landon told me of an extraordinary encounter he'd once had there when eating lunch. He became aware of a fellow customer staring at him unashamedly. He was quite used to this; being a famous conductor and a public figure it happened to him quite often. However, this starer was unusual in that he was definitely the ugliest man Sir Landon had ever seen in his life. Moreover, he became aware that just as the man was looking at him, so he was returning the stare, absolutely fascinated by this most dreadful face.

Eventually, the other man finished his meal, came over to his table and said: 'I do hope you'll excuse me staring at you, it is Sir

Landon Ronald, isn't it? I'm always being told by my friends that I look exactly like you . . .' He dined out on the story for days.

Another part of my education concerned standards of behaviour—perhaps it would be more accurate to say that I learnt how to be a gent. If Max Mossel was always immaculately dressed, so was Sir Landon. He insisted that all the students at the Guildhall should dress properly; senior students were even expected to wear suits to set a good example to the younger ones. But Sir Landon and Max Mossel were more than well dressed; their suits and shirts and shoes were the best you could get, made by the finest craftsmen. That kind of workmanship made all the difference and gave them that aura of elegance.

Of course tailoring was something I knew about, and my mother had always counselled that shoes had to be of the best quality you could afford. 'You should never save on shoes, it's the worst economy you can make.' She was right, as invariably people who bought on the cheap found their shoes fell to pieces all too quickly. But my mentors at the Guildhall proved that there was a purpose to dressing well and I've always gone for the best tailor and bootmaker that my pocket allowed. I don't remember ever having bought anything 'off the peg'. I think they both felt that caring for one's appearance meant that one had standards on other issues. They argued that if one was tidy and well turned out in everyday life, there would then be room to be creative and expansive in one's art.

My great hero Heifetz also insisted on this same kind of attention to detail. His female pupils were expected to come for their lessons in a skirt and blouse, or a dress; the boys had to wear a jacket and tie and have their hair cut properly. He was a stickler for punctuality too. If you were expected for a lesson at three o'clock and you rang the doorbell even at one minute to three, he would open the door and say you were too early, and shut it again until the exact time. If you were late, he might not open the door at all! His students used to synchronise their watches with the speaking clock before setting out for their lessons!

Max Mossel also introduced me to a whole new world of style and comfort. During the General Strike, when there weren't any buses, and several times after, he gave me a lift home in his Rolls from the Guildhall to Bank Chambers in Jermyn Street, where he lived. Sometimes he would stop off briefly at Adelphi Terrace to talk to a friend at the Savage Club where both he and Sir Landon Ronald were members. I would wait for him in the lobby, watching people go in and out, listening and looking and taking in absolutely everything around me. I'm sure it's no accident that I'm now a member of the same club.

However busy he was with his conducting career and the Guildhall work, Sir Landon knew all his students and what they were up to. If we worked hard to learn all we could about being professional musicians, as we were expected to, then the school and Sir Landon himself would help all they could to find us jobs. Many of the singers went on to work in the D'Oyly Carte Opera Company, and he would put in a word for instrumentalists and soloists with the right orchestral managements. By and large, I think we all felt that we were being well looked after.

I'm happy to have been part of the Guildhall's history and it made me proud to read my name in the list of 'distinguished' past students mentioned in the programme for a gala performance to raise money for the new school. They had picked out quite a selection for that evening in 1982: Fred Astaire, Chris Barber, Edna Best, Honor Blackman, Claire Bloom, Owen Brannigan, Mrs Patrick Campbell, Noel Coward, Peter Cushing, Jacqueline du Pré, James Galway, Henry Hall, Myra Hess, Dora Labette, Dudley Moore, Peter Skellern and me!

It took me back to 1930 and the Guildhall's fiftieth anniversary celebrations. There was a Queen's Hall concert, when I led the second violins while Sydney Bowman led the orchestra, playing for a perfectly ridiculous revue. The music was written by the pianist Sidney Harrison who had only recently been appointed to the staff as the youngest teacher ever. The title was terrible—'Would Jubilee'v'it!' (That's the awful kind of pun which seems to have dogged me through life. A name like Jaffa is asking for it. 'Hello Max, Jaffa good time?' people would constantly say to me—and worse!)

When I was studying I had no idea that my fellow students included such names as Noel Coward and Fred Astaire, who were struggling to learn a little formal musical technique. There was also Sybil Thorndike, who found that her acting showed greater promise than her music lessons. You find out about your fellow students much later on in life.

However, I knew all about the other string players; we tended to stick together according to the instrument we played. Pianists knew pianists, and singers watched other singers. But even as a first-year student, thirteen years old, I knew the school was humming with the news that a young violinist called William Primrose was going to make his Queen's Hall debut at the age of nineteen. This was an internationally famous concert hall and one of our colleagues was going to star. Years later, William Primrose gave up the violin and turned to the viola after he'd heard Nathan Milstein play the violin. He knew he could never play as well and would only torment himself by trying. He went to audition for Arturo Toscanini in New York and then made a tremendous career as a soloist and chamber music player. And if he couldn't play the violin as well as Milstein, he was certainly good enough to play the viola alongside Heifetz in chamber music and in Mozart's Sinfonia Concertante.

The other sensation of the Guildhall was Albert Sandler, the very same player whom my father had taken me to see leading the orchestra at the Lyons Corner House in Coventry Street, a job he'd found at the age of sixteen. Albert had won a scholarship to the Guildhall after years of earning his living playing in the silent cinema. Three years later, in 1925, he become a household name with the BBC broadcasts from the Grand Hotel, Eastbourne.

Well, as it happened, Father had been right to point him out to me; I seemed to follow in Albert Sandler's footsteps for a very long time — from the cinema to Lyons, and from *Grand Hotel* to playing trio music with his very own colleagues Jack Byfield and Reg Kilbey. It's hard to know if I could have been influenced directly by Albert Sandler, but I'm sure what he did gave me some ideas when it came to thinking about how I could earn money to keep myself at my studies.

For all Sir Landon's good intentions, I'm not sure that we took much notice of the professional musical world beyond the Guildhall, though of course we all knew about violinists. We all went to the Royal Albert Hall to hear Yehudi Menuhin make his debut in 1929 at the tender age of thirteen, and of course any concert by Heifetz or Fritz Kreisler would see us there in force. During the summer holidays, there was the Promenade season, again at the Queen's Hall, where Sir Henry Wood was busy introducing as wide a range of music as he could. Meanwhile, on the BBC (still the British Broadcasting Company until 1927) there was more music than anything else, although dance bands had more air-time than 'serious' music.

61

However, time off to go to concerts became a rare luxury for me. I had to remember that the family were still counting every penny at home to make ends meet and to give my brother and sister the same kind of chance that I'd been given—not that either of them appeared to be the slightest bit interested in learning any musical instrument (although my brother David is very knowledgeable and has amassed a large record collection). My family had launched me at the Guildhall and were prepared to help me with very basic expenses. For example, lunch was never more than a small packet of cheese, biscuits and a cup of coffee; my proper meal would be waiting for me at home after school.

Though my father must have been impressed by the attention that was being given to me, I expect he was equally concerned by the realisation that my scholarship didn't cover my keep or any of the necessary extras like strings for the violin, re-hairing the bow, buying music and of course the bus fares. If I felt I ought to have more to spend on extras or luxuries, it was made quite clear to me that I would have to earn it myself.

CHAPTER FIVE

First Jobs

Perhaps it was nothing to do with Albert Sandler, but the first place I could think of that might have a job for me was in a cinema. They were opening up everywhere and films were all the rage: Charlie Chaplin for some people, while the girls went wild over Rudolph Valentino.

Each new cinema tried to be better and grander than its rivals and the idea of the 'Super cinema' began to spread all over London once the Tivoli in the Strand had set the trend. Of course it was bigger—there were more seats, they were more luxurious, the decorations more exotic and the music they played to go with the films was much more sophisticated. Super cinemas boasted a small orchestra, all in uniform, which gave them that touch of class.

I first tried my luck at the Bloomsbury Super Cinema, presenting myself to the musical director—who rejoiced in the name of Raymond de Courcy! Obviously he wanted to know what I could play and I was very grand about my talents: I was a violin scholar at the Guildhall, which proved I could play the fiddle. But he looked me up and down, saw this young lad of fourteen and offered me a job in the back desk of the violins, but without pay—as he said: 'For the experience.' For that I was to work between two in the afternoon and ten in the evening, with the odd break in between film showings! The management provided the musicians with red jackets, though they were expected to supply their own evening trousers. Being just fourteen I had to have my first pair of long trousers made.

All young players have to start somewhere, and naturally music directors took advantage of us to fill out their little orchestras with students and youngsters. On the other hand, de Courcy knew very well that I didn't know anything about the job—and in the five months that I stuck it out in the back desk I acquired a considerable education, learning the tricks in playing bits and pieces of music to fit the films. In between the main showings we'd also give a little concert, playing everyone's favourite pieces, like the overture to *Orpheus in the Underworld*, with perhaps a popular ballet suite like the *Ballet Egyptienne* by Luigini and a medley of tunes from an opera. That was another kind of repertoire which never saw the light of day at the Guildhall.

So I learnt about light music, film music and the bitter facts of musical life too. I found out quite by chance that I should have been getting paid whilst acquiring all this knowledge. The official union rate for orchestral players in the cinema was a pound a day, but although I was on the payroll paid by the management to de Courcy, de Courcy never paid me. That was very common; many people made their way in the business by taking advantage of others. There was absolutely nothing I could do about it—after all, it was my own fault for agreeing the terms, to do the job 'for the experience'.

It was time for me to do better for myself. The next step came from reading the musicians' newspaper, *The Era*, which was published entirely for players, and advertised all sorts of jobs. The Station Hotel, Richmond, wanted a violinist for their trio, evenings only, between half past seven and ten. That was ideal, because it gave me plenty of time for practising.

I rang up, found the job was still vacant and was invited down to Richmond so they could have a look at me and try me out. I found myself playing with two ladies of the old school, a pianist and cellist. I can clearly remember sawing my way through a selection from 'The Vagabond King', one of the popular pieces of the time. They were marvellous old dears, who belonged to quite another age. They were probably rather good players, too—and nothing like the image we have these days of 'the teashop trio'.

I got the job immediately; it was six evenings a week for three pounds' pay. That was good, because my finances were improved, and I had all day to go to the Guildhall, to practise, rehearse, and have lessons as I needed to. I could even enjoy a bit of life again.

It is amusing, given what happened later on in my career, that we played in the Palm Court of the Station Hotel, Richmond! There were palms everywhere; they created a pleasant ambience, and it was a very social place. People came there in the evening to meet their friends, drink and listen to us play. It was my introduction to the idea of the importance music has in other people's lives and that you could give people pleasure by playing.

Indeed, the audience would sometimes try to make friends. There was one young man who was very attentive. He used to come to listen two or three times a week, and would always offer to buy me a drink. At that stage, I didn't drink alcohol, of course, as I was far too young and ginger beer was my great favourite. But my lady musicians became very agitated about this friendship, they were in a dreadful state, trying to warn me against this young man's intentions. We had an extraordinary conversation all about 'It'; I must beware of 'It'. What 'It' was all about never dawned on me until much later when I had long gone from Richmond. They were too genteel to bring themselves to say the word 'homosexual' or 'sex' or anything so direct. And I didn't know too much about the facts of life.

The Richmond job kept me interested for about three months and then again I wanted a change and a new challenge. At the Guildhall I was stretching my playing every day, trying to reach new goals, to achieve new technical skills. The trio music didn't really test my technique, and after a while my playing began to get automatic. It would then have been a short step to slide into some very bad habits.

So it was back to *The Era*, where I saw another job advertised, again leading a trio, at the Super Cinema, Hoe Street, Walthamstow. This time I came armed with a recommendation from a cousin by marriage, Harry Joseph, who was already a professional violinist. Somewhere he must have heard me play, and his word got me the job. All I had to do was telephone the pianist to let him know when I could start. What's more, I now received the official union rate of a pound a day.

I discovered that Harry Joseph was not the only other musician in the family. Another distant cousin, Leslie Jeffries, was also a fiddle player, and strangely enough he worked at the Grand Hotel in Eastbourne. I even met him about twenty-five years ago, when he was still working in the hotel.

The pound a day from Walthamstow Super Cinema meant there was money to give Mother to help the household finances. I took what I needed to get me through the week and gave her the rest. It was a marvellous feeling to be independent. I didn't owe my father anything now, because I was both paying for my own expenses as a student and also doing my bit to help the family. The result was that

I no longer felt I had to bow to Father's authority—I was my own man.

The Walthamstow management taught me that there was a commercial side to music which had nothing to do with art. I had thought it was most important to please the audience by playing the right kind of music to go with the pictures; and to change the music at exactly the right time. You can't really have a galloping chase to accompany the death-bed scene. On the other hand, there was a lot we could do to whip up excitement even though we were only a trio of piano, fiddle and drums. The drummer was our special ingredient—he could make up all kinds of splendid sound effects with his range of percussion instruments.

But there came this wonderful moment one day: the pianist and I were swooning away with music for a romantic love scene when the little curtain behind me, that screened us off from the audience, was rudely drawn back, making a terrible noise. The owner was hissing in my ear, pointing at the drummer. 'What's the matter with him, why isn't he playing? Why is he taking a rest?' I hissed back out of the corner of my mouth (I still had to keep my eyes on the screen and keep playing the right kind of music to go with the pictures). 'It's a love scene, you don't have drums beating in a love scene, he'll come in again when it gets more exciting . . .' But the owner would have none of it. 'I'm paying him to play, aren't I, and you all know what the hours are. I want him to play.' So play he did—there was nothing else we could do. I expect we beat up more passion than anyone ever before—or since.

By 1927 the writing was clearly on the wall for silent films. Al Jolson's *The Jazz Singer*, the first full-length talkie, took the whole film business into another dimension; audiences would never be satisfied with a trio of musicians once they heard full-blown orchestras and real voices speaking. Only a year later, talkies had more or less taken over, and the best directors were inviting good composers to write music specially to go with the pictures. Any music that was left in cinemas was simply to entertain the customers between features.

I left the cinema as soon as I could and began going down to Archer Street—the musicians' street, where people would go every morning to see what jobs were available for the day. Luckily someone I knew persuaded me that I'd be much better off trying for a job with J. Lyons and Co., the catering company which had opened teashops all over the country, reputable places for anyone to have a meal or a cup of tea when they went out.

The Corner Houses were a British institution, with their famous 'Nippies' as the waitresses were called. Some of them were really teashops which served light refreshments and quick snacks, beautifully presented of course. They were nothing like today's cheap and tawdry fast food places. A Lyons Corner House was immensely respectable and indeed rather glamorous. Many of them were lavishly decorated with marble pillars and marble floors specially imported from Italy. In the West End of London, the Trocadero, the flagship of the company, was among the smartest places in town to go for dinner and dancing. It was patronised by high society, with a restaurant of the finest quality and a floor show of some of the best talent in town.

More importantly the Lyons company employed a vast army of musicians to entertain the customers. At the Coventry Street Corner House, music was played all day long. The building had four floors with two orchestras to each floor playing alternating shifts of three hours each, from twelve noon to midnight. That made eight groups of musicians altogether. The Trocadero had two ensembles, one in the restaurant and the other in the Grill Room. So did the 'Pop'—the

Entertainment at the 'Pop' Café   My uniform for lunchtime concerts at the 'Pop'

The Strand Corner House (a 1957 drawing)

Popular Café (which was where Simpsons department store now stands)—and Maison Lyons in Oxford Street, a very smart rendezvous for luncheon and tea (now Lilley and Skinners shoe shop). There were four ensembles at the Marble Arch Corner House, three orchestras at the Strand Palace Hotel and two 'salon' orchestras at the Regent Palace Hotel.

I had to impress Mr Grant and Mr Alexander, who had an office round the corner from Archer Street. They were employed by Lyons to book the musicians for the orchestras, and they reported upwards to Charles Tucker, who planned all the entertainments and extravaganzas like the C. B. Cochran shows at the Trocadero. At the top, there was Major Monty Gluckstein who was part of the management of the firm, and a member of the family which owned Lyons.

Having looked me over, Mr Grant and Mr Alexander suggested that I might start by leading the orchestra at the Corner House in the Strand (there was a dance band playing there too). Of all the Corner Houses, the Strand, on that corner just before Trafalgar Square, is the one that most people remember. This meant a definite improvement in the musical quality of my working life: I would be with a group of musicians who were among the better players in town. The Lyons Company expected high standards and needed a good reference before they employed you.

It was quite an experience playing at the Strand Corner House. The orchestra supplied the music to all three floors of the restaurant at the same time. We played on a sort of shelf on the central floor, but there was an open well through the middle of the building, so the sound could reach the higher and lower floors too. It was a hard day's work as we started at quarter to four in the afternoon and finished at a quarter to midnight, with two half-hour breaks.

This was a world of music-making which has long since disappeared. We were expected to mix 'serious' pieces with the odd solo turn. The conductor, who was known as 'Oskaro' (his proper name was Oscar Thomas), happened to be a very fine cello player, and would play a couple of solos during each of our sessions. His encore and party piece was to play the Musical Saw, which was fascinating to watch—and indeed to listen to, because he chiselled a remarkable sound out of it. But when he started to do the knee-trembler, the whole restaurant would stop to watch him. He would put the handle of the saw under his right thigh and bend it from the other end with the left hand to get the right notes while the right hand pulled the bow—exactly as with a cello—across the edge (the blunt edge, not the teeth). But to get a decent tone or a vibrato, the right knee had to work up this trembling action which was mesmerising to watch. He looked as though he'd suddenly developed an incurable nervous tic.

The hours we played at the Strand Corner House left me enough time for my lessons, classes and practice at the Guildhall. Because I was the youngest player in the orchestra, I was well looked after by the band and the staff. Everyone was kind to me, which was just as well because a final flourish of patriarchal authority was to come that could have finished my London musical career.

One of my better friends at the Corner House was a sweet girl who worked as a cashier. She was very pretty and certainly very kind to me. We soon found that we lived quite close to each other in the Langham Street area, so we walked home together after we'd both finished work at night. We'd just stroll through the streets, gossiping about who we'd seen and what they'd done. In 1927, the Bright Young Things were in full swing, letting their hair down and enjoying themselves, the more outrageously the better!

I don't think she could have been much older than me, and as far as I was concerned she was just a good friend and good company. Unfortunately, Mr Oskaro, the conductor, was rather sweet on this girl but she would have nothing to do with him. So he was more than a little put out that she allowed me to escort her, and worse, to take her home every evening! His revenge was to write to my father to warn him that I was having an 'affaire' with his cashier, and that, in view of my tender years, my father might like to give me some good advice about the possible consequences of such an alliance!

Well, the only way my father knew to hand out good advice was to beat me about the head. He was absolutely livid, even more livid than usual. This situation had to stop, he said. I tried to get him to understand that there was nothing to stop in the first place—but meanwhile thanked him very much for putting the idea into my head. I hadn't realised that something interesting could happen if I went about it in the right way!

In the evening, after I'd come back from the Corner House, he confronted me with Oskaro's letter, but things didn't stop there. The next day Father suddenly appeared at work. He marched right up to the little platform on which we were playing. I was astonished; he'd never been there before and now he was all dressed up and talking to one of the 'Nippies'. She then came up to Oskaro and said that Mr Jaffa senior, Max Jaffa's father, was waiting and would like to talk to him.

It was normal practice for a conductor to leave the stand from time to time and let the leader get on with the music, so I was left in charge while Oskaro and Father disappeared into the back of the restaurant. The trouble was that Oskaro didn't come back; he completely disappeared for the rest of the evening. All Father would say when I got back home that night was that I'd know what he'd said 'soon enough'. Which of course set my mind racing as to what he could possibly have done.

The next day, the management told me that Mr Oskaro would not be returning to the orchestra in the near future. In the meantime would I please take over the music. But the worst part of it was to discover that Oskaro wasn't coming back because he had been set upon and beaten up and was not in a condition to be seen by the public.

My father's hand again. But he was unashamed: 'I did it because I don't want any tales to be told about my son. If he's behaving badly

Major Monty Gluckstein

and there's anything to be done about it, I'll do it. It's nobody else's business.'

The players in the orchestra were not at all upset about Oskaro's fate, as they disliked him intensely. Each and every one of them came up to me separately to tell me that he'd got his come-uppance at last! Like many conductors of modest talent, he was very pleased with himself and lorded it over everyone even though most of the players were older than him and rather more distinguished. For example, his pianist was a fellow called Otto Mann, who turned out to be related to the famous German writer Thomas Mann, and who certainly didn't enjoy being denigrated in public.

The strangest part of it was that this fight gave me the promotion I really wanted. After I had been conducting for two or three days, Major Monty and Charles Tucker appeared in the balcony above us to see how things were going, and about a week later I was summoned to the Trocadero to see Major Monty.

It was the most marvellous interview. Major Monty had noticed that I was doing very well taking charge of the orchestra at the Strand Corner House—but Mr Oskaro was now much better and was about to come back to his old job. Would I therefore be interested in another position, leading one of the two orchestras at the Popular Café—the 'Pop'? This meant promotion and a pay rise: I would be earning ten pounds a week!

There was another argument soon after I arrived at the 'Pop'—a musical argument which emerged after a directive arrived from the management. Charles Tucker, who was in charge of all the entertainments at Lyons, liked to believe that he had been quite a showman in his performing days. He was an American who had an act in the music halls as a vagabond gypsy violinist. He didn't play very well, but he had a certain charisma and enough charm to marry an actress called Violet Essex who was very friendly with the Salmons and Glucksteins.

Tucker had been considering the performance style of all the orchestras and decided that there was something rather untidy about the gaps in between the pieces they played. These pauses didn't bear any relation to the music; sometimes they felt too short, sometimes too long—so he sent a directive to all the leaders to say that we should note the duration of each piece of music played, and then ensure a break of half that length before we played the next piece! I thought this was absurd, as did every other leader. The normal practice was to get on with the next piece of music as soon as we were ready, having tuned our instruments and so on. But the management wouldn't listen. So I set out to prove it wouldn't work.

There were often spot checks on how we were performing; we'd suddenly see either Mr Grant or Mr Alexander sitting at the back of the room. When one of them next turned up while I was playing, I decided to act. We started to play the first movement of Schubert's 'Unfinished' Symphony, with the repeat included. By the time we reached the end we must have clocked up something like eleven or twelve minutes of music. Then we sat back and took a six-minute break before the next piece. Well, of course, he was up at the platform pretty quickly wanting to know what had happened. Why wasn't there any music, why had we stopped playing? So we won our argument, to applause from all round the company. I felt very pleased with myself, learning to stick up for what I wanted—and fast.

I must have been at the 'Pop' for about a year, when there was a further promotion to the Trocadero—the top establishment. I started by leading a small ensemble in the restaurant while the large orchestra in the Grill Room had Alfredo Campoli at its head. He liked to play excerpts from various concertos every now and then, and I would sneak off from my ensemble to go and listen. I took over from him when he left.

This was before Alfredo decided that he really wanted to become a serious concert artist—and indeed he had a wonderful career, he played beautifully. But before that, he was a session musician along with the rest of us, playing in restaurants, for records and in film studios. Many years later, there was an amusing moment down at the Beaconsfield Studios when a group of fiddle players were all standing around chatting about the Heifetz film *Melody of Youth*, where Heifetz plays with the San Francisco Junior Orchestra. There was Antonio Brosa, a distinguished player and teacher, and Hugo Rignold who became the conductor of the City of Birmingham Symphony Orchestra, but Campoli rendered us all speechless: 'I saw that film . . .' he said as though he didn't think it was particularly special. 'If only I had his looks.' We all marvelled at him, amazed that he could seriously think it was only his huge head and double chins that separated him from the same kind of playing as Heifetz!

My role model Albert Sandler had also played at the Trocadero. He joined the Lyons musicians in 1922 when he was sixteen and was soon playing at the 'Troc' as a star violinist. The 'Troc' was the most extraordinary of restaurants; partly an eating house, partly a show-place. It was one of the oldest of the Lyons establishments, opening long before the famous chain of Corner Houses. In 1924 the great impresario C. B. Cochran staged in the Grill Room the first of a series of cabarets which featured the best talent in London. Dancers like Frederick Ashton and Balanchine appeared, and there were sketches by a very young Noel Coward, with the finest of set designers and costume-makers. However, when I was there, my job was to lead the orchestra which played while the guests dined. Someone else played for the floor show. We played background music for the restaurant trade; selections from favourite operas like *Carmen* or *La Bohème* and Gounod's *Faust* used to be very popular. People would ask for the widest possible range of music—from the Largo from Handel's opera *Xerxes* to the patter songs in Gilbert and Sullivan!

I had never been anywhere so elegant. People came in full evening dress, white tie and tails. Some came to dine and dance, while others arrived later just for the dancing, after dining somewhere else. Evening dress wasn't a rule, you were welcomed regardless—but it was rare to see anyone in a dinner jacket, let alone a suit.

Dancing was confined to the restaurant—and the music was someone else's business! The 'Troc' was a place to while away the night hours and no one turned a hair at the strangest of sights among all the elegance. People were dancing away the effects of the First

World War; once it was all over, everyone wanted to forget the misery of it, to have fun—and sometimes to anaesthetise themselves. The older generation looked on in horror at the Bright Young Things, calling them callous and insensitive, and the women fast and immoral, because they painted their faces, cut their hair short and threw themselves at men to get a husband. Dancing was a way to forget your cares and enjoy yourself—and it was a craze that went on and on. It still hasn't stopped.

The Grill Room, however, was not the place for the real antics— these happened later in the evening when it was time for the stage show. The place would fill with groups of friends who all turned up together, often very merry already, demanding a table from where they would enjoy themselves loudly and freely. As skirts went up, dances went mad and many people completely abandoned their inhibitions, flouting convention at every turn. Young men came out with their boyfriends, other handsome fellows in full white tie and tails turned out to be handsome young ladies, and Nancy Cunard had the town agog for days when she turned up with her black lover.

And though the older generation disapproved, we noticed that they were also out for a good time in their own way; more often than not with people of the opposite sex—but who were married to someone else.

The glamour of the Trocadero

The Trocadero Grill Room

CHAPTER SIX

A Trip to Buenos Aires

I'd just finished playing a lunchtime session one day at the 'Troc', when a waiter brought me a visiting card from a fellow called Reiss, who asked if he and I could have a word. He ran a general entertainments agency which also supplied the orchestras for passenger ships and he offered me a surprise invitation. Would I like to play the violin with a five-piece band going to Buenos Aires?

He was booking players for the Blue Star Line's *Avelona Star*, bound for Buenos Aires via Rio de Janeiro, for a fee of sixteen pounds a month all found. It was certainly not riches compared to the twelve pounds a week that I was then getting from Lyons, but an extra bonus was promised. I would leave the ship in Rio to play a five-day guest spot with the ship's pianist at the Copa Cabana Hotel. The fee for those dates would be negotiated on the spot.

But I didn't hesitate and signed then and there. I didn't care about the money, it was the excitement of going so far away that really interested me. South America sounded the most exotic place on earth and we would be leaving at the end of the month. I gave notice to J. Lyons and spent the rest of the day dreaming about sailing off to this fabulous new world. It felt as though I was really on my way—until I went home that evening.

Mother wasn't at all pleased with my great news: 'You're not going!' She was very definite. I argued that it was the most wonderful chance; but she knew or had read that the place was full of unspeakable evils, just waiting to ensnare me. 'There are women there,' she said, 'who stand in the doorways and pluck you off the street.' (I'm sure she said 'pluck'.) 'And before you know what's what, you'll be dragged off into white slavery.' It hadn't occurred to her that they might not be interested in boys for white slavery, but no child of hers would be allowed to take the risk . . .

I thought the trump card was mine since I'd signed a contract, but she was as sharp as a knife: being seventeen I was under age and the contract would definitely be invalid. It didn't mean a thing in law. We argued, I cajoled, she wept, I sulked. We must have gone through the complete range of family emotions over the next few weeks. In the end, she came round to the idea, and even saw me off at Tilbury Docks—still weeping gently, convinced it would be the last time she'd see me.

The crossing was tremendous fun. I'd never experienced anything like it. The only sea I knew about was from holidaying at Westcliff-on-Sea, where I learnt to love cockles and whelks and other seaside treats. But I'd never seen anything like the *Avelona Star* and its sumptuous staterooms, even more luxurious than the decor I'd come to take for granted at the Trocadero. She wasn't a large ship, mostly carrying freight. However, there was nothing but the best for her select band of passengers. They were all in stunning quarters, the cabins actually large suites with private bathrooms and their own sitting rooms. As soon as we boarded I went off to explore, since someone had warned me that once the passengers arrived their section of the ship would be strictly out of bounds to us. I discovered a world that I never knew existed, except perhaps in the films.

The passengers looked as though they were the richest people in the world; owners of great Argentine cattle ranches, or mines—

The Avelona Star

wherever they got the money from, they proclaimed it. Their clothes were in the best of taste, their jewels huge, and the women the last word in beauty, dressed in the latest Paris fashions.

We watched them at dinner. This was the grandest affair with everyone in full evening dress, while we played discreetly in the background. The passengers were absolutely marvellous, really enjoying the music we gave them, which obviously added to their feelings of escapism and romance. They loved asking for requests which they would write on the backs of large, crinkly five-pound notes (I grew very fond of those notes). We shared them out between us, and each extra pound made a considerable difference to our miserable wages.

Life was easy, as we didn't have to play much during the day. The evening was the time for music and dancing, so we could lounge about in the sun when we weren't working. Once we got to the tropics they rigged up a canvas swimming pool for the crew which we were allowed to share. It was a very pleasant way to pass the time.

However, there was something new for me in the job. It was the first time I'd really had to learn any dance tunes, as the Lyons establishments always employed separate groups for dance music.

On the *Avelona Star*, the most important music was the tango, surely the national dance of Argentina. Luckily, someone in Mr Reiss's office had had the wit to make sure that on board was the sheet music for the most popular tunes. The first and probably the only rehearsal we had together was spent running through a selection of these new tunes. 'La Cumparsita' was one favourite request, but nowhere near as popular as 'Jealousy'. We must have played that tune at least twice a night on the voyage both out and back. Of course we changed the name immediately to Ja-Lousy because of the French spelling of 'Jalousie' on the sheet music. No musician will ever call a piece by its proper name if there's the slightest excuse to find an alternative!

I had taken the job in search of adventure and a new view on the world; and it was an adventure right from the start. First of all I shared a cabin with the pianist who was a perfectly pleasant man, except that very early on in the day, every day, he became blind drunk. I was fascinated. I'd never seen anything like it and I was curious about the effect that drink would have on him. I still thought ginger beer was a great drink and hadn't yet touched a drop of alcohol. However drunk he became, he still managed to play the piano; we sort of wheeled him to it, poured him on to the seat and off he went without a single wrong note. It was hilarious when we hit rough weather, because the piano wasn't fastened down so it slid around the saloon with him still pounding the ivories. Some bright spark had obviously put his mind to securing the instrument so it wouldn't roll around the room, but instead of attaching it to the wall or the bulwark or whatever it's called, he'd attached the piano to the stool—and the whole thing would take off with the rest of us in pursuit.

Getting off at Rio to play my five days in the Copa Cabana was the next shock to my system. This place was unbelievable. The Copa Cabana Hotel was, and is, one of the most famous hotels in the world. Jean and I went back there in the early 1980s and I remembered most of it (though naturally nobody there remembered me).

If the Trocadero's image had been slightly dented by the luxury on board ship, the Copa Cabana eclipsed it completely. Of course Rio was a different world; even though we were looking at the same kind of rich people who made the Trocadero so smart—the men in white tie and tails, the ladies in beautiful gowns—there was a different feeling in the air. Perhaps it was the heat, the language, or the smell of exotic flowers that decorated the hotel and its gardens. The women all looked magnificent, sultry and dangerous, while their men appeared to own them as they might a magnificent, highly strung racehorse.

These people looked straight through us. We were way below their level, probably on a par with the waiters, who were simply ignored—they were merely servants to bring the food and clear the tables to the orders of all sorts of higher-ranking flunkeys who busied themselves about the room. A man could lose his job simply by dropping a spoon. This was quite another culture, arrogant and rich.

We played during dinner at the Copa Cabana, but for three nights rather than the five I was promised—and we came and went without causing the smallest sensation. Looking back, I wonder how we did it at all. The pianist was pretty well liquored as usual by the time we played in the evening and my eyes must have been out on stalks drinking in every detail. Unlike playing through the evenings at the 'Troc', I wasn't going to miss anything going on around me here. Alas, as I didn't and don't speak Portuguese, many of the dramas must have passed me by!

However, Brazil was a country of violent contrasts: people richer than one could possibly imagine with others suffering an equally grotesque poverty. There was astonishing cruelty and callousness too. When we eventually got to Buenos Aires, we had a few days' wait before the *Avelona Star* turned round for home, and I used to sit on deck to watch her being loaded with unripe, green bananas, which were dropped into the hold in huge bunches. All around the four sides of the hold, there were great iron hooks that stuck out from the wall and as they dropped the bananas down, they were caught on these hooks and wired up. On one dreadful occasion, one of the banana throwers forgot to let go of his bunch and was swept down into the hold with them. He was torn to shreds by the hooks. I'm not sure what was more shocking, his dreadful accident or the attitude of some of the crew who were also watching. They were quite nonchalant about it, since it happened all the time to 'these stupid fellows'. I had to be led away, sick at the sight.

Nevertheless, Buenos Aires was a most exotic city, full of extraordinary sights. There were the cafés and restaurants of the Boca, almost on the docks, and famous because Rudolph Valentino danced a seductive tango in one of them. Each café had somebody playing the accordion or the guitar to entertain the patrons — but halfway up the wall, on a kind of balcony, they also had an 'orchestra', entirely of girls, five or six of them, who looked as though they were playing the instruments they held. But they weren't: these 'musicians', I was soon told, were prostitutes. If you caught the eye of one of them she would put down whatever instrument she wasn't playing and come and join you. Mother, I thought, you don't know the half of what goes on here. Who needs to stand in a street doorway, when the white slave trade comes with your meal!

I thought it might even happen at the barber's. I went to get my hair cut because I'd seen these fantastic hairdressing salons in the Avenida Florida, the most elegant of shopping streets, where many of the best stores in the world have a branch. Every afternoon it was closed to traffic between two and four o'clock so people could parade up and down, window shopping to their hearts' content.

I wasn't much interested in the shops in those days, however marvellous they all looked. What fascinated me was the local scenery; the women were so beautiful, and even at the age of seventeen I thought they had exquisite taste and dressed so well. I was taken out to the race-course on just an ordinary race day—and it looked like our Royal Ascot, everyone was so tremendously smart.

But the barber shop in the Avenida Florida was too much of a temptation. Again there was an orchestra playing, they brought me a cup of coffee, a man whisked my coat away to brush and press it, someone else shined my shoes, they gave me a manicure, a scalp massage—all sorts of attentions. It was quite wonderful, and it's still the best haircut I've ever had. When it was all over I counted my change and tried to work out what it had cost in real money rather than Argentinian, and was horrified that the total was just under two pounds. That was a fortune to me. In London it would have been eightpence—and that's old pennies. Had I missed out on anything else that was on offer in the shop and included in the price? Could I have been entitled to one of those young ladies in the 'band'?

But I couldn't have coped! I found that out on the night before we sailed for home, when three of my good friends from the crew promised they'd take me out for a very special evening in a wonderful house that they knew about. And indeed it was absolutely magnificent. We were shown into a graceful drawing room where, set into the centre of the floor, most unusually, was a strange circle of clear glass. Arranged around this were several small tables with parties of men and women all in very high spirits—fuelled of course by a constant flow of drinks. We found ourselves a free table and sat down, and drinks were brought immediately. It was whisky all round for the men and lemonade for me.

Everyone was waiting for the cabaret which they promised would be rather unusual. As the lights went down, the glass floor was lit up from below and twelve ladies tripped on to the circle, absolutely naked. Or rather, six of them were naked and the other six had the added adornment of what looked like male sexual organs. I couldn't believe my eyes; these people were female from the waist up and male from the waist down. Of course they were artificial organs—dildos—and all part of the show, which involved the performance of every sexual contortion that you could imagine.

I hadn't a clue such things were possible, as I hadn't even reached lesson one. I was the complete innocent abroad. Well, I suppose I knew about the birds and the bees and the basic facts of life, but this was something else again . . .

While it was all going on, one of my chums said to me, 'Whatever you do when it's over, look anywhere in the room but don't look at any of the girls.' That was a little difficult as my eyes were glued to the show and when it was finished they were still glued, my mind in an absolute ferment. And of course, one of the girls saw me and came over like a shot to sit in my lap.

That was far too much for me: she was absolutely revolting. What's more, she was obviously quite willing to teach me all she knew. I couldn't cope with that at all. Mother was right, I was much too young to be exposed to such experiences. Everyone thought it was terribly funny as I excused myself and rushed from the room. They thought I couldn't cope with all the excitement—but I left that house and was as sick as a dog.

Thank goodness I haven't gone through life saying: 'Sex makes me sick'. But I couldn't return to that house, and instead made my way back to the ship. I felt much better when the others returned and I discovered that they too had found the experience a bit extreme. I've never seen anything like it anywhere else in my travels.

CHAPTER SEVEN

The Piccadilly Hotel

Caution had been thrown to the winds for the Buenos Aires trip, and I hadn't a care about what I would do for money when we came back to London. Something would turn up, I was sure of that—even if it wouldn't be quite as grand as the job I'd left behind at the 'Troc'. In money terms, it had been a very successful adventure; there was twenty-five pounds in my pocket, which was remarkable considering they had only paid us thirty-two pounds for the two months we'd been away! In 1929 twenty-five pounds was a large sum, especially for a young man of seventeen.

Nevertheless, it wasn't going to last for ever, and there were bills to pay to keep me in the style to which I was becoming accustomed as a bright young student at the Guildhall. So, like any prudent musician, I went down to Archer Street, to let people know that I was back in town and ready to work again. And since I was there in the very same street, I thought I might as well tell the Lyons people too— Mr Grant and Mr Alexander. It couldn't do any harm to call in at their office; if I hadn't blotted my copybook by leaving the 'Troc' so suddenly, there might be a job for me somewhere.

But no such luck. Mr Alexander was a decent sort of chap, a retired cellist who had some sympathy with musicians and their problems. Mr Grant, however, took a perverse pleasure in being thoroughly discouraging to any player who came his way looking for work. He was very sarcastic: 'You know of course that the job you should be going for—given your experience—is at the Piccadilly Hotel. Their Mr De Groot is leaving and going out to tour the music halls.'

This was ridiculous advice. De Groot was one of the most distinguished players in London, the only real star violinist (before

Albert Sandler stole some of his thunder). He ruled the musical roost at the Piccadilly Hotel, one of London's best and smartest establishments.

Grant went on to say that the Piccadilly Hotel believed they were engaging one of the Lyons players to take over, a gypsy fiddler called Mottelinsky. 'But they can't have him because he's got a contract with us—to which we're going to hold him. He thinks, and they think, he's accepted the job at the Piccadilly, but we shan't let him go. This could be the chance you are waiting for!' (Grant's sarcasm was pretty familiar after a while.)

Most musicians who played for Lyons worked without a contract. They offered you a job through recommendation, and you kept it if you played well enough. The only reason that Mottelinsky got a contract out of them was because they had brought him from abroad. At one point, Lyons were very enterprising and went over to Budapest to engage three or four gypsy musicians. Whoever chose them did a good job; they were all fine-looking, dark young men, who played this wild and romantic gypsy music, and they were an immense attraction at the various restaurants. However, after several months had gone by, women started turning up at all the establishments where they were playing, bringing with them an assortment of fine, dark babies—all claiming that one or other of these gypsy musicians was the father. That became a bit too much for J. Lyons and Company who had a respectable reputation and their gypsy fiddlers were sent back home.

Grant's sarcasm about the Piccadilly Hotel job only made me all the more determined to see if I could get it. After all, it wouldn't really be that different from leading a Lyons orchestra—but the place itself was considered more prestigious. It would definitely be a step up the ladder for me and too good an opportunity to let slip. So, with the blissful arrogance of youth, I walked out of the Lyons' office, across Piccadilly Circus, and into the Piccadilly Hotel. Marching straight up to the Commissionaire, a grand and formidable figure in a wonderful uniform, I had no time to be nervous: 'Could you please direct me to the person who is responsible for engaging musicians and orchestras?'

The Piccadilly Hotel was another family business, owned by R. E. Jones Ltd who were once dairy farmers. Now their business was a strange combination of the delivery of fresh milk around London and running this most elegant of hotels. Colonel Elwy Jones, one of the family, looked after the entertainments.

As luck would have it my timing was perfect; Colonel Jones had just finished lunch and was upstairs in his office, feeling rather generous to the world. Certainly I had no problem in being allowed to see him and found a charming man, very courteous, very genuine—who knew absolutely nothing at all about music, other than the fact that the great De Groot was leaving the Piccadilly Hotel.

I dived in head first: 'I hear that you will be needing a new leader for one of your orchestras, so I've come to apply for the job.' I could see that he was slightly bemused by this because he thought he had a leader all lined up. But I went on: 'I can tell you on good authority that if you think you've engaged Mr Mottelinsky, you haven't. He is still under contract to another employer, and I know for a fact that they're not intending to let him go yet.'

Colonel Jones may not have known anything about music but he knew about contracts, and I played my trump card. 'His present employers told me themselves, but they suggested that I should come across to see you to offer my services instead.' If Grant had been sarcastic about my chances, that was his business and Colonel Jones didn't have to know. In the meantime, I could tell him a great deal about my previous experience with Lyons at the Corner House, the 'Pop' and the 'Troc'. No one had a written CV in those days—but it was quite a good catalogue, with Buenos Aires and the Copa Cabana as icing on the cake!

In those days, this corner of the entertainment business relied on good, efficient musicians rather than stars. Elwy Jones made a quick phone call to check my story, and invited me to do an audition that very evening, leading the musicians who were playing in the restaurant! Of course I agreed. 'But,' I said, 'I'd rather have a trial engagement for something like two weeks. That would give me time to get used to playing in the right way for the hotel's atmosphere, and would give you time to see what I can do.' That original fortnight's trial eventually lasted over four years!

As I've said, the Piccadilly Hotel was one of London's best, truly in the luxury class. One side opened on to Regent Street, and the main entrance was on Piccadilly, about a hundred yards or so from Piccadilly Circus. There is still a hotel there but it is now called Le Méridien. In the twenties and thirties hotels like these were among the most fashionable places in town, favourite venues for people to

Myself around 1928

meet and enjoy themselves; the public rooms were sumptuous and the restaurant boasted some of the best food in London. At lunchtime, it was a popular rendezvous for people talking business, or up in town for a day's shopping. At night, it was an elegant place to dine and dance. In both the restaurant and the Grill Room, a small salon orchestra played light music while people were eating, then at nine o'clock a dance band would take over.

I started in the restaurant and was then promoted to the Grill Room, which was reckoned to be more serious about its eating and presumably the quality of the music that went with it! The other orchestra was directed by 'Leonardo'—Leonard Kemp was his proper name—and Jerry Hoey led the Grill Room dance band.

De Groot wasn't the only big name who worked at the

Piccadilly. The band in the restaurant was conducted by one of the great names in the dance band world—Al Starita. There were three Staritas, Rudy, Ray and Al, Italian-American brothers who were all involved in playing for restaurants or hotels or night-clubs. They started off with their own band in the States, copying Paul Whiteman. Eventually they came to England and Ray was the first to get a job leading the Piccadilly Revels Band at the Piccadilly Hotel, with Rudy in the line-up. Al meanwhile was leading Jack Hylton's band at the Kit-Kat Club.

In 1928, they all changed around. Al took over at the Piccadilly while Ray went off to new pastures at the Ambassadors Club. But Al's reign didn't last long; one night he was caught with a customer in one of the hotel bedrooms and was sacked on the spot.

The next night there was a new leader, Sidney Bright, promoted from his usual job of playing the piano in the band. He came from another musical family. His twin brother was Gerald Bright, otherwise known as Geraldo, the band leader who became famous in the forties. While Sid was conducting from the piano at the Piccadilly, Geraldo was at the Savoy Hotel with a group of musicians all dressed up in Latin American style suits as Geraldo's Gaucho Tango Band.

They may have been twins, but they couldn't have been more different; Gerry was the epitome of the tall, dark and handsome band leader, while his twin brother Sidney was short, fat and myopic. Sid, an excellent pianist, was certainly the better musician. After the war we met up again when he joined the BBC's London Studio Players. We often worked together and became good friends and colleagues.

Dance bands and band leaders were highly popular. Carroll Gibbons at the Savoy Hotel had led the way through the twenties; Ambrose first made a name for himself at the Embassy Club, and in 1927 was invited to become Musical Director at the Mayfair Hotel. With the enormous salary of £10,000 a year and a weekly spot broadcasting on the BBC (which he had not been allowed to do at the Embassy), it was an offer he couldn't turn down. Every Saturday night, tens of thousands of listeners tuned in to Ambrose from ten thirty to midnight and he became a national figure.

The BBC broadcast dance bands from all the better-known night spots every evening of the week for this hour and a half. They also broadcast a great deal of 'light music' during the day: small orchestras, operettas and light musicals, cinema organs and ballad recitals. Far more air-time was given to this than to 'serious' music.

Lunchtime, Monday August 19th 1929, was my broadcasting debut. It was a very casual arrangement. Someone in the BBC's Outside Broadcast department in Savoy Hill invited me in for a chat and I came away with an agreement to broadcast once a week. There was to be non-stop music for an hour, with no announcements, and I was asked to submit my programme well in advance so they could check it. On the day, there was no fuss at all, compared with what they get up to these days. A man arrived at the hotel some time during the morning and merely stuck up a single microphone above the orchestra. At one o'clock, when it was time to start playing for the broadcast, he just popped his head around the side of our platform, gave us the 'thumbs up' and we were off.

The hotel was absolutely delighted because so many people listened to the radio that this was worth thousands of pounds to them in free advertising. The BBC were also aware of the impact, but their worry was 'plugging'. As a form of advertising, band leaders were being paid to play tunes specially for music publishers. In those days sheet music had enormous sales, just as records and CDs have today. By playing a tune on the air, you could certainly boost those sales.

Unfortunately, paying the band leaders wasn't part of the BBC deal; their argument was that the conductors or leaders didn't need a fee since we got the kudos of having our names mentioned on the air. So we weren't paid a penny while all the players were given an extra ten shillings. They even booked in a harmonium player at the Piccadilly to boost the sound from our quintet.

Naturally, any leader was fair game to a song plugger, and soon they came around to see me. The first one was Tolchard Evans, composer of, among other tunes, that huge hit 'Lady of Spain'; he also ran a music publishing business. He was quite open about what he wanted—if he arranged a tune specially for my orchestra, and I played it during a broadcast, he would be waiting there for me at the end with a pound or perhaps thirty bob, in cash.

The tunes were always specially arranged for each band, because we all played a different kind of music. A tune that was better for a dance band needed a certain amount of doctoring before we could play it with our quintet and make it sound a natural part of our repertoire. It was easy to side-step the programme planners at the BBC who were busy checking our lists of music. We always sent in programmes that were slightly shorter than the broadcast time of sixty minutes, so there would be room for extras on the day. You had to be clever about it, but if you worked out your timings very carefully, you might fit in three or even four of these lovely little two-minute extras. They were gone before any BBC ears took them in, but the avid listeners at home heard exactly what the publishers wanted.

The BBC became extraordinarily worried about it, even though at that stage there were no rules to stop us playing the tunes. Some people clearly thought it was immoral; we were taking bribes, since it was possible to make between four and six pounds a broadcast—a very welcome addition to one's salary. But band leaders felt the BBC could hardly complain since they paid us no fees at all.

However, the big evening programmes were in a different league altogether. Those bands broadcast with singers and soloists, with announcements for each and every item so you could make sure what tune was being played. Song plugging was big business, and many band leaders made a great deal of money out of it. Word had it that some publishers even bought them houses and cars.

Eventually the BBC decided it had all got out of hand, and even considered banning band leaders from talking to the audience, to leave the introductions to announcers, as they did with their own BBC Dance Orchestra directed by Jack Payne. He brought most of his players across from the Hotel Cecil, where it was rumoured that he and the pluggers had done the best business in town.

The dance bands were the really popular programmes; my kind of music at the Piccadilly Hotel had nothing to do with the favourite tunes of the day. The programme for that very first broadcast was strictly the light classics, with nothing modern or jazzy. We played the waltz 'Etincelles' by Waldteufel as well as the usual mix of entr'actes and overtures and an operatic selection. It was hardly going to make me a household name. However, there were two great advantages; the music wasn't difficult to play (except when I decided I'd wake people up by launching into some gypsy fireworks), and it was in a style that didn't interfere with my studies at the Guildhall.

De Groot had left behind an extraordinary library of music. It had everything you could possibly want: musical comedy selections, novelty pieces, entr'actes, ballet suites, operetta selections, opera arrangements, all the overtures you could think of—Verdi, Rossini, Meyerbeer and even Wagner. It also went as far as the Beethoven symphonies (though I don't think the Choral was included!).

Of course the music was all arranged for a small ensemble. It's a tricky business with only five players: two violins, a cello, a bass player and a pianist. (There were never any violas in ensembles like this. The piano was supposed to add the middle parts, and all the other important bits.) The cellist was Samehtini, a brilliant player. As well as having one good eye and one glass eye, he had a most peculiar sense of humour. Occasionally he arrived late, or just in time to start the session with us. He would apologise, using the same excuse every time—that his glass eye had fallen out somewhere near the Piccadilly Hotel—but he always managed to find it.

I think the most memorable of his numerous practical jokes was played outside the front entrance of the department store Swan and Edgar, a popular meeting place. There was always a crowd of people waiting for their escorts to arrive. Sammy had managed to secure a cow's udder, which he had secreted down the front of his trousers. He joined the throng, and after a few minutes undid a couple of front buttons, to reveal the udder. When he knew that this had been noticed, he produced a pair of scissors, and cut the udder so that it fell to the ground. Imagine the scene: hysterical women, general pandemonium. I believe one or two fainted. In the general melee Sammy slipped away round the corner and entered the Piccadilly Hotel.

All kinds of composers put their hand to making arrangements, as this was the accepted way of earning some extra money. It was also the way most people heard things like the Beethoven symphonies and Verdi operas in the days before recording and broadcasting. I got to know De Groot's library very well indeed and had a lot of fun with it too. If I'm honest about the job, it was hardly the most absorbing work. After a short while, I could put the music together almost without thinking and make a balanced programme. We all had folders of suitable music from which I would choose the pieces according to the atmosphere in the room. Somehow, playing fast pieces when the restaurant seemed a little quiet never really worked.

We started at precise times, regardless of whether there was anyone in the restaurant. At lunch we played from one o'clock until two thirty and began again at seven for dinner, finishing at nine. Of course, we'd often start performing to an empty room; all the tables were set, the waiters ready, and not a guest in sight.

On one of these dull starts to an evening, we decided not to go into a selection of novelty pieces straight away. The empty room gave us a chance to get our teeth into a really big piece of music and I had the very thing in the Beethoven symphonies which I'd just found in the De Groot library. I'd put them in the folders to amuse the others.

We decided to play the first movement of the Fifth Symphony. We would each take an appropriate orchestral part and then play everything else we could remember from the music, such as the woodwind parts. Things soon got quite out of hand; it seemed fairly easy when we started off, but we didn't know the music as well as a player would know it today. In 1929 the Beethoven symphonies weren't played on the radio and in concert halls as often as they are now.

We had to concentrate very hard indeed to get through it and remember all the extra cues. We were staring at the notes like mad and sawing away at our instruments, completely absorbed until we finished the movement. Even though we were enjoying ourselves, it must have sounded pretty horrible to anyone else listening; I don't think the waiters enjoyed the joke very much.

At the end, there was great relief all round. We stopped, mopped our brows, had a breather—and realised that there was considerable applause coming from one corner of the room. It was more than applause, there was laughter too—from three people in evening dress who from a distance looked very familiar. I felt I ought to go and say something about why they had just been listening to this terrible noise, even though they were obviously enjoying the joke.

When I got close to them I was horrified to see that we'd been serenading the most famous piano trio of the day, the violinist Jacques Thibaud, the pianist Alfred Cortot and Pablo Casals the cellist. They were the top musicians of their time, wonderfully sensitive chamber music players—and I'd subjected them to this dreadful parody of Beethoven. But they had loved it; there were tears rolling down their faces and they had 'never heard a better performance!' I liked the exaggeration.

Cortot, Thibaud and Casals were taking an early dinner before going on to give a chamber recital, probably at the Queen's Hall at the top end of Regent Street. I never had to look at a newspaper to see which musicians were in town because most of them seemed to stay at the Piccadilly Hotel, and sooner or later all the great international concert artists would appear in the restaurant. I met Rachmaninov, the composer and pianist, and the whole

Rachmaninov family. He was a tall man of some six foot or so, his wife was a tall woman, also about six foot, and the two daughters were almost the same height. These four giants made a wonderful, stately sight as they walked into the room. Rachmaninov was well known for being a silent sort of chap. Artur Rubinstein on the other hand was charming and very outgoing. He'd always have some pleasant remark for people. The violinist Mischa Elman was another frequent guest; he had the most extraordinary technique, beautiful tone, and a bowing arm so smooth that the bow sounded as though it went on for ever—you couldn't hear it change direction. However, when he ate celery, he made more noise than anyone else I have ever come across. The trouble was that Elman wasn't a sophisticated violinist; he could play very crudely at times. But I liked him as a person. I felt an affinity with him because he too had started from humble beginnings and had made his own way to success.

The best advice anyone could ever hope to have on being a musician came my way at the Piccadilly Hotel. One day, to my consternation, I saw that the great Austrian violinist Fritz Kreisler was sitting very close to the little stage where we were playing—so close that there wasn't even the chance that distance might add a little bloom to our sound.

To many people, Kreisler is one of the supreme violinists; he is one of two players (the other being Heifetz) who tower head and shoulders above the rest in the history of the violin this century. His hallmark was the most wonderful sound imaginable. Many people have said: 'Oh, Kreisler used to play so out of tune . . .' I have a great number of Kreisler records which I've listened to often over the years. While it's true that there were times when he played out of tune, even on records, the sound he made was always glorious. It was easy and elegant—there was never any distortion. Even his out-of-tune notes were beautiful.

When I saw Kreisler sitting there, I thought my nerves would get the better of me at any moment. To be playing exactly the kind of music at which he was so brilliant was terrifying. Worse was to come, because after a while I saw him giving a note to a waiter, who brought it straight to me: 'Fritz Kreisler sends you his compliments and would like you to join him at his table!' Well, I thought I was going to be told some home truths about my playing—and as soon as I got to him I immediately apologised that such a great player as he was should have to listen to my efforts.

But he wouldn't have any of that. First of all, he was complimentary about my playing, but then said: 'Whenever you play, you must give a performance. Whatever you play, play it to the best of your ability. You must always give the music the best possible chance. Now, if it happens to be a piece of music that you don't particularly like, then you must give it an even better performance than you feel you might want to. Then, the music will always be enhanced and your playing will never suffer.'

I've always thought that was the most perfect piece of advice a young musician could be given. I have tried to follow it whenever I play. One should never go on to the concert platform and just play through the notes of familiar pieces of music that the audience will automatically like. In my mind I always hear Kreisler's advice and treat every melody I play as an important piece of music.

CHAPTER EIGHT

A More than Musical Education

It did us a power of good to know that at any moment we might be playing to some of the most famous musicians in the world; if Fritz Kreisler could be eating caviar about ten feet away, you made sure that you played properly. The Piccadilly Hotel was probably the best job I could have had as a student, and my teachers at the Guildhall definitely approved. It was a top date as far as playing was concerned and although we might not have been as fashionable as the hotels which featured great dance band leaders, the Piccadilly had a name for quality which was doing no harm to my reputation.

For Max Mossel, it was an ideal place to check up on my playing. The hotel happened to be his favourite lunch spot—and he'd often eat there with Sir Landon Ronald who was another regular. They could slip in unnoticed and listen to all the bad habits that had crept into my playing. Neither of them minded that I had a job outside the Guildhall as they were both well aware of the pressures on a music student in those days before the grant system. They knew that most of us had no choice, we had to earn money in our spare time in order to survive.

However, juggling studies with work made life complicated. Many young students couldn't cope with the demands of both and all too often opted out of their remaining studies to earn money. But the better one plays, the more one ought to understand about music; and as I became increasingly senior at the Guildhall, I was expected to take in orchestral playing, chamber music groups, sonata playing—all very important in a serious musician's education. As I've already said, Sir Landon Ronald also made me take conducting classes. As he

Playing during the Piccadilly Hotel period

pointed out, I was already leading an important salon orchestra, so who could predict where that would take me next?

The trouble was, it all left very little time to learn how to play the music properly. I have always learnt new pieces by practising them, working over the notes again and again, to get them into my fingers. That way, I felt that the music was truly under my skin—that I was living and breathing it. But with so many distractions there were often occasions when I flew into one of Max Mossel's lessons having barely looked at the music I was supposed to be studying. All I could do was to play through the piece with great panache and hope he wouldn't notice. But he always did. 'You sight-read very well . . .' he'd say. He noticed everything. However, he was wonderful about it; he never lost his temper, never made a scene. He must have had enough students distracted by the pressing need to earn some money.

We all knew, deep down, that we were the only ones to suffer if we didn't work properly—and it wasn't a pleasant feeling when it caught up with you. The Guildhall knew perfectly well that most students would succumb too easily to those temptations outside. So it was the rule that we each had to give a public recital every three months or so. We were expected to play a short programme of about forty minutes, playing from memory and treating the occasion as if performing in a concert hall. The audience was composed of students and teachers (all very critical). This system still exists today.

I was bound to get caught out sooner or later—it had to happen. One term, I was so busy that I found myself staring at my imminent recital date, knowing that I was nowhere near ready to play my pieces, let alone perform them from memory. The notes were barely in my fingers. This was dreadful. I was a scholar, and year after year the top playing prizes had come my way. Now, as a very senior student, I was about to shame myself in front of everyone! I must have spent hours trying to work out a way to get round the problem. It was my piano partner who, thank goodness, came up with the ideal plan to save the day. (She was the daughter of Mr Achille Serre, the owner of a chain of dry-cleaning establishments.)

Accompanists always play from music—this is an accepted concert tradition. She cleverly worked out that if she moved the score to the right-hand side of her music desk, I should be able to get a clear view of the notes over her right shoulder. The piano music always has the violin part printed with it, and luckily I was long-sighted enough to be able to see it at a distance.

After that, it was down to showmanship. The great performer had to act the part. I took up my position behind her and tried to look like a famous musician deeply concentrating on the playing, with my eyes shut, communing with the muses. Actually I was squinting furiously over my left shoulder, trying to see what was coming next.

Playing without the music makes all the difference to a performance; there's nothing to get in the way of the notes which should just flow out from you to the audience. When musicians peer at a music stand while they're playing, I often think they've forgotten there's an audience in front of them: an audience who have come to the concert to listen to a performance, not a read-through. Music can only 'speak' for me when it has become an integral part of me.

The Piccadilly's hours were ideal: I planned to get to the Guildhall first thing in the morning, to warm up properly before the day's work started. That meant either a violin lesson, chamber music, or a rehearsal. On Fridays, as I've said, we always had a full orchestral rehearsal. The lunchtime session at the Piccadilly left the afternoon clear for more study, rehearsals or practising. But all too often, I have to admit, there was dreadful temptation at the hotel to skip my own work. If the top fiddle players in the world made a point of staying there, it was difficult to resist sneaking upstairs to listen at the door while they were practising. Naturally, any idea of listening at the door was strictly forbidden by the management. Employees like me were not even allowed to go upstairs to the guests' part of the hotel; the rules said we were to keep to the public rooms downstairs.

The way musicians work should tell you a great deal about the way they understand the music and find a way around the difficult bits. If you listen very closely you can then appreciate all kinds of technical details: the fingerings they use, bowings and phrasing. I suppose it's rather like industrial espionage—you find out all their trade secrets. However, it's not as underhand as it sounds, for many musicians make a point of passing on their knowledge and the benefit of their experience. The great Czech teacher Ševčík made a complete book of studies out of the tricky passages in the Mendelssohn and other concertos, breaking them all up into eight-bar phrases and creating technical exercises around them.

It all became too much for me the day I found out not only that Kreisler was again staying in the hotel, but also that there was an empty room next to his, linked with his room by a connecting door. I begged one of the managers to let me go in there to listen secretly, promising not to make a sound and not to talk about it in the hotel.

It was the most extraordinary experience: Kreisler was playing so badly that I could not believe what I was hearing. He was in London to give a Queen's Hall recital in which he was playing Tartini's 'Devil's Trill' sonata. This is a fiendishly difficult piece, which got its name because the Devil is supposed to have appeared to Tartini in a dream, where he snatches his fiddle from him and plays this unplayable music.

Something fiendish was going on for Kreisler; he was not only playing out of tune, he couldn't even play the notes of the piece. He was fumbling, missing simple changes, doing dreadful things with the bow. It was so appalling and the piece was such a mess that I couldn't for the life of me see how he was to play it in public.

I couldn't wait to discuss it with Max Mossel. 'I expect,' he said, 'that Kreisler was practising how *not* to play it!' That sounded so absurd and so wonderful—but somehow Max Mossel was right. At the concert, Kreisler's playing was superb. Everything was in place, the fingers worked, the bow worked and his glorious sound was as perfect as ever.

Max Mossel was never interested in people blaming their failures on nerves or putting bad behaviour down to temperament. He would say: 'There's no such thing as temperamental; it's simply half temper and half mental.'

As we finished playing at the hotel a little before nine in the evening, there was usually plenty of time to catch the second half of concerts. The Queen's Hall was at the top of Regent Street and if I really hurried, I could arrive there just as the second half was about to begin. It was easier at Lyons because I could always swop times with people in the other orchestras, or do a double stint to get away early. Listening to other people play is an essential part of any music student's education—but I confess I was more interested in hearing violinists than other musicians. Occasionally Max Mossel would take me off to hear Sir Landon Ronald conduct the Queen's Hall Orchestra, but I made the most effort to hear Kreisler, Mischa Elman or of course my great hero Jascha Heifetz.

Funnily enough, the very first record I ever bought was of piano music: Chopin's *Fantaisie-Impromptu* played by Irene Scharrer. I heard her play it and simply had to have that music. But from then on it was always violinists; I certainly have every record that Heifetz made and some on the third or fourth copies. I've played them all so often they wear out.*

Meanwhile, the more I found out about the Piccadilly Hotel, the more I enjoyed myself there. It became much more to me than just a means of earning my living. In many ways it was my finishing school, or my university. In the musical line, the players with whom I worked were always teaching me something new; they were older than me, had seen everything and played every sort of music imaginable. They taught me what to do, how to work with them as a group, even how to play the music. Nothing worried or distracted them. They'd have gone on playing if the roof had fallen in.

My musical education was also helped by the waiters, as they were mostly Italian and loved their opera. They knew all the librettos, the arias and all the names of the great Italian opera singers, while I knew only the staple 'light' adaptations. Having decided that I was shamefully uneducated, they taught them all to me.

The waiters also turned their attention to my clothes. Since we worked in one of London's best hotels, there was an understanding

*Now my replacement problems are solved by the wonderful and everlasting CDs.

that we should look after our appearance. Some of the best dressed people in London paraded before us every day and you'd have had to be blind not to learn anything from the way they looked, how they carried themselves and the cut of their clothes. But there was an art in knowing what to look out for and at the start I needed guidance.

After sartorial elegance, there were further lessons in how to enjoy the finer pleasures of life. I'm sure my love of food started very young with my mother's and grandmother's traditional Jewish cooking. However, I had begun to branch out in my tastes when I went to the Corner House, but there was nothing to beat what I learnt from the people at the Piccadilly Hotel.

There was a Greek waiter whose only job was to wheel around a trolley which boasted a kilo tin of caviar and a side of smoked salmon. All he ever did was serve this to the guests; he never waited on tables. But most days, at two thirty when we'd finished playing, he would make me a special lunch which was always a couple of sandwiches, one of smoked salmon and the other of caviar. It was absolute heaven and a very expensive taste to acquire so young. I'm happy to say that I've never lost it—when I can afford it at today's prices!

It was easy to become more and more interested in food. I used to ask the waiters about the dishes they'd just served. I would study the menus before lunch and dinner and find out what all the French terms meant and how to tell the difference between various styles of cooking. The Piccadilly's restaurant was as famous as the hotel, and the chef was renowned for the best of classic French cuisine.

There was a style to it, which was all part of the showmanship of the place. Food was presented with great panache; flocks of waiters fluttered around the guests, serving plates, taking away plates, pouring wine, lighting cigarettes, etc. Just like a ballet! There were also great machines and trolleys from which spectacular dishes were created. For example, Canard Sauvage à la Presse used a duck press, a great chromium-plated dome with an enormous handle on top—rather like a large tap. You sometimes still see them in restaurants where they've ended up as part of the decor.

The duck would be lightly cooked so the flesh remained pink. The breast was then carved off and put into a pan to be finished with a knob of butter and a little brandy. The rest of the carcase went into the duck press; the handle was turned and the poor beast squeezed till all the juices ran out. These would be poured on the duck in the pan and then flambéed. Of course, it had to be wild duck (canard sauvage) which tastes quite different from the farm-fed variety—and it was absolutely delicious. Whenever I see one of these machines in a restaurant, I always ask the waiter for Canard Sauvage à la Presse. They usually look at me as though I'm talking rubbish, because as far as I know the machines are never used now.

It was the most extraordinary time for me. Everything I knew changed faster than you could think possible. All the old values of the family and Father and the Langham Street community became sadly irrelevant. As my own circumstances altered I found myself leaving my parents' world far behind. My father earned very little money, whereas for that first year's contract at the Piccadilly Hotel my salary was sixteen pounds a week, with two free meals a day if I wanted them. This made me quite a rich man.

Naturally, I began to grow up very fast indeed. It was tremendously exciting to be in this smart, fashionable, moneyed world—like finding yourself in a story or on an extravagant film set. It was a fantasy world where things happened that I could only have imagined before. Moreover, the further I was drawn into the music world, the greater were the possibilities to explore experiences that 'nice' boys like me could never have believed would come their way. After music, food, manners and clothes came sex. The Buenos Aires trip may have started me thinking, but the Piccadilly Hotel certainly provided the opportunities.

The musicians were served their meals along with the head waiters, in what was known as the couriers' room. Each orchestra had their own special table and one of the chaps warned me almost as soon as I arrived: 'There's a wonderful waitress who looks after us, she's away on holiday at the moment—but when she comes back you're in for a very pleasant surprise . . .' And indeed I was. She seemed much too young and too good-looking for the tricks she knew.

Not something I could easily cope with when it happened— which was all part of the fun for everyone else. We had all sat down for lunch, waiting to be served, when I suddenly felt a hand coming up between my legs in a more than familiar manner. It was extremely intimate. It was absolutely electrifying . . . and I just couldn't believe what was happening to me! She had been under the table waiting for us to sit down, when she would turn her attentions to whichever pair of legs she fancied the most to enjoy our discomfort. She had a great laugh doing it and so did everyone else. It was really more fun and games than naughty behaviour.

However, hotels don't have that seductive aura of assignations and affaires about them for nothing, and in the fashionable slang of the day, the Piccadilly was known as rather 'fast'. We used to call it a bit of a knocking shop—though naturally a very high-class one. Occasionally I'd go in for the afternoon session when the band were playing for a tea-dance and there would be the ladies of the night all out for the day, sitting drinking their cups of tea, dressed most beautifully and carrying their fox furs. They were wonderful, brilliant butterflies and later several became great friends. One of them even tried to take me under her wing; she was very grand and very particular about who she would have as her regular clients.

Being young and still somewhat innocent, I asked her how she'd got into this game and she told me her life story: 'Well, I could have been a maid, or I could have washed up dishes in a restaurant, but I have a young brother and sister and I wanted them to go to a decent school. Doing this I can send them to school and look after my father and mother too. And what the hell, I dress well!'

And they did. They all had their fine clothes, furs and hats—but they couldn't have supported themselves in that kind of finery in any other way except by getting married. And, as we tend to forget these days, so many young men died in the First World War that women had to fight really hard to find a husband. They also had to go out to work to support themselves—even society ladies knuckled down and started shops and businesses. People tried everything and perhaps the most famous businesswoman of all was Kate Meyrick, who took advantage of the way people wanted to have a good time. She opened a tremendously successful series of after-hours drinking clubs; she spent some time in jail, but made enough money to send her children to the best schools and it was said that each of her four daughters married into the peerage.

The Piccadilly ladies were very classy, with upper-crust clients. They were indeed great characters, teaching themselves to speak well, look good and behave impeccably. But practically all of them chose that way of life because they'd come from very poor, deprived families. Most of the ones I knew were London girls, although occasionally one would be the Marlene Dietrich type who spoke with a slightly foreign accent. They were all glamorous of course, and didn't have to walk the streets, but plied their trade in the top hotels.

However, they didn't use the hotel rooms; they all had flats of their own nearby where they took their clients. One of them often invited me round to her flat in Maida Vale—it was a gracious and elegant place and we would have tea and talk.

They had a strange code of behaviour, often offering me their favours. They might have taken a night off from 'business' if they'd done well during the day, or if a regular client cancelled. But I never accepted these favours. I hated calling them prostitutes, as I felt they deserved better.

Another group of Piccadilly habitués didn't care too much about how they behaved in public. These were the flat-racing jockeys, who used the Grill Room as their favourite meeting place. All through the winter, they would gather to gossip and eat at a long table set up just in front of the bandstand. They were 'resting' after the summer season, and came to the hotel to enjoy themselves. Frequently they'd be joined by some leading racing person—Sir Harry Preston who built Preston Park in Brighton was often to be seen mixing with the lads. They would eat like kings, drink like fishes and then troop off around the corner to the Turkish baths in Jermyn Street to sweat off their lunchtime indulgences. (During the season, of course, some jockeys didn't just diet, they 'starved'—or, as they say, 'wasted'—to get their weight down.)

There are various flat-racing seasons: in the southern hemisphere these start during our winter, but there's also a Swiss winter season, when fashionable resorts such as St Moritz have flat racing on the frozen lake. Years later, when I started taking winter holidays at St Moritz, I met a crowd of jockeys again and it was like going back thirty years. I used to joke that I had had the same kind of conversations with their grandfathers who introduced me to racing, now one of my favourite pastimes.

In the Grill Room, the jockeys couldn't have been better friends even though they were the deadliest of rivals on a race-course. I liked playing for them, and chatting to them at the end of our stint when they would sometimes give me tips and talk about 'form' and technical details about horses. But on broadcast days, they made us very nervous. Their language was appalling, littered with non-stop graphic four-letter words and worse, which were delivered at top volume. The orchestra always thought that the management put their table so close to us in the hope that our music would drown out some of the language before it reached the ears of the other patrons.

There would have been dreadful repercussions if the jockeys' table was left where it normally was on a broadcast day. The BBC always put their microphone directly above it and listeners would have been shocked by what they heard. So the jockeys were banished to the far end of the room—where they carried on in their normal way, at exactly the same volume, even though we were on the air. I often wondered how much of their talk was broadcast.

It was most important to broadcast 'from' a recognisable place, and make the audience at home feel that they were there too. Broadcasts encouraged people to come along and be part of the show. The band leader Ambrose remembered that after five and a half years of regular Saturday night broadcasts from the Mayfair Hotel, people came from all over the country specially for a grand night out 'live on air'. But when that happened, high society patrons no longer felt it was their kind of place and went elsewhere.

CHAPTER NINE

The Scottish Orchestra

All good things have to come to an end, and by the summer of 1931 it was time to think ahead and to decide what I was going to do when I left the Guildhall. I was nineteen and had a year left to choose a job that would be interesting and appropriate to the kind of musician I had become.

My records at the Guildhall show that I'd had quite an impressive career; I'd kept my scholarship all through and also won every single prize there was for violin students. You weren't allowed to compete again for the same prize once you had won it, so I must have gone through the list, picking them off one at a time! It was the kudos that mattered more than the money; most prizes brought you about five pounds but the Lord Mayor's prize, a violin bow, was really useful, particularly as the winner was allowed to choose the bow at Hill's in Bond Street. This had lasting value, because I'm sure most of us spent our prize money in ways that had nothing to do with music!

Sir Landon Ronald had kept an eye on me during my last two years. I was totally bereft after the death of Max Mossel and felt my world had come to an end with the loss of my only true mentor. My new professor, Louis Pecskai, was also a distinguished teacher but his approach wasn't the same. There wasn't that fine attention to detail, and he didn't know when I was only scraping the surface. In fact, he never probed my technique at all: 'Let's just concentrate on the repertoire,' he would say, which was a marvellous invitation to sight-read my way through every lesson.

Sir Landon, however, was more eagle-eyed. As Principal it wasn't his business to become too directly involved with the students, but as he and Mossel had been close colleagues, he already knew a

103

good deal about me. I think he also cared about what would happen to me. He always said that the school couldn't just train people to play, act or sing and then throw them out into the profession to find their own way. Sir Landon kept abreast of what was going on in the music business. As one of the country's leading conductors he was well placed to help all the instrumentalists end up in the right jobs.

I'm sure he knew that financially it was out of the question for me to make a solo concert career, as by this time I was supporting both my studies and my family, and they would have been in dreadful difficulties without the extra funds I brought home. That made quite a problem for my future; I'm sure that Sir Landon didn't want one of his better students to end up playing only in a salon orchestra — yet that was nearly all I knew of the music business.

Sir Landon had a good idea of what I could do, since I'd been playing right in front of him for some years on the first desks of the Guildhall Orchestra which he conducted every Friday. At the 1930 May Jubilee Concert at the Queen's Hall Sidney Bowman was leader and I led the second violins. The following term I took over when he left for Glasgow to lead the Scottish Orchestra.

At the time, without knowing it, I was being watched and assessed and singled out for promotion. At the start of my final year it was lovely and rather moving to find that I'd come out of this strange education with the top prize of all. At the Students' Annual Concert at the end of October 1931, I played Kreisler's 'Tambourin Chinois' (fellow students on stage included the soprano Gwen Catley and Churchill's daughter Diana doing a recitation), and collected the Guildhall School of Music's Gold Medal.

However, the prize I treasured most was the Principal's Prize. This was a measure of Sir Landon Ronald's own opinion and no one ever knew who was going to get it before he made the announcement. You couldn't compete or lobby for it and he didn't always give it; there were several years when he said publicly that none of the current batch of students came up to his required standards. The citation made me proud: 'Awarded to a Student considered by the Principal most likely to distinguish himself or herself in the Musical Profession.'

We all knew that the prize itself was a copy of Grove's *Dictionary of Music and Musicians*, the musician's bible, containing all the information on music that anyone could possibly want. I kept mine for years and years, until it was stolen the day our house was

The Scottish Orchestra

PROGRAMME.

SONGS ... ... (a) "At the Mid Hour of Night" }
(b) "Border Ballad" } ... ... *Frederic Cowen.*

CHARLES MAYHEW.

A Sam Heilbut (Major) Scholar. A Sir Frederic Painter Prize; The Bearne Prize;
The Sir Charles Wyndham Prize; The Knill Challenge Cup, 1931. Pupil of
Mr. Walter Hyde, Sir Frederic Cowen, and Miss Jenny Hyman.

SONGS ... ... (a) "Silent Noon" ... ... *Vaughan Williams.*
(b) "Spring is at the door" ... ... *Roger Quilter.*

MARIE FISHER, A.G.S.M.

A Corporation Scholar. The Sheriff's Contralto Prize, 1924; A Special School Prize, 1925;
The School Contralto Prize and The Max Hecht Prize (divided), 1926; The Elkan Prize
(divided) and The G.S.M. Gold Medal, 1927; The Associateship (Gold Medal), 1928;
The Musical Union Prize (divided), 1929. Pupil of Mr. Bantock Pierpoint and
Miss Jenny Hyman.

VIOLIN SOLO ... ... Tambourine Chinois ... ... *Kreisler.*

MAX JAFFE.

The Gibson Memorial Prize and The Urch Prize, 1928; The Katharine Wattson Memorial
Prize, 1929; The Lord Mayor's Prize, 1930; The G.S.M. Gold Medal, 1931.
Pupil of Mr. Louis Pecskai.

RECITATION ... ... "The Biscuit" ... ... *H. M. Gordon.*

DIANA CHURCHILL.

A Corporation Scholar. The School Elocution Silver Medal, 1931. Pupil of Miss Kate Rorke.

QUARTETTE ... ... "A Regular Royal Queen" ... ... *Sullivan.*
(from "The Gondoliers")

GWEN CATLEY.   MARIE FISHER.

A Corporation Scholar. The Liza Lehmann
Prize, 1927; The Lord Mayor's Prize, 1928;
a Sir Frederic Painter Prize and The Pearse
Morrison Memorial Prize, 1929. Pupil of
Mr. Walter Hyde and Miss Jenny Hyman.

MARTIN BODDEY.   NORMAN MEADMORE.

A Sam Heilbut (Major) Scholar. The Alfred
and Catherine Howard Prize, 1930; a Sir
Frederic Painter Prize, The Rudyard Kipling
Prize, and The Dove Memorial Prize, 1931.
Pupil of Mr. Walter Hyde.

A Sam Heilbut (Minor) Scholar. The Bearne
Prize, 1930; The Fitzherbert Lord Prize, 1931.
Pupil of Mr. Walter Hyde.

Accompanist - - - - - - JENNY HYMAN, F.G.S.M.
(Professor.)

Concert Grand Pianoforte kindly lent by the Chappell Piano Co., Ltd.

The programme for my final students' concert at the Guildhall (they misspelt my name!)

burgled. I think I was more upset about losing that than anything else. It always reminded me of the doors Sir Landon kept opening for me, and the help he gave me throughout my student days.

Sir Landon had put me well on the road to success by the time I left the tender care of the Guildhall. However, notwithstanding all my playing at the Piccadilly Hotel, I knew practically nothing about

105

the world of serious music. At this point a wonderful opportunity beckoned from Glasgow. Away from home, the hotel and the distractions of London, I would be able to concentrate on making music among seasoned players and with internationally famous conductors. I certainly needed total immersion in serious orchestral playing in order to decide which path to take in my career.

In September 1931, the Scottish Orchestra announced their forthcoming winter season, with a new leader. As the programme book reported, Sidney Bowman, my predecessor from the Guildhall, hadn't lasted long. 'Mr Bowman having intimated that he will not be available for re-engagement as Principal First Violin, Mr Max Jaffa has been engaged in his place. Mr Jaffa comes with the very highest recommendation.'

That can only have been from Sir Landon, so he obviously believed I could do the job. Nevertheless, he was thoughtful enough to hedge his bets and negotiated a leave of absence for me from the Piccadilly Hotel, so I had a job to come back to at the end of the season to carry me through the last weeks at the Guildhall. Whichever way I looked at it, there could be no argument. So I packed my bags and left for Glasgow.

A week after that prize-filled concert at the Guildhall, I played my first concert with the Scottish. My contract ran from November 7th 1931 until February 6th 1932. However, nothing was really resolved and the pull from the lighter side of music was still strong, even on the very morning that I took the train to Scotland. I had just been to the Abbey Road Studios of HMV, to make my first ever gramophone record: playing the solo violin on 'Gypsy Idyll' with Constantine Vladescu, a Romanian cimbalom player, and his gypsy orchestra. He'd heard me play something gypsy at the Piccadilly Hotel and had more or less fixed the session on the spot. There was one rehearsal, and I arrived at the studio with my suitcases packed, ready to rush off to the station by taxi. We were recording only two tunes—one on each side of a 78—so it didn't take long. They were still ringing in my ears as I got on the train to Glasgow, my mind full of the experience for the whole journey. It seemed such an easy thing to do; I wasn't at all intimidated by the microphones or the techniques, we just set up and played until everyone was satisfied.

The recording business was nothing like as technical or as perfectionist as it is today. The public wanted a steady stream of music and the record companies were always looking for something new to bring out, and to bring out quickly. They wanted popular favourites and things that were new and different. The dance bands recorded non-stop, because of their radio popularity—but Mr Vladescu no doubt added the exotic element for the week.

My arrival at the Scottish Orchestra took me into another world. In that very first concert, the programme included Dvořák's *Carnival* Overture, Debussy's *Prélude à 'L'Après-midi d'un Faune'*, a Strauss overture, a Haydn symphony and Mussorgsky's *Night on the Bare Mountain*.

The concerts we played were given by the Choral and Orchestral Union of Glasgow. This was an institution founded in 1898 to support the Scottish Orchestra and the Glasgow Choral Union; so the season boasted a good mix of choral and orchestral pieces, liberally sprinkled with soloists. The 1931 season promised six conductors whom I'd never met before: Basil Cameron who was Scottish, and Constant Lambert, a young Turk of British music, who'd been 'discovered' by Diaghilev when he was still only twenty. He was to be very rude about the English musical establishment in his book *Music Ho!* which he wrote in 1934. But his most famous composition, *The Rio Grande*, was a great favourite with concert audiences who loved the jazz and Latin American rhythms.

There were four distinguished foreigners: Robert Heger, well known in the Vienna, Berlin and Covent Garden opera houses; a Dutchman, Albert Van Raalte; Issai Dobrowen, who had left Russia and worked mainly in Germany and America; and the unnerving Nicolai Malko who had trained under Rimsky-Korsakov in St Petersburg. Malko had the most phenomenal powers of concentration. I once sat opposite him on the train from Glasgow to Edinburgh where we were going to give a concert. By the time we arrived he'd memorised a complete score of music that he had never seen before—a last-minute change to the programme. I'm almost sure it was Vaughan Williams' overture to *The Wasps*. He more or less went straight from the train to conduct the piece at the concert, without rehearsal, and from memory—amazing!

Looking at the programmes now, I'm astonished at the wide range of music we played in that short season: promised highlights included Beethoven's Choral Symphony, Elgar's Second Symphony, Mjaskovsky's Fifth, Sibelius' First, Bruckner's *Te Deum* and Handel's *Semele*.

As for soloists, I was very proud to be playing with some of my

107

musical heroes. Artur Rubinstein played a Tchaikovsky concerto and brought his own piano stool with him, insisting that he couldn't play the piano without it! The cellist Antoni Sala played two concertos in the same programme; people often did that, but one of his pieces was Strauss's *Don Quixote*. Most players think that enough for one evening, but he also gave us a Haydn concerto. I was fascinated by two very distinguished violinists, Zoltan Szekely and Joseph Szigeti, both of them Hungarians, and intrigued by their approach to playing the violin since they came from a completely different tradition from my heroes of Leopold Auer's Russian school. They weren't interested in violin fireworks and playing for its own sake—it was the music which always came first.

I was twice booked to play a solo. The first came just before Christmas, with Warwick Braithwaite conducting, when I played the solo violin in Mozart's Serenade in D (K.203) in a programme of Gluck, Elgar, Bach and Berlioz. Then at the end of January, there was Bach's Brandenburg Concerto No. 5, conducted by Issai Dobrowen, with no less than Professor Donald Tovey of Edinburgh University playing the solo piano.

Tovey educated generations of musicians with his detailed musical analysis of the major pieces in the classical repertoire. He was probably the most serious musician in the country and yet his behaviour in the Green Room just before we went out to play was quite extraordinary. He strode up and down, spouting Bach all the time, humming, singing, tapping out the rhythms. He was quite the loveliest of lunatics I've ever worked with and there was no problem playing solo violin with him.

I also made my own symphonic conducting debut and had much to thank Sir Landon Ronald for his training in those conducting classes. Naturally the occasion was nothing so grand as a public concert. I was let loose on the orchestra for what I suspect was an unwilling audience of schoolchildren dragooned in for what used to be called 'musical appreciation'. I wonder whether my efforts got through at all—so many others failed at it!

The Scottish Orchestra worked quite hard; we played some twenty-eight concerts in the twelve weeks that I was with them and not only in Glasgow. We also went to Edinburgh every week and out to Stirling, Perth and Dundee too. The programmes were full of music which was new to me, like the *Don Quixote* variations, and Strauss was never an easy composer to play. In the same concert, conducted by Malko, there was Stravinsky's *Firebird* suite, still a very modern piece of music to many ears even though it was first performed back in 1910.

But the worst experience of all, and there's been nothing to beat it since in all my playing experience, was that first meeting with the orchestra. A cold shock hit me when I faced these hardened professional players and felt their hostility towards a young unknown upstart. There was a deathly hush when I walked in to the rehearsal, and the hush grew even more hostile (if a hush can do that) when I sat down next to David McCallum, the sub-principal violin. I didn't know anything about him—no one did outside his native Scotland and the Scottish Orchestra; but I soon discovered he was a wonderful violin player and had already proved himself a fine orchestral leader. And yet over his head they'd been sent this raw kid from London who not only wasn't a Scot—and that was enough cause for resentment—but was also a Jew.

It was very difficult to know what to do. For four whole days McCallum said not one word; he didn't even acknowledge me, let alone greet me. Mind you, he turned over the pages beautifully and did everything right by the music and for the conductor. After all, he was a professional. On the fourth day of this endless silence—by which time various members of the orchestra had decided that I was all right and had begun to talk to me—I turned to him and said: 'Is there something the matter? Do I smell?' or words to that effect. 'Are you never going to say hello?' To which he replied, in a very broad Scottish accent: 'I'm finding out whether you can play the fiddle or not.' I was a bit taken aback; there was a pause, a pregnant silence, and he growled: '. . . You can play.'

That meant we could both relax and work together. We became very good friends once the ice was broken. And Scottish ice is something to break, rather more difficult than breaking a haggis! (And I do like haggis—especially when we have it stuffed inside our Christmas turkey. Delicious!)

As an experience, the Scottish Orchestra widened my horizons; it was really my musical finishing school, a serious and different world from the student fun at the Guildhall. And yet I enjoyed myself far more with silly little things. For a while, tram travel gave me the best pleasure, whatever the line I took, the blue car or the yellow or green. Fares were very cheap, a round trip of twenty-six and a half miles for a penny ha'penny. It had nothing to do with sightseeing although I gave myself a terrible thrill from what I could see. Inside the tram, all round the top of the wall, were lots of advertisements: 'Zam Buk will remove that ugly bump', 'Glaxo builds bonny babies', and the slogan that made my heart beat faster: 'Scottish Orchestra, Leader Max Jaffa'. I'd never seen my name advertised in print in a public place, and I used to go on those long rides just to sit and look at this amazing legend: 'Leader Max Jaffa'. I felt like poking my fellow passengers in the ribs and saying: 'Do you know who you're sitting next to?'

That sense of achievement helped me to get through the horrible start to the Scottish experience. But once everyone relaxed and I felt welcome, it became boring reading about Max Jaffa and I took up golf instead. I was staying with an old friend of my mother's, Millie Behar, whose family owned a carpet shop in Sauchiehall Street and they were all mad keen golfers.

Soon I became serious about the game and went down to Lumleys in Sauchiehall Street to learn the secrets of playing well from Mark Seymour, the Scottish Open Champion, who was advertised as giving lessons in the store. I had a pair of plus-fours made and within a few weeks was playing to a handicap of twelve. Naturally the orchestra approved heartily that I was obsessed with a Scottish game and I found myself with plenty of partners. They took their golf as seriously as they took their music; and when I left them, my farewell present was a beautiful set of clubs.

Sadly, once I was back in the whirl of London's music, it became too difficult to get out of town to play and the set of clubs disappeared during the upheavals in the war. But I took the game up again in the sixties when I got to Scarborough, where it became a favourite form of exercise. I never got back to my handicap but enjoyed golf in the fresh air — particularly approaching the nineteenth.

The Scottish experience was an interesting experiment—but I didn't want to go on with it. The season there lasted only a few months and once it stopped, there was really nothing to do in Glasgow musically speaking. The hotels and clubs already had their own full-time players and there wasn't any work in recording. So everyone packed up and left town for summer jobs at resorts and spas all around the country. About half of the Scottish Orchestra players in fact went down to the Spa at Scarborough, so it's rather pleasing that I eventually ended up there too; and also found myself engaging young players whose grandparents had once played in the Scottish Orchestra with me. Talk about wheels coming full circle!

But it wasn't just Glasgow—I felt this symphonic life was not for me. Even if I pursued it in London it wouldn't have the fun and high spirits I was used to, and certainly not the excitement and glamour. So I thanked the Scottish Orchestra's management and gave notice that I wouldn't be returning for the next season. I also pointed out that there was no need for them to go around the country looking for a leader to replace me. They had their man in David McCallum, a first-class leader already sitting in the front desk. David took over from me, and became one of the longest serving leaders in British music. He was a marvellous player and justifiably well respected.

I packed my bags again, said my farewells and went back to London and the Piccadilly Hotel to see how the world had changed while I had been away. After all, there was a contract waiting for me and I was honour bound to go back to it.

In 1934 I had another opportunity to gain experience north of the border. I was asked to join a concert tour with Joseph Hislop, at that time Scotland's most famous tenor, known as 'The Scottish Caruso'. He was celebrating his fiftieth year and I think he must have been winding down on the opera stage and had decided to remind the folks back home that he was still a voice to be reckoned with in concert. There were some thirteen stops. We started with a week of concerts just north of the border, then travelled up to the Highlands for another five before finishing in Edinburgh at the end of the month.

I was probably invited on two counts: the first was obvious— 'Late Leader Scottish Symphony Orchestra', as they described me in the advertisements—but the second could have been the Guildhall connection. Hislop taught singing there, and must have been told what kind of a person I was. Singers were notoriously particular about who they were seen and heard with: you had to be good, so that your performance enhanced theirs—but not so good that theirs was eclipsed!

In those days, no singer would take on a concert tour by themselves; people expected variety on a night out. They certainly got it with Hislop's programme, which was a clever piece of dramatic planning! The evening started, quite soberly, with pianist Alfred Roth playing some Chopin, which was followed by an operatic aria or two from Verdi's *La Traviata* sung by the guest singer, Marie

Gluck, 'Soprano, from the Italian Opera Houses' as her billing went. Then it was the turn of Max Jaffa to play the slow movement and finale of the Mendelssohn Violin Concerto.

Now the last movement does whip up the tempo—and of course it raised expectations for the star of the evening, who then came on to sing a group of arias ranging from Handel to Verdi, including several of the favourites. For his second group, Hislop pulled out all the Scottish stops with songs like 'Bonnie George Campbell' and 'My Love She's But a Lassie Yet'. But there was more to come: for the climax of the evening he brought back Marie Gluck, and they performed the end of Act One of Puccini's *La Bohème*—from 'Your Tiny Hand is Frozen', right through to the passionate duet which the lovers-to-be sing as they walk off stage . . . Hislop proudly informed everyone that Puccini himself had told him he was the best Rodolfo he had ever heard.

But I fear that the message in that duet wasn't received quite correctly. At least, Marie Gluck never confused Hislop's warm stage presence with any off-stage possibilities—much to the poor man's chagrin. On the other hand, I was having a very pleasant time with her indeed!

We'd become firm friends almost the instant we met at the start of the tour, and got to know each other very well during the three

On tour with Joseph Hislop. Marie Gluck is standing between Hislop and myself

weeks or so it lasted. We travelled by car, in a vast machine which easily accommodated the four of us, our luggage and Hislop's manager, Captain Illingworth—so we had to be on our best behaviour in public during the day, when we were together all the time. But once we'd found our hotel for the night, it was quite another matter . . .

Marie Gluck obviously felt that as the baby of the party, I needed to be taken under her wing. Anyway, I was more than a little surprised a couple of nights into the tour, when there was a knock at my bedroom door, and in she came to see how I was getting on. I was amazed: we'd hardly met beyond the rather formal pleasantries in rehearsing and travelling together; yet here she was, in my bedroom, and, as I soon found out, wearing very little under her wrap. Her breasts were an extraordinary and a glorious shock to me—I hadn't imagined that women could be so wonderfully endowed!

As far as I was concerned, her care was magnificent—and I don't think I ever learnt so much in such a short time! But I'm not sure that our happiness added much to Hislop's pleasure. After the tour I lost touch with him for a long time—he had a Swedish wife, and disappeared for years to teach in Stockholm. But as so often happens, we did meet again in a London restaurant some time in the late sixties. I was with my wife Jean and he was with a very dramatic-looking lady, to whom we were introduced. She was Birgit Nilsson, the greatest Wagnerian soprano of her day. Jean was absolutely thrilled to meet her—but I have to say, I wondered a little whether she'd ever done a Hislop concert tour.

CHAPTER TEN

The Family Style

The months with the Scottish Orchestra made up my mind about which way I was going to earn my living. I was grateful for the engagement but came back to London without any wish to repeat it—or to go any further down that particular path.

In 1932 London offered more opportunities for orchestral players than ever before. There was the new BBC Symphony Orchestra, then two years old, with a large and hand-picked band of the best players in the country who were fully employed all year round on a regular salary: that was a new and welcome approach to employment and the kind of job contract that no other orchestra could match. Even so, the word was about that Sir Thomas Beecham was out to rival the standards of the BBC orchestra with his own London Philharmonic, and he spent the year collecting together his own fine band of players.

Obviously both orchestras had their attractions. The excitement of working with great conductors and top soloists, of playing the very best symphonic music, of travelling and giving concerts abroad was very tempting. And yet, there was a very definite minus as far as I was concerned; if I was to work as an orchestral player, even as the leader, I would no longer be my own boss.

That was the key factor which sent me back to the Piccadilly Hotel, even though it was a small world and one that I probably knew far too well for my own good. Nevertheless, I could do what I wanted with my group of players, just so long as the patrons were happy and kept coming back to the Grill Room to spend their evenings out on the town. The only time anyone ever looked over my shoulder was when I sent my programmes in to the BBC for our weekly broadcast, and that hardly cramped my style.

Above all, of course, it was a job that was actually waiting for me, with a very high income for a young man just into his twenties. No one would turn down that kind of a job lightly in 1932. There was the most terrible unemployment throughout the country, and every day we heard stories of dreadful hardship for people who had once had valued skills and good jobs. In the music business, hard times had come some years earlier for those people who worked in the silent cinema, who hadn't seen the change coming with the talkies, and didn't get into other work soon enough. And yet (and it's hard to believe), the times were also very good for some musicians, the lucky ones who kept up with a changing profession. I sometimes marvel at my luck. I always seemed to find myself in the right place at the right time—and with work which gave me the chance to enjoy life as well.

In the high society world of the Piccadilly Hotel, we hardly noticed what was going on outside; it was business as usual, with fine food, fine clothes and an air of elegant enjoyment. Perhaps one or two of the regulars quietly disappeared from the social scene, perhaps others cut back on going out so often, but there was no wholesale decline in the numbers of guests coming to the hotel every day. Of course we knew that when times are bad, people want to escape from reality: they danced away their cares in the First World War, through the years of the Depression—even the dangers of the Blitz couldn't stop them. So long as that feeling remained, musicians were happy to play.

However, luck wasn't all, and Sir Landon Ronald was absolutely right about musicians; there was more to success than just playing your instrument well. In my musical world, it was just as important to get on with the group, to be part of the team—part of the band. If you were temperamental, behaved badly or turned up to play half cut with drink, then you were a liability. You might mess up the job for everyone. What people liked was to see someone who worked with a smile, a sense of humour, a way of shrugging off the bad moments.

Now that also happened to be the cornerstone of Mother's view of life: she taught us all to be polite and considerate and to have a sense of humour, however difficult the circumstances. If Father went overboard with his temper, Mother calmed us all down with her advice and counsel. She knew that we'd have to get on with people in order to get on in life. For me she was the model influence, the centre of reason; Father was just too volatile, too unstable—and ultimately, too unreliable. Furthermore, he was a disaster when it came to money and finding the means to keep the family going. Father always thought he was on to some new business deal or other, but somehow only became an expert at getting himself into debt.

At heart he was really the great romantic. He idolised my mother, he would do anything for her, wanted everything for her—and that often caused the trouble. He'd dream of giving her lovely presents and things that would make her life more comfortable. Then he'd fall behind on the payments and that would be that. The truth was that she actually controlled the purse strings, otherwise we would have been in dreadful trouble.

As soon as I started to earn a decent wage at the Piccadilly Hotel, I was able to change life for Mother. It was easy to give her a regular supply of money: I simply split my weekly earnings with her, half and half. But I wanted to do more than that for her. The house in Langham Street was too crowded, the area too noisy and dirty, and we all knew that out in her favourite area, Cricklewood, there were houses for sale which were both comfortable and pleasant. There were trees in the streets and the open spaces of Gladstone Park were only a short walk away. We looked at houses which were light and had enough room for each of us—with four bedrooms, sitting rooms and, particularly, a bathroom. Mother and I could even have the dogs we both wanted. Above all, Cricklewood was such a respectable Jewish area that the community even called it Cricklevitch!

Naturally most people want to better themselves. In our community, people struggled to move out from their rather difficult living conditions in the inner city. The East End people moved out to Stamford Hill, but our neighbourhood chose Cricklewood or Golders Green. It was a natural progression, a well deserved reward for hard work. It was also expected that people showed the world the measure of their success.

Life was certainly treating me well. In 1929 my starting salary at the Piccadilly had been fifteen pounds a week, going up by degrees to twenty pounds, with extras from the occasional bank notes sent across with special requests and of course that weekly thank-you from publishers for playing their tunes on the BBC. The total was a considerable amount of money for the start of the thirties and the years of the Great Depression—actually it was a fortune, considering that many people were in dreadful poverty and literally starving. We sometimes forget that life was so bad that in 1932 people took to the streets to protest, walking many miles in the National Hunger March. But it's rather dreadful to look back and realise that very little of the horror of that time ever came close to the dining and dancing world of the hotel. The stock market may have crashed, people may have lost what they thought were their fortunes—but there were still those with money enough to spend on having a good time.

Nevertheless, after the great stock market crash in 1929, there was considerable talk in the couriers' room about the best way to look after one's savings. It was the first time I heard the word 'mortgage' and several people urged me to consider putting a bit of my earnings into buying a house. It would hardly cost any more than the weekly rent at Langham Street, they said—and it would still leave enough over to support the family and to enjoy life. Nowadays, it might seem a great responsibility to take on; there are not many eighteen-year-olds who bring in a large proportion of the money to support their family. In those days, in 1929 or 1930, youngsters were expected to do their bit to help as much as they could. I was very pleased that at last I had some status in the house, that I was my father's equal.

It was a marvellous adventure when we actually bought the house. Mother and I took the bus up the Edgware Road to see the estate agents Dutch and Dutch (who are still the top firm in Cricklewood) and we signed the papers for No. 2 Ivy Road, an Edwardian terrace house just off the Cricklewood Broadway, for the enormous sum of eleven hundred pounds. In 1930, Cricklewood was definitely a neighbourhood in demand!

Ivy Road was a quiet street which ran right down to the park; our house was at the end of a terrace with a small patch of garden in front and a bigger spread behind. It wasn't a vast space, but there was more sky visible than we'd ever seen at the Langham Street house. Father didn't have anything to do with this development, which was all dreamt up between Mother and me. Life carried on exactly as usual for him: of course he moved out with us, but he still had his business in Middleton Buildings, off Langham Street, he still had his circle of friends, and he wasn't really interested in looking for anything new.

However, the rest of us found ourselves liberated by the move. The local community worked hard to welcome newcomers and the synagogue in Walm Lane was the focus of an active social life. This was mainly organised by the Syder family, the oldest family in the community and people of consequence; they seemed to be behind most of the parties and gatherings in the area and I soon made friends with their daughter Gertrude. We played tennis together and suddenly there were invitations and social functions, parties and dances, and I was expected to go whenever I wasn't working at the hotel.

Life was very different from the closed world we'd been used to in town. As I was coming up to my twentieth birthday and my sister Anne was a very pretty and vivacious teenager, I suspect a good deal of this activity was designed to lead up to romance and good Jewish marriages! For my young brother David, the change was marvellous: his school was just down the road, he had a green park only yards away and plenty of new friends. I think that park was the best part of Cricklewood—I used to walk my dog there every day.

The dogs were important additions to our family. Both Mother and I had longed to have a dog but we couldn't come to any agreement on whether we should have a big one (which was what I wanted), or a little one. In the end we bought two. In Cricklewood that was no problem since there was masses of space for them both to have as much exercise as they needed. Karl, the Alsatian, was a special character and we became the greatest of friends. I probably spent more time with him than with anyone else. He was always there for me, waiting for a walk, waiting to play.

Karl and my mother's dog Pat—a highly improbable cross between a whippet and an Irish terrier—had an endless routine at feeding time. They were fed at opposite ends of the garden because Pat, being a little dog, was given only a small amount to eat compared to Karl. But that small amount also went down rather more quickly than Karl's food and Pat would then rush off to his dish, to sneak a second helping. Karl would pick him up by the scruff of his neck, carry him back to his own plate and his own corner and go back patiently to his waiting dinner. But it would be only a matter of moments before Pat was back again, pushing Karl out of his own dish. And again he would be carried back to his place. So the routine would go on until Karl had swallowed his last hard-won mouthful. He was such a good-natured dog, never losing his temper, never snapping. The new house was a source of great pleasure: I loved sitting out in the garden on a sunny day, while Mother would plant flowers and look after the lawn. Mother became the best girl in my life—I thought she was wonderful, with a lovely character and great natural beauty. It's only now, while thinking about her as I remember those early years, that I realise I must almost have been in love with her. As she was only eighteen when I was born, she was so young as I grew up that we became very close. I loved to be seen with her. She wasn't very tall, but she had a good rounded figure and a beautiful face with very fair hair, almost blonde.

She was a highly moral person with a strong sense of what was right and proper and how a gentleman ought to treat people. But she must also have been a very understanding woman because there were occasions when I certainly tried her patience. I remember when I was about thirteen, I somehow got hold of a condom (it must have been one of those dares which wind schoolboys up into a ferment and I half remember working up the courage to go into a barber's shop to ask for one). Of course, I was delighted to have this object, to know what it was for and to feel that it was all very secret; but I was also desperately worried about where to put the thing, to hide it safely until the day it was supposed to be produced at school to prove to everyone that I'd done the deed. For some extraordinary reason, I decided that under my pillow was the best place. Of course Mother found it!

That evening, when I got home from school, there was a terrible confrontation. I'd hardly walked through the door when she grabbed my arm and propelled me into the kitchen, white with indignation and waving this dreadful object in my face. Funnily enough, she wasn't concerned about what I might be doing with a condom, what kind of a secret life I might be leading with girls—it was the object itself which roused her fury. She was adamant; never again was I to have anything to do with such a thing (which shows how times have changed today!).

There was nothing I could say or do to calm her. She even threatened to tell my father, which she knew would be an absolute torment to me. I can still hear myself pleading with her not to, desperately trying to think of a way in which we could come to some arrangement to avoid my being punished by him. The threat of Father was obviously a very effective way of keeping us all in check. However, I now wonder how Mother would have known what a condom was, because she didn't seem to be very communicative about sex—we had certainly never had a conversation about it.

The only other time I ever saw Mother cross was when we played cards together; we often did this, and there were several two-handed games that we enjoyed. She could get very worked up if she was losing a game and thought I was cheating or pulling a fast one on her. She even went so far as to swear — the first time I ever heard her use a word like 'bloody' was when we were playing cards. Then she'd throw down her hand and refuse to have anything more to do with the game. Since she was usually so mild-tempered it was sometimes fun to egg her on to see how far she would go.

That was really unfair, since she was a very gentle woman, the complete opposite of my father. Her whole life was taken up with looking after the family and producing good meals for us at the right time. If I have a mental picture of her, it's seeing her shopping for food and cooking. The centre of her life was Father; she was devoted to him. Meals were never a question of: '*We're* going to have such-and-such for dinner', instead she'd say: 'Tonight we're going to have something your father likes to eat.' She always cooked for him.

But meals were never peaceful, unless they were at my grandparents'. Father and I always quarrelled at table. Anything would start it off, any opinion that I might have that was different from the one he held would be a good enough excuse for an argument. The rest of the family sat silent, staring at their plates; Mother would never join in, nor would she try to stop us.

We didn't talk much about serious matters. She wasn't particularly interested in what I was doing at school or what I got up to with my friends; even the music wasn't that important to her. Mother's world was the family, the house and our close relations, and she expected us all to value that kind of relationship. She seemed happy to leave the musical business to Father who appeared to be quite proud of what I was doing — and especially proud of what I was earning.

However, I didn't discuss my musical life with him either: what was important to both of them was that I was successful. When I was working for Lyons at the Corner Houses, the two of them sometimes came to hear me play; they'd make an outing of it and sit at the back somewhere having their cup of tea. They wouldn't tell me they were coming beforehand, but I always felt very pleased when I looked around during a piece and saw them. Sadly, they stopped these visits when I worked at the 'Troc' and they never came to hear me play at the Piccadilly, though Mother listened to the weekly broadcasts. And so, while it was satisfying to be able to show that I'd made a success of things, was a responsible son and played my part in supporting the family, I soon realised that I'd have to work out my life for myself, on my own terms.

My struggle for independence also became embarrassing because Mother wanted to show me that she understood what I was doing. Her method was to lavish attention on me when I came home for my meals, which were generally at different times from everyone else's. She would set a place for me with the best silver (the only set of silver we had in the house) and the best china and glass, and she'd wait on me while I ate.

Though Mother never came to the Piccadilly Hotel to hear me play, she would meet me there every Wednesday afternoon at two thirty. We regularly had a meal together after I'd finished the lunchtime session. She'd wait for me in the lobby and we would go off to one of the Lyons Corner Houses which served food all day and where one could sit and chat for hours for the price of a cup of tea. I used to look forward to those afternoons when I could be her escort; we always had great fun together, window shopping along the way and discussing the people we saw. With her I felt something of a man about town, pleased to show off some of the new ideas and experiences I'd discovered from the people at the hotel.

Mother didn't follow all the Orthodox rules about food, but she was still quite strict about buying from proper Jewish suppliers—and she wouldn't eat meat in a restaurant that wasn't Kosher. However, she would always eat fish, which made things easier.

One day, feeling rather daring, I said: 'I'm going to have bacon and eggs.' (This was a regular favourite of mine, though the last thing any Orthodox Jew would dream of eating.) I waited for what I thought might be a shocked response. However, Mother knew better than that, and let me get on with it. But I could see she was fascinated by this dish; as a wonderful cook herself she couldn't have failed to be tempted by that mouth-watering smell. I offered her a forkful and urged her to try it—which to my great delight she did. She loved it, she absolutely adored it, and I said: 'Well there you are, you are a sensible woman after all!' But I think she drew the line at cooking the dish herself back at home; eggs and bacon were strictly for escapades.

There was one Wednesday afternoon when without any warning she didn't turn up. I looked for her in her usual place and waited around, yet there was no sign of her—nor was there any message for me. I was worried and rang home to see if she had left as usual. And there she was, answering the phone.

Naturally I was a bit taken aback and asked her if she'd forgotten that it was the day for our weekly date. But she knew perfectly well that it was Wednesday and that she'd stood me up. She was very mysterious about it, saying: 'I'll tell you only if you're coming home tonight.' That made me very suspicious; there was obviously something on her mind and it sounded as though it had something to do with my social life. I didn't always go home after the evening session; if there was an early start the next morning, or if there was a concert or a party to go on to, there was always room for me to stay at my grandparents' house.

However, this particular evening, I made sure that I returned to Cricklewood; in fact I couldn't wait to get there to find out what had happened. Eventually, after a lot of quizzical looks, she said: 'I hear that you've been seen riding around in a white car with a black woman!' It was a statement that suggested a great many unspoken questions, for which *I* wanted some answers as well. It was a disturbing experience to be reminded that there were curious eyes everywhere, reporting back to the family network.

As with most gossips, their report was inaccurate. Staying at the Piccadilly Hotel at that time was a rather large Indian family, who were all absolutely charming. They often came into the restaurant and would always come up to the bandstand for a little chat.

I was particularly taken with their teenage daughter, who I thought was lovely; she looked beautiful in her sari, very delicate and feminine and yet full of fun. She was intrigued by our playing and I was fascinated by her stories of life in India. She was about my age and we became friendly enough for her to invite me occasionally for an outing in their white Packard car. We'd drive around London between the lunchtime and evening sessions, with the chauffeur and her maid. Of course, it was all very innocent—there wasn't even a flirtation involved.

Her family were obviously very well off. There seemed to be so many of them that they must have taken a whole floor of the hotel. As far as I was concerned, the really interesting part was to see their quite astonishing lifestyle. And for their part, my life must have been interesting in a different way.

For Mother, this was a very dangerous liaison. Her imagination no doubt working overtime, fuelled by what she saw in the cinema, I think she imagined that I was being introduced to all kinds of exotic Eastern practices. Perhaps she thought it was the white slave trade all over again. Thankfully, it wasn't that difficult to talk some sense into her. In fact she came back to lunch the following Wednesday and the whole episode became something of a family joke. She'd say: 'Who was that girl I saw you with last night—was she Jewish or white?'

CHAPTER ELEVEN

The End of the Family

The summer of 1932 was golden: I had left the Guildhall with every prize that I could possibly have won during my career there. Walking off at the end with the Gold Medal and the Principal's Prize, it seemed as though I'd really been given their blessing as a professional player. I stopped outside the door for a moment on my last day to savour that feeling of walking out as a 'graduate': I took a deep breath and knew that my days as a student were finally over, I could now get on with the serious business of making a life for myself, and that anything was possible. Even better, I felt that it was the end of having to prove myself to my father. He could feel tremendous satisfaction in having started me off on the fiddle all those years ago, but from now on I wouldn't have to justify myself to him any more.

At this time Father started a new chapter in our family life. After more than twenty years of working in the tailoring business, he suddenly gave up his workshop in the Langham Street area and moved out to Cricklewood. One day he was a tailors' presser, and the next he'd decided to go into the delicatessen business and set up a shop. Naturally he knew nothing about shops or the food business, and I don't suppose he had much idea of charming the customers. His shop closed almost as soon as it opened. It was a mystery to me at the time as to why he should have gone into this line of business, but I can see that there must have been some kind of trouble—to do with either work or the family.

Grandfather had died at the end of the summer in 1931: he was a kind, sweet man, but really far more interested in preparing himself to meet his Maker than in providing the comforts and necessities of this life. They used to say of him that Morris Makoff only came out of the synagogue to make a suit when there was a pressing bill to pay;

he would never have dreamt of working to build up his savings for old age, or for a rainy day.

Poor Grandmother was left with nothing except her memories of a man who was one of the gentlest of people. Luckily, one of her three daughters, Katie, was very happy to join her in her little house in Middleton Buildings. Katie's husband Harry, a ladies' tailor, was able simply to move his entire business into Grandfather's workshop which was there ready and waiting. Father's workshop was next door at No. 7 Middleton Buildings: and I have no doubt that almost as soon as Harry moved in there must have been arguments and a general agreement that Father should leave. At the time, I'm sure everyone thought it was a good idea; but somehow, it now feels as though we were blindly walking down a road, totally unaware of what we were doing.

One day I shall never forget was December 14th 1932. I'd been playing in the evening as usual at the Piccadilly Hotel and my only concern was to finish a little early as we had a family party at home. Some cousins were staying with us and Mother had specially asked me to come back and join them. It took just over half an hour by bus to Cricklewood, and the house was only a five-minute walk from the Broadway.

As I turned the corner into Ivy Road, I became aware of a dreadful screaming, high-pitched and wild—and saw my sister Annie out in the street, completely hysterical. It was a shocking sight with people everywhere coming out of their houses, wondering what to do with her, and how to calm her down. When she saw me she rushed into my arms and I realised that she was screaming, 'Mummy, Mummy, Mummy . . .' Soon I was screaming back: 'What about her, what's the matter, what's she done?' Meanwhile more and more people came out on to the street, also shouting, also trying to get some sense out of her. Eventually, with no more breath in her, poor Annie—white and gasping and staring at us all wildly—could hardly whisper the dreadful words: 'She's dead, I think she's dead.'

At that point, I'm afraid I pushed Annie into a neighbour's arms and rushed into the house where I found everyone standing around in a state of shock, with my mother's body slumped on the floor in the dining room. Five minutes earlier everything had been normal. Now, the world was spinning off in a frightening new direction. I could feel that icy grip of fear in the room, freezing us all.

They had stayed around the table, talking, after they had

finished eating. It had been a calm and happy meal with no arguments from Father. Mother was pleased to have the family around and she'd been quietly sitting at the end of the table, smiling at everybody, enjoying herself. But suddenly, she had stood up and urgently called Father: 'Israel, Israel . . .' and staggered towards him round the table. He stood up and rushed towards her, and caught her just as she started to fall. A moment later, she was dead in his arms.

When you read about a sudden death, there is no way you can imagine what it feels like in reality. I had no idea that Mother was ill in any way. She didn't look ill and always seemed to be the same wonderful, kind person — but that shows just how much we can take a person for granted, and not see the signs or take any notice of the changes that must have been happening to her.

We soon found out that the doctor had been treating her for some time for a kidney complaint which eventually became the cause of the massive heart attack which killed her. We knew nothing at all about it, because she had sworn him to secrecy. I think some of her Russian blood must have come out, and she must have threatened him within an inch of his life if he said anything to anybody in the family.

However, the time for wondering how it had all happened came later: for Jewish burials take place very quickly and there's really no time to think before the funeral. Unless death happens on the eve of the Sabbath, people are supposed to be buried the following day. There is a highly efficient organisation run by the synagogue which copes with the arrangements for the family, who are often too shocked to know what to do next.

Even so, it was all a ghastly experience. Father and Mother were Orthodox Jews, though I wasn't, and it was still necessary to go through the traditional — but for me, terrible — period of official mourning, being visited by all the friends and the community.

Jewish mourning is a tremendous ritual; a mixture of prayers, torment and reliving memories. For the people in mourning, there's a seven-day period of sitting at home, on specially uncomfortable chairs which are provided by the synagogue. These are low and hard, to remind you of the weight of sorrow. At the same time, the house is full of a stream of visitors who bring the family offerings of sweet things to try to make them feel better. But since the mourners are not allowed to offer visitors anything to eat or drink, these also bring their own refreshments, and may sit around for hours, gossiping.

Even if you want to be alone with your grief, it's not in the tradition.

The second part of the mourning ritual is the prayers. For seven days, first thing in the morning every morning, the sons of the deceased person have to go to synagogue in order to join in at the end of the seven-thirty service where they have the prayer for the dead. More prayers are said in the house while the visitors are there. Twice a day, the cantor or the rabbi comes to the house for an afternoon prayer and an evening prayer.

But I wasn't quite the dutiful son that I ought to have been. I couldn't come to grips with the whole business—I'd grown away from the serious Orthodox traditions after my Bar Mitzvah and after Grandfather had died. Moreover, with the kind of life I had to lead playing the violin it was impossible to keep to any of the rules. It was impossible for me to observe an entire week of mourning because of my work at the Piccadilly. It wasn't a Jewish company and I didn't feel I could go to the manager and ask for a week off, even for a death in the family. It didn't occur to me to try.

In fact I have no doubt that it was going to those twice daily sessions at the Piccadilly Hotel that kept me sane. I was devastated by Mother's death, shocked and numbed by a feeling of the loss of my best friend as well as my mother. We had been very close, but without being over-demonstrative, since we weren't a family that touched and held each other. When we came back to the house on the day of her funeral, I realised that I couldn't remember when I'd last kissed her.

It was the end of the family. Mother's calm, loving influence and her good advice had been the anchor for all of us, and now that she was gone we quickly fell apart. The first one to leave was her dog Pat who was utterly distraught from the moment of her death. As we left the house for the funeral, he ran out into the street and disappeared—and was never seen again. As animals know these things, he must have sensed there would be changes to come which he couldn't bear.

Then, we all found ourselves facing the reality of Father's dreadful business sense. When the delicatessen shop folded, he found himself not only without any work but also owing a great deal of money. Soon it became impossible to keep up the running costs of the house: the ten pounds a week I'd given Mother weren't enough to support the whole family and the mortgage.

So Ivy Road was sold, we moved out to a flat in the Harrow

Road, and I said goodbye to my dog Karl. It would have been cruel to keep him cooped up in a small flat with no garden so I gave him to some friends in Cricklewood. Needless to say, I also felt cooped up in the flat which was neither big enough for us nor a family home without Mother to keep things going. Father was like a child again, helpless and needing a great deal of attention. Poor David, who was just ten years old, had to compete for the kind of love and support which he ought to have had as his right. Annie became even more flighty than she had been before; she developed a rich imagination, telling tales of tremendous fantasy, but when she began to believe in these fantasies they caused considerable altercations in the family. There was no malice in what she said or did; but she was unhappy and when old enough she left home, marrying as quickly as she could.

Of course, it was difficult for me to escape. As the eldest son, earning a good living, I had a duty to stay at home and support Annie, David and my father. Yet I knew that unless he picked himself up and started again, the whole family would come unstuck trying to look after him and cope with his self-pity. After all, he was only in his mid-forties.

Father didn't want to marry again, but I persuaded him to look for a wife. Fortunately after some years (during which time he worked intermittently) he met a widow named Sadie and married her. They moved (with her financial assistance) to a larger flat in the Willesden Green area.

Sadie had two sons from her first marriage, who, extraordinarily, were also called Max and David. Sadly, her son David was killed in the war. Her Max decided that he'd change his name to Martin—he didn't think it was right to have two Maxes in the same family. (Martin emigrated to America and the last I saw of him was on our tour of the USA and Canada in 1962, when he came to a concert we gave in Buffalo.)

But I'd left the flat long before that, in order to preserve my sanity. Getting married to Betty Joseph seemed to be the answer to all my prayers. It was as though she made my dreams come true. Betty came from Stamford Hill, the other side of London, but we had met at a party given by the Syders in Anson Road, Cricklewood—she was a good friend of Gertrude Syder. Betty was bright and sparky, full of fun. She had a wide circle of friends, many of them very 'stagey' since they'd all met through acting in the Apollo Dramatic Society. Betty's mother was a clever businesswoman, running what was called a 'Madame' shop, selling quality coats and dresses to ladies. Their family lifestyle seemed so much more attractive than ours.

We were married on October 7th 1934 at the New Stamford Hill Synagogue, and I splashed out on a *thé dansant* reception at the Empire Room at the Trocadero (which I remember cost two shillings and sixpence a head!). There were lots of guests: the Raznicks and all the old Langham Street community came; her mother's friends and business clients, the acting group, and I invited those musicians I knew who were able to give up their afternoon. It was a tremendous party—and they gave us a fabulous send-off to our first night, which we spent at the Pastoria Hotel in Leicester Square before leaving for the honeymoon in Bournemouth.

But our marriage was an absolute disaster from beginning to end; we might have been good friends but as husband and wife we were hopelessly incompatible. We did have a daughter, Elizabeth, who was born in January 1936—but from that moment on, it was a marriage in name only. Obviously, it was some years before I realised what we'd done to each other; meanwhile I was stuck with supporting a wife and a child, and stuck in a marriage that wasn't going to give me the kind of life that I wanted or could enjoy. I'm sure that Betty felt the same.

CHAPTER TWELVE

Playing with the Bands

As always seemed to happen, luck came to my aid. I'd said goodbye to the Piccadilly Hotel shortly after Mother's death; the charm had gone out of the job, it was becoming dull and repetitive. But just before I left, one of the top band leaders, Jack Harris, sauntered up to the stand one lunchtime, introduced himself, and invited me to come and join his organisation as his right-hand man. I didn't have a moment's hesitation in saying 'Yes'.

When I started playing for Jack, he was at the Café de Paris—a high society night-spot that was very popular and just as fashionable as the Mayfair Hotel, which was where Ambrose ruled both the music and the customers. Every night-club and restaurant had its special band: there was the 400, and the remains of the Embassy which was slowly going downhill—bands came and went as fashions changed.

However, Jack Harris did far more than lead a band at a London night-club. His musical operation was considerable, providing all kinds of bands to play for society's big private functions: royal parties, coming-out dances for debutantes, Hunt Balls and fashionable Balls of the Season like the Caledonian at Grosvenor House, and the Chelsea Arts Ball at the Royal Albert Hall.

Jack and Ambrose shared the party market between them, but unlike Ambrose, who became famous through the radio, Jack wasn't at all interested in broadcasting, so perhaps he did more on the social carousel. For a while, they also shared the music at Ciro's night-club, which they owned together, playing alternate seasons there.

Ciro's main business was eating, drinking and dancing—there was a large dance floor in the main part of the club, surrounded by tables and chairs for the people having their food and drink. It was elegance itself, decorated in white and gold with flowers everywhere; gentlemen wore tails and ladies exquisite evening gowns. Ciro's also had a balcony over the dance floor reached by stairs from the foyer. People loved to sit up there, watching the dancers—and no doubt avidly taking note of who was dancing with whom and which couples were likely to provide the column inches for the gossip writers.

The dancing stopped every evening for the cabaret, another ingredient in the great rivalry between clubs. People went for the band leaders, the dancing and the decor, but the attractions had to be kept up when it was time for the band to take a breather. All kinds of acts were booked as cabaret, but for my money the best of all were the Adagio Dancers. They performed a wonderful, ultra-slow kind of ballroom dancing: cheek to cheek, belly to belly, everything to everything—it was unquestionably highly erotic. There was one outstanding pair who were star attractions at Ciro's; an American husband and wife team called Veloz and Yolanda who were the height of glamour as they took to the dance floor. It didn't matter what they danced to, a tango, a waltz or whatever, they danced with such beauty and such passion that it was deeply moving. Looking at them dancing, one knew that they were in love and probably miles away from all of us in their own private, dazzling, physical world.

Another favourite at Ciro's was Frances Day, a vivacious platinum blonde with an extraordinarily sexy singing voice— everyone loved her. But I think the outstanding musical talent came from a jazz pianist who mesmerised audiences whenever he played: Art Tatum had this stupendous technique, he could do absolutely anything on the piano and he packed the club. Not surprisingly, people are still buying his records which are never out of the catalogue.

Jack Harris was what was called a 'great' fiddle player. This didn't mean that he was a particularly good player, but he played with large expansive gestures and reckoned that he made a sound that no one else could drown. He would boast that for a Chelsea Arts Ball at the Royal Albert Hall, he had a sixty-five-piece band, which included something like twenty-five saxophones and fourteen trumpets plus other brass. No strings. He claimed that his fiddle playing drowned the lot.

The Chelsea Arts Ball was meat and drink to the Jack Harris operation. It was non-stop music all night long, right through until five in the morning. Players took their breathers in shifts and the music would go on without a break. Non-stop music was his hallmark.

A lot depended on the size of the band. With an eight- or ten-piece band it was quite easy to get a break of about half an hour because you could stagger the players—most of whom, incidentally, doubled on other instruments. That meant we always covered the lead instruments and could even change the musical colour of what we were playing. We never allowed two of the top line players to break together, nor could the pianist leave at the same time as the bass player—but apart from that, two or three could go off at a time without affecting the music. Those left would just carry on, filling in any solo bits they knew would be missing. All this was worked out before we started so that there were never any obvious holes in the sound.

With a small group of musicians, perhaps five or six all told, it was impossible for a player to slip off because every note counted. So we'd just play on for as long as we could bear it—often for about three hours—then snatch a quick fifteen-minute interval.

It was a curious and a hectic business doing society dances—

Giving a prize at Ciro's

132

Jack had a big office in Regent Street with a wonderful secretary called Miss Ash who did his paperwork and sorted out all the pay packets every Thursday. I'm sure she was the only one who knew exactly what was going on and where. Jack would invariably begin the evening playing at the Café de Paris while my job was to be his stand-in, either starting the evening off for him or taking over from him. He usually came on from the Café de Paris to take over wherever the dance happened to be that night—it was rare that there wasn't another dance at which we were playing. We'd often synchronise our watches at the start of the evening to get our timing right for the switch-over. The attraction in booking a band was the band leader; the musicians were only incidental. They got paid their standard union rate but the band leader commanded a special fee. It wasn't the music that interested Jack though; it was the business side of things. At one stage, Jack also looked after the music at the London Casino. This was both a restaurant and a theatre, where people would eat at tables arranged around what had been the stalls and the circle, and watch a lavish floor show or a revue every evening, before the dancing started. These were huge stage shows, produced by a man from America in true Busby Berkeley style, from the movies or the Folies Bergères in Paris. There was a second band for that, which Hugo Rignold conducted.

Rignold was a tremendous musician, a top London session player who went from playing the fiddle in all kinds of dance bands and jazz bands to conducting the Liverpool Philharmonic Orchestra and the City of Birmingham Symphony Orchestra, and became Musical Director of the Royal Ballet. But that was after the war. Before the war, we'd often work together on recording sessions— once I remember we joined forces with Eric Sidey, a jazz specialist and arranger, to record for the legendary Ambrose, when he wanted three fiddles.

For the London Casino spectacles Jack had to be ready to turn his hand to anything. There were show dancers and specialist acts, comic and serious—they were the real attractions of the evening, and went on long enough for the rest of us to leave the theatre for the café-cum-bar immediately opposite the stage door. (Which is how I learnt to play snooker: above the café there was a snooker hall, owned by a man with only one arm—who nevertheless was the most astonishing player.)

The London Casino shows were all part of the frenetic pace of the thirties; it wasn't enough any more simply to dine and dance the night away—people wanted other attractions. Paul Whiteman brought his orchestra over from America and they caused a sensation, especially when three members of the orchestra, the Rhythm Boys, started to sing. (One of them was Bing Crosby.) Then Jack Hylton produced a 'show band', employing musicians who not only played their instruments but sang as well: Billy Cotton picked up that idea too.

Meanwhile, Jack's presence at the Casino was as intermittent as it was anywhere else—he would rush in just to make sure we were doing what was expected of us, and then disappear to some other fixture. One evening he arrived and handed me a package wrapped up in brown paper and asked me to look after it. This parcel was about six inches by five inches and I stuck it under my chair and promptly forgot about it. Jack certainly never came back to pick it up.

At three o'clock in the morning my phone rang: it was Jack wanting to know about the parcel. I couldn't even remember what he was talking about—but he ordered me to get up, get dressed and go round to the Casino immediately to find it. This seemed a bit excessive at that time of night and I asked whether it couldn't wait till the morning. But steam was pouring out of the telephone at my end—Jack was more than apoplectic. It was bad enough that I'd been so casual about the package in the first place, but to leave it behind was unforgivable: there was a cool one thousand pounds in bank notes there, a fortune in those days. I was round to the Casino like a flash—and thank goodness, the package was still where I'd left it. If we'd waited till morning the cleaners would have found it and might have had a bonanza.

Jack's temper was proverbial. If you were sensible you didn't argue, you just got on with what he wanted for the sake of peace and quiet. But one evening, a trombone player called Miff Ferrie decided that he would argue, and the two of them had the most unlovely and very public verbal exchange, before Miff walked off the stage. Jack of course followed him and the argument continued right up to the band room on the fourth floor. I was supposed to carry on with the music, but felt sure that something dreadful would happen if someone didn't go up to stop the row. So I left Monja Liter in charge at the piano and rushed after Jack and Miff—to find that Jack had thrown off Miff's glasses, pinned him against the wall and was slowly throttling him. Jack was terribly strong; however, I managed to get an armlock round his neck and stop the attack. I yelled to Miff Ferrie: 'Get out—I can't hold him much longer!' Miff was off like greased lightning. Jack burst into tears and thanked me for saving him from 'committing murder'. Needless to say, Miff Ferrie didn't return.

Years later I heard that there was trouble brewing for me as a result of having saved Miff. He'd given up trombone playing to become an agent—and Tommy Cooper (then unknown) was one of his very first clients. Ferrie had stitched Cooper up in an unbreakable contract. So when Tommy became very successful, he found that it was Miff who was making the money and there was nothing he could do about it, much as he tried. Tommy put out the word that he was looking for Max Jaffa and had a bone to pick with him. The message went that Miff Ferrie should have been killed.

In the thirties people spent fortunes on their parties, each host trying to outdo the others in lavishness, and there were extraordinary goings-on from the guests to match. As musicians we were simply considered part of the scenery. People out for a good time carried on just as though we weren't there; it was as if the music we were playing made us invisible. But we were forever amazed at what went on, hissing to each other under our breath: 'Did you see that? Did you see her?'

I remember one particular occasion when we were playing at a party given by Cecil Beaton at his home down in Wiltshire. The house looked absolutely glorious, as you'd expect from one of the best designers of the time, and the party was held in a vast marquee which he'd had decorated in a fantasy of flowers and lights. It all looked very special and magical.

I'd gone down there to start the evening at about nine thirty or ten—it was important to get the atmosphere going, to create the party spirit and to keep it up through the evening. However, on this particular evening, after we'd been playing about three or four hours, we were told to take a break because all the guests were going off to have supper and wouldn't be dancing for a while. They'd also laid on supper for us with champagne and the same food that the guests were having.

But it wasn't in the Jack Harris tradition for his band to stop playing, whatever the excuse. We were about halfway through our supper interval when he arrived from London and exploded with rage: 'Why isn't the f—ing band playing?' He and I usually got on well together, but he often used the most terrible language and you never knew when his temper would boil over. There was no reasoning with him, even though I explained that we'd actually been told to stop playing. As far as he was concerned, the Jack Harris Band had been booked to play and that was what it should be doing, especially when he himself had turned up—he wasn't going to stand around doing nothing for his large fee.

Once Jack arrived, I was more or less free but kept in touch, my main task being to make sure that Jack had his glass full: he couldn't go on without a drink and always had a supply of neat whisky on stage which he drank from a large tumbler as though it was lemonade. If everything was running smoothly, I'd go off to the bar or chat to some of the guests. It was a marvellous opportunity to see how the other half lived and look at all the beautiful furniture and paintings people had in these houses. I used to look forward to that part of those evenings enormously.

All band leaders of the day could tell you racy stories about the social side of their work. People were completely uninhibited, they wanted to experience as much as they could and consequently the most unexpected conversations and friendships developed. At that Cecil Beaton party was a guest I'd come to know quite well, or as well as one could know a society lady from chatting to her when she came to Ciro's or to dances where I played. But there she was, Lady Deirdre Guthrie, looking utterly charming and making a determined path towards me. 'Come and have a drink,' she said. 'I want to talk to you. Let's find a private corner.'

Now Lady Deirdre had the sort of determination which was very difficult to resist: having secured a bottle of champagne she led me off to a quiet corner of the garden, clearly knowing exactly where to find a spot well away from the other guests. We ended up what seemed like miles away from the dance. When we had sat down she said: 'I must talk to you.' It was half a command and half a desperate plea. Well, not unnaturally, I thought she could mean only one thing—it did happen to a lot of band leaders, and it seemed as though my time had come. Things were looking up.

She fished around in her evening bag and suddenly produced a piece of paper and a pencil—I really didn't know where this might be leading. 'Now,' she said, 'I want you to tell me every single swear word and obscene word that you know and what they mean, and I'm going to write them down as you say them.'

My mouth must have dropped open because this was not one of the possibilities that had crossed my mind. All I could say was that I couldn't do it. 'Yes you can,' she said. 'You must, because I want to use them. There are some of my friends who think they know a lot, but I'm sure that you must know many more. And you must tell me.'

Well, a command was a command. So I started: after all one heard a fair selection from other musicians, who'd learnt some pretty ripe language in their time. I remember starting off gently to see how far I could go without causing offence. But she was way ahead of me and turned out to know far more than I did. It ended up with her enlarging my vocabulary considerably.

In fact, underneath the evening dress and sophisticated veneer, I was very naive. I liked to think that I looked like a band leader and dressed like a man of the world, but I was really only a beginner. And compared to what some of the top names got up to, I hadn't even started.

Jack Harris was the number one stud. He was an American who'd been brought over to London by Lew Aronson, to lead the band at the Embassy Club. Aronson's business was night-clubs and entertainment of that kind and eventually he went on to buy the 400 Club as well. He knew the value of publicity, so before Jack arrived he'd prepared the ground for him by telling everyone that Jack Harris was America's top band leader, the most famous, the most fashionable and the most attractive. Not surprisingly after all that publicity, Jack became very successful in England.

Goodness knows why though. Jack Harris was one of the most badly behaved people I ever knew—much as I liked him and got on well with him myself. Even at a private gig he was quite likely to be as rude as he could to everyone, particularly to the host who'd booked his band.

Most of the time I worked for him, he was heavily involved with a society lady, Bridget Paulet. They never bothered to keep their affair a secret. She used to come to the club in the evening with her husband and a group of friends and as she danced past the band she'd stick her tongue out at Jack and he'd stick his tongue out at her. It couldn't be more obvious what sort of relationship they were having and of course everyone knew. Except Jack's wife. She was an absolutely charming woman. I was often given the job of taking Jack's fiddle back to his flat at the end of a gig, when he was off doing something he oughtn't to have been. So I had to make excuses to his poor wife that he'd been caught up with some Americans he used to know and was off talking business with them. She didn't seem to mind a bit. Perhaps she knew exactly what was going on. Surely all wives know what their husbands are up to, even though their husbands think they don't?

What I do remember quite plainly about those early morning visits to Jack's flat in Bryanston Court—usually at about 3 a.m.—was that there was invariably a particular car parked outside. It was a black Humber, with, if my memory serves me, the registration number ALB 1. Of course, the scandal hadn't yet hit the headlines, but at Bryanston Court there lived a Mrs Wallis Simpson who'd set up what the papers would call a 'love nest' for herself and the Prince of Wales, since obviously she couldn't be seen visiting the Prince.

What is extraordinary is how he could be so open about parking the car outside night after night. After all, ALB 1 was the sort of number plate that would easily stick in the memory and readily be associated with the Prince of Wales who liked to be seen in public a great deal. But then, the Prince's and Mrs Simpson's affair was the most famous secret of the day; we all knew about it, but no one ever talked about it publicly.

Playing at so many of these parties, we saw absolutely everything that was going on while people danced around. We could chart the course of relationships and love affairs, we knew who was cheating on their husband or their wife, and we could sniff when an engagement was about to be announced.

But we loved following our regulars, such as Mrs Horlick of the Horlicks bedtime drink company. She had a favourite tune called 'My Romance', which she adored from the minute we'd introduced it as a brand new number from America. Every time she and her husband took to the dance floor, we would immediately launch into it—and they'd glide past us, smiling their thanks. Then there was Mrs Albertini, who wore diamond bracelets from her wrist to her elbow: the boys would mutter threats about chopping her arms off—one arm's worth and all their financial problems would be over.

One deep friendship which developed during my time at Ciro's was with the American heiress Barbara Hutton. It was both glamorous and sad. Barbara always made a stunning entrance: her favourite gown was a black velvet décolleté which had fifteen or sixteen inches of the richest band of sables around its hem, which she wore with a long single strand of pearls. It was simple and the height of elegance—but it made a stark contrast to her face which was so pale it was almost white. She was in London in 1936, building a sumptuous mansion in Regent's Park, Winfield House (which she later gave to the American Government to be the London residence for the American Ambassador).

Poor Barbara, as heiress to the Woolworth fortune, was one of the richest women in the world—but she was not a happy person. She was always rather silent, talking only about the places she'd visited. If she smiled, it was a thin-lipped, tight smile which showed her small teeth, but never really touched her eyes. It was obvious that she was highly strung, very temperamental and liked to be surrounded by a party of people. But they, alas, were not so much friends as hangers-on, people out for a free meal. Men pursued her mercilessly for her money and she had a succession of unhappy marriages. At that time she was still married to Count Reventlow, but they were already drifting apart.

We met quite by chance one evening, when Jack Harris was in charge of the band and I was standing around the bar—the rapport was instant and we became close friends. And I mean friends: the idea of marrying Barbara couldn't have been further from my thoughts—I was already married and a father—and she seemed to appreciate having a friendship without pressure or fuss. For quite a while, we would spend the afternoons together out in her car, or walking—and once in 1937 she took me round to see Winfield House just as the work was finishing. I think I must have been the first 'outsider' to see it.

The house was simply astonishing, like a Hollywood film set. I had never imagined that people could live in such opulence. The entrance hall was like a theatre, all done in black and white marble with a beautiful sweeping staircase up to the first floor. The rooms were huge, with high ceilings and enormous chandeliers. Since we went during the day, they weren't lit—but the effect at night must have been wonderful. Above all I remember the marble—it was everywhere—and the bathrooms had gold taps. All most impressive and quite unreal.

Sadly, the relationship suddenly changed. One day Barbara gave me a surprise present, the most elegant and expensive gold and platinum banded cigarette case which came from Cartier. I don't know what she meant by it—but everything my mother had ever told me about accepting expensive presents came flooding into my mind: I knew it would change our relationship, and that I'd become somehow beholden to her. So I could only thank her very much, appreciate the gesture enormously—and give back the case.

Of course she was desperately upset and angry that I'd rejected her present; in her eyes it was just as though I'd rejected her as a person, that I didn't appreciate her. She never contacted me again. It was all very sad, because she was soon involved in another unhappy marriage which, like the others, ended almost as soon as it had begun.

I don't think any of us really wanted to be part of this glittering but nervous world. Most of the musicians were happily married and loyal to their long-suffering wives—any musician's marriage was constantly under terrible strain. The hours we all kept, especially if we were playing in a number one band, were absolutely crazy. Most evenings we'd start playing around nine thirty and we wouldn't stop till two or three in the morning. That was gruelling enough, but most days we'd have started work at 9 a.m. with a session in the recording studio and often a second session in the afternoon. There was rarely the chance to go home before the evening stint except to dress; we just had to keep going from one job to the next. Exhaustion caught up with most of us at one time or another.

What a life! I wonder if people outside the business ever thought about the kind of existence we led, in order to eat and pay the rent. We didn't even stop on Sundays; that was the day players went off to do concerts which were put on in theatres when the current show had a day off.

There was a marvellous occasion when I was booked by Maurice Winnick, another band leader who had once worked at Ciro's. 'The sweetest music this side of heaven' is what he thought he played. Others were less impressed by his musical talents and thought him more a businessman than a musician. Jack Byfield always said of him that he'd 'studied at the Gas, Light and Coke Company—and failed.' This particular concert was in Epsom, and I had been engaged to play six violin solos along with a pianist called Stanley Black and a singer named Sam Costa (these were early days in the profession for them too).

Maurice was perfectly competent conducting the strict tempo dance music, with tangos and waltzes, but straight music was another matter. Since this was a concert where patrons expected a little variety, we were all aware that the music wasn't going down too well. But then it was time for my solo spot, and the atmosphere changed completely; Stanley Black launched off on the piano with the introduction to 'Torna Sorrento'. They loved it.

Maurice Winnick was absolutely thrilled. 'Wonderful, marvellous,' he said. 'Quick, go back on again, have you got anything more to play? Go on and do it.' So on we went and played another three tunes or so—which was the selection I'd planned to play in the second half of the evening. That meant I'd done my bit according to the contract.

Maurice was aghast when he realised that he was left with a great hole in the second half of his programme or he'd have to pay me an extra fee. However, I could pull any amount of tunes out of my hat thanks to my long career at the Piccadilly, Stanley could follow anything at the piano, and we saved the second half of the show too. I don't think Maurice was a happy man having to pay out twice what he had bargained for.

Despite the hours, band life had the promise of being very exciting. If you made it to the top, there were plenty of good times to be had. Take Ambrose, for example, probably the greatest band leader of them all and a tremendous favourite with high society. He was a personal friend of the Prince of Wales who'd actually sent him a telegram to come back from New York quickly because everyone missed his playing.

They often played golf together, but Ambrose, who was also a great gambler, wouldn't play any sort of game unless there was money involved; with golf it was usually two pounds a hole. As if that wasn't enough, he wouldn't fix a day to play until he'd first had a bet on what the weather would be like—five pounds that it would rain or five pounds that it wouldn't. I'm surprised he managed to find any partners who could afford to play with him apart from the Prince of Wales.

One story that went the rounds was that in one night at Monte Carlo, Ambrose lost twenty-eight thousand pounds at the gaming tables. His father told me a bizarre tale about his Bentley. He'd driven to see his parents in Stamford Hill one day and spent the time listening to their good advice about curing his gambling habits. When his father asked if he could borrow a tenner he was amazed when Ambrose said: 'No, I haven't got any spare cash—but I'll leave you the bloody car!' And he did just that: he left the Bentley in

Stamford Hill, went up to London and bought himself a Rolls-Royce. He'd been wanting to change to a Rolls for ages and this seemed like a good excuse.

I don't remember how we musicians felt about the strange state of things, with all the partying on the one hand and appalling poverty and unemployment on the other. In a way, the band life created split personalities for us: by night we watched the indulgence and excesses of the privileged, and then we went home to a life where we had to count every penny.

There was also a strange divide between the fast life and exhibitionism displayed in the clubs and restaurants and the formality of private parties. People would swing like mad in a public place, dropping all the conventions of nice behaviour, while at the big private parties the good old-fashioned Viennese waltzes were still the great favourites!

The King, George V, loved Viennese waltzes too. I remember playing at Buckingham Palace, standing in for Jack Jackson, another great band leader who used to play at the Dorchester. I was booked simply to start the music off for him at the Palace because he was flying down from somewhere or other and coming on later. But he never arrived at all. It was wonderful to see dear old King George dancing with Queen Mary. Whenever he danced past the band, he would say: 'The Blue Danube . . .', his favourite of all Viennese waltzes. And of course, we immediately went into 'The Blue Danube'. We played little else for hours.

Gallons of champagne were drunk on these occasions; people drank far more than they ate. There was always food laid on and guests went into supper intermittently and would consume a couple more bottles to wash down the meal. They'd carry on drinking champagne all night long, right through until breakfast—which was also accompanied by popping corks.

When we played at the Palace, we were told that supper would be waiting for us at the appropriate time. After two and a half hours of solid playing we were delighted to see footmen carrying all kinds of trays into the room behind the bandstand. But goodness knows what they did with them; all we found were three cases of champagne to drink with a meagre tray of sandwiches to be shared between some sixteen people. We may still have been hungry by the time we had to go back, but we were definitely very jolly!

We all loved playing for Hunt Balls where the high spot was the breakfast once all the dancing was over. It was absolutely sumptuous: champagne, caviar, lobsters galore, kedgeree . . . What we were asked to do musically didn't matter a bit: the only change from the normal mix was that we'd play endless Scottish reels as well as the famous Viennese waltzes. Everyone seemed to think that there was nothing better than whirling around and the merrier they became the more we were asked to play a reel. And they did get very merry: at one party, the Duke of Gloucester decided to drop his trousers and do a jig on top of the piano.

Carroll Gibbons of the Savoy Hotel was yet another top band leader. Though I never worked in London with his Savoy Orpheans, I spent a marvellous summer season with them in Monte Carlo in 1937—the last easy summer before we saw the shadow of war looming. We played at the newly opened Summer Casino, a beautiful development outside the centre of the town, right on the shore, with a glass floor lit from under the sea.

While Carroll did the strict tempo dance music, my job was to conduct the orchestra which played for the cabaret. This had to be flexible enough to cope with anything from Adagio Dancers to singers or comedians. It was a marvellous job, because I didn't have to do anything until quite late in the evening and then we didn't play for long.

About six months before we went, I'd signed on at an agreed rate of twenty pounds a week, to be paid in sterling which was the clever part of it. When we signed, the exchange rate was a hundred and fourteen francs to the pound—but when we arrived, we found we were given a hundred and forty-two to the pound, so we had quite a bit of extra spending money to enjoy. I found myself a wonderful room at the Hotel Terminus for three shilllings a night. It was on the first floor with a bathroom and balcony overlooking the sea and the price included breakfast.

But talk about gambling: when we came to collect our wages for the first week, we found that Gibbons had somehow lost the lot at the tables . . .

It was an idle time for everyone in the band: since there was nothing else to do but play in the evenings, we could get up late and relax around the pool at the Hotel de Paris or the Summer Sporting Club. In fact I lazed around so much when we first arrived that I fell asleep in a deck chair and got dreadfully sunburnt. This was followed by acute dysentery and all I was allowed to eat for a week was boiled lettuce and grilled veal.

Since my work on the cabaret didn't start till around midnight, there wasn't much to do until supper—which I had with the rest of the group. Once they'd gone off to do the main music, I'd go upstairs, change into evening dress and amble gently up to the Casino. Carroll Gibbons would be sitting at the piano and playing away in strict tempo for dancing; sometimes our vocalist Anne Lenner would be centre stage with a selection of hits and favourites.

After the cabaret I'd hang around while there was more of the strict tempo dance music. And every night after we'd finished at about 2 a.m., we'd all go off to the Tip Top Bar to have hot dogs and champagne for the equivalent of ninepence. We occasionally went over the top; at one point Anne Lenner was to be seen standing in the middle of the square shouting for a carriage at the top of her voice. 'Fiacre, fiacre!' she was bawling—except it didn't quite sound like that in her accent.

There was a great group of friends in the band—Frenchy Sartell, Sam Acres, George Melachrino, Paul Fenoulhet and of course Anne Lenner. We had marvellous adventures together. There was the famous occasion of the Cinéma Bleu in Nice, the one and only time I've been to such a place. The Cinéma Bleu was the great fashion in naughty films at the time and someone had discovered a private house which showed these films. So we went.

Everyone had to be accompanied by a partner. Frenchy and Sam had their wives with them, Anne Lenner had her boyfriend and I took the daughter of a Madame Hassan whom I'd met during the evenings at the Casino. She was probably under the legal age, but she didn't seem to suffer unduly. Years later I met her mother again, and she roundly ticked me off for introducing her daughter to such a place—but then admitted that she and her husband had found the detailed confession of the events of the evening as hilarious as we had found the experience of being there.

We were all ushered into a drawing room containing a number of tables and sofas, with a dozen or so people sitting and drinking. They then showed us three films, in flickery black and white and rather scratched prints, only one of which I remember because it reduced us all to hysterics.

It opened with a scene of three girls in sailor suits playing ball in the park around a statue of a naked man—and being watched from the bushes by a real man, who was obviously extremely interested in getting to know these three girls a little better.

As the game goes on, naturally a ball is dropped and rolls past the statue, which the girls seem to look at for the very first time. They certainly notice its sculpted manhood and dissolve into fits of coy giggles at the sight. This gives the man in the bushes an idea; as soon as the girls move away, he's out of hiding, removing the statue from its plinth and tearing off his clothes to take its place.

Of course the girls come back, having decided to examine the statue a little more carefully. One of them is slightly bolder than the others and decides to touch its male nakedness, and then touch it again. Of course there's a 'miracle' as it was described in the French sub-titles. The statue's organ starts to grow and rise to the horizontal. At which point the film ended—which we all thought was a decided let-down.

At the end of the season, having had such a good time we didn't want to go home. The Sartells, the Acres and I decided that we had enough money left over to prolong the trip and spend a few days in Paris. I'd never been there. The Paris Exposition was on and it seemed too good a chance to miss; we could explore a new city and enjoy ourselves before falling back into the London rat race.

But I lost a day by being too curious. I remember it being surprisingly hot, so I stopped at a café for a drink. The trouble was that I didn't know the French for what I wanted but saw a young lad at the next table having a cool and refreshing lemonade. There was a tremendous pantomime with the waiter as I tried to place my order. Much later on, through the haze of a terrible headache, I realised that I had not been served 'lemonade' but instead had been given what the boy's father had been drinking—pastis. This does look cool and refreshing but is very alcoholic. The end result was that I couldn't remember anything of that day. But I suppose I learnt something!

CHAPTER THIRTEEN

Breaking into Films

Carroll Gibbons always called me 'Max' until he got too drunk, when inexplicably I became 'Dave'. As 'Max' I was getting to be well known in London, only a couple of rungs away from the top of the ladder and joining that select band of freelance players who never had to look for work and who were never out of a job.

Once in—and it was very difficult to gain admission—you were part of a charmed and jealously guarded circle. My breakthrough came as a complete surprise, when I was booked one day to play for Louis Levy.

Usually, Louis Levy was to be found in film studios; he was a composer and conductor and he supervised the music production on all the films made by Gaumont and Gainsborough for about twenty years. (If you were in with Louis, you could work in films all day and every day.) They asked me for this particular gig which turned out to be an extraordinary party arranged by Lord Beaverbrook, who wanted Louis and his orchestra to play a selection of 'music from the movies'.

Obviously it was a very special occasion and Louis wanted to arrive with a brilliant orchestra—so he booked several extras, including me, to make up the numbers. It all went well when we were simply playing the movie tunes, but consternation broke out after we had finished. Beaverbrook sent a message to say that now the guests would like a few tunes for dancing! This wasn't in Louis' repertoire. I don't think he'd ever done the kind of strict tempo music that dance tunes require. It was a dreadful moment for him, because he knew the request was impossible. He had no music for us to play and worse, he didn't know what to do about it. But this was my lucky moment; Alex Blackford (married to the actress Betty Ann Davis) was the pianist that evening, we'd worked together several times in dance bands and I was certain that he knew exactly what to do.

After a few seconds we decided on a string of tunes to start people off, and we set to, busking our way through many pieces. We weren't the only ones with a dance band past; many players from the orchestra joined in and we saved the night. Louis meanwhile gave a marvellous impression of conducting. He was delighted to receive everyone's compliments for making the evening such a success!

Louis thanked me by asking if I'd come and play for him in the film music business. So the evening proved to be my passport out of the dance band world. I wasn't sad to say goodbye as there seemed little pleasure in sawing away at those strict tempo tunes, to say nothing of the late nights followed by rushed studio recordings the next day.

Recording film music was a very different world. Matching music to film needs a precise sense of timing; composers not only have to get the mood and correct atmosphere to match the action on the screen, but also the music has to fit the film perfectly—to a split second, and to an exact number of film frames. It was a tricky business getting us to play the right notes; we were always working with new scores and at the same time watching the screen and the footage counter. Since the technical side was behind the orchestra, we had to concentrate solely on the music and the accuracy of the beat. My only regret was that we never saw the films we worked on!

People asked some difficult things of film musicians—but the most extraordinary feat that I remember involved the legendary Austrian tenor, Richard Tauber. He came in for what we were warned was a very complicated piece of re-recording for the film of Lehár's operetta *The Land of Smiles*. He wasn't happy with the key in which he'd originally recorded one of his main arias and he wanted to raise it a semitone.

This wasn't as simple as it sounds. First of all he had to watch the film to remind himself of his facial movements. At the same time, he needed to listen to the original sound-track so that he would get the music to fit. On top of all that, he was listening to the orchestra and recording a new sound-track a semitone higher than the music that was coming through on his headphones.

Now that is tremendously difficult to do; in fact I'd say that it was almost impossible. It was a feat of immense concentration and musicianship and everyone was asked to be on their best behaviour (session players were known to take their work fairly casually at times). Tauber of course was a charming man, and such a great singer and musician that he didn't have to throw his weight around to make everyone appreciate him.

He proved the point by doing his recording in a single take, which impressed us all. I remember complimenting him on this extraordinary achievement. He just smiled gently and said: 'You know, it wasn't so hard—I have sung Schoenberg, and after that, nothing's so difficult!'

My strangest experience in the film world actually happened years before all this, in 1927, just after I'd come back from Buenos Aires—and before starting my job at the Piccadilly Hotel. People knew I was back in town, and after a couple of weeks picking up the odd job here and there I got a telephone call from a man called Zeitlin, one of a whole family of Zeitlins who were all theatrical agents.

He wanted a 'violinist'—he didn't say whether he wanted a good one or a special one, but I was to go round to his office in Charing Cross Road to find out more. First of all, he gave me a warning: it was going to be a very odd job. He didn't know for how long it would last but I might be working for ten days or more. And then he told me that the client was Pola Negri, one of the top stars of the cinema until the talkies came in and her Polish accent ruined her. Now she was in England to make a film directed by Dr Paul Czinner.

However, Pola Negri had a peculiar obsession: before she could take a single step on the set, she needed a violinist to play for her. So whenever she was to be on the set, they had to organise a fiddle player to be there, otherwise she couldn't act at all. They were also prepared to pay a great deal for the music—Zeitlin promised me a fee of one pound ten shillings per day. I couldn't imagine how an unaccompanied violin would help her, but Zeitlin told me: 'Just go to Elstree—be there at ten o'clock tomorrow morning and ask for Dr Paul Czinner. Oh, and take your fiddle!'

Which I did. Paul Czinner took me off to meet Miss Negri, who spoke a lot of Polish, a bit of German, but practically no English except 'You know song called "Ramona"? This you play. Every time.'

Naturally I knew 'Ramona'. This was one of the top favourites of the day; everyone was singing and playing it. And each time Miss Negri came on to the set, as soon as they called 'Action' off I went into 'Ramona' (off stage, off camera of course). I played 'Ramona' for the first take, and the second and the fifth . . . I played 'Ramona' all day, and I played 'Ramona' every bloody day for ten days. I played it in every key, making up little arrangements and trying different ways to attack the tune. It was driving me slowly crazy!

However, there was a bonus: I didn't have to find my own way to Elstree every morning. On the second day Miss Negri asked if I would like to drive down with her, so thereafter I presented myself daily at the Berkeley Hotel and was picked up by her Rolls-Royce. By the end we had become 'very good friends', as they say. But nothing 'untoward' happened—which was a pity!

I thought Pola Negri was very beautiful, but wouldn't know whether she could act or not since I was so busy playing bloody 'Ramona'. She was a leading lady in German cinema and audiences loved her—but there were some very silly moments in this particular film, which made me laugh so much I nearly split my sides. Perhaps that's why there had to be so many takes.

Most of the action was set inside a small country cottage. From what I could make out, the hero had been injured in some way; he was bandaged and was sitting slumped at a table. Then Pola Negri came in dressed in country dirndls and with rustic charm started to cook him bacon and eggs. She had to go across to a very old-fashioned kind of stove, find a frying pan and put in rashers of bacon and the eggs. Then while they were cooking she would turn round to comfort her young man.

As soon as her back was turned, quick as a flash one of the stage-hands would switch frying pans for one with ready-cooked bacon and eggs. This must have gone on for seven or eight takes, by which time I started wondering what was happening to this endless supply of bacon and eggs. Who was eating them all? You could get very hungry on a diet of nothing but 'Ramona'.

I was fascinated by the whole business of filming—there were so many people involved and so much machinery and paraphernalia. Everyone was busy on what looked like important activities, and all I was doing was playing this tune which wasn't even going to be part of the end product. I don't think my 'Ramona' was ever given the treatment she ought to have had—we never got so much as a credit. But then, there are a few people who will still remember me saying: 'After that experience, the one piece I will *never ever* play again in my life is "Ramona".' And I haven't.

We were lucky in the film music world: once we were booked to play for a film recording, we knew that there would be three or four sessions involved as we worked through the entire film. More often than not, many of us would then move on to the next film. We were almost like a permanent orchestra and a world away from the daily market-place in Archer Street which is where most players found work.

Every weekday, at around ten in the morning, you could find a vast number of freelance players gathered there, with their diaries at the ready for the 'fixers'. Fixers were—and are—the people who engaged the musicians for gigs or jobs. There was always someone around looking for musicians for an evening's work playing for a dance band or a deb's party. By lunchtime they'd have got what they wanted and the street would be deserted.

I used to go down there from time to time, because it was great fun and you could meet many of your friends. On the whole musicians are very sociable, and even though scattered around town playing in small groups, we liked to know what was going on, to find out the gossip and the rumours. 'See you in the Street,' we'd say to each other when we'd finished a job, though it would probably be months before we would meet again.

Nowadays, a gig might mean a performance at the Royal Festival Hall or one of those huge outdoor rock concerts and the booking of musicians and their venues has become highly sophisticated. There's so much music and so much variety that fixers are now specialists with a network of musicians whose playing they know very well indeed.

Getting started in the freelance pool was difficult; you couldn't just turn up in Archer Street as a student and hope to get a try-out. The fixers never booked anyone they didn't know personally or know about from other players, so young performers tried first to get themselves a reference from other musicians. Sometimes a teacher helped but more often youngsters would go direct to a band leader and ask to play a few sessions free for experience. That way, several players would hear how good they were and might even pass the word on to their fixers.

There were a few musicians in regular work, playing for the bands organised by Ambrose, Carroll Gibbons, Jack Payne and the others. However, most players freelanced, working on recording sessions, signing on for a few voyages on the liners going out East or across the Atlantic, or making up small bands for hotels and restaurants. The ad-hoc gigs, getting together a group for a single evening's work, were actually considered quite a good form of business. Although these jobs weren't paid well and the hours were fairly unsociable, starting at nine o'clock at night and finishing at two in the morning, at least everybody got paid immediately and in ready cash—which was always welcome. Few people thought about income tax in those days: earning a living was precarious enough.

CHAPTER FOURTEEN

Joining Up

Though we did speculate on Edward VIII's abdication we didn't think too hard about the stories that were coming across the Channel in the late thirties. We played on regardless: as long as there were people who wanted to enjoy themselves, to dance the dark news away. Just as we didn't really notice what was happening during the years of the Depression, we still didn't take serious account of what was going on in the news. If I'd worked with a different crowd of musicians I might have been more concerned: many artists were active in left-wing politics, some of them even going off to fight in Spain. But alas, the entertainment world in which I worked had other interests, principally earning a living.

I was adamant there would never be a war, although it was obvious that people were preparing for something. There were air-raid precautions and the Foreign Secretary Anthony Eden resigned from the Government, which was quite a headline. Gas-masks began to be issued and in 1939 the sky over London started to fill with strange sausage-shaped balloons, a daily reminder that they were expecting hostile planes to fly over and bomb us as they did in the First World War.

Nevertheless I still refused to believe there could be a war. For me the most exciting event of 1938 was when England beat Australia at the Oval and Len Hutton beat Bradman's test record by thirty runs.

Betty and I began our married life living in Mount Royal, a brand new block of flats just off Marble Arch which wasn't even properly finished when we moved in. I'd met the estate agent for the block and had been offered a wonderful deal whereby our down payment was greatly reduced if we took the flat early and were prepared to put up with the mess of the builders in the other flats around us.

About a year later we moved on to Hillcrest Court, further out of town in West Hampstead, right on top of the hill between Kilburn and Cricklewood. It was a spanking new block, and with more space as there was going to be an addition to the family. Best of all, it was in a prime position for the film studios which were just a few miles further down the road in Denham and Elstree—and anyone who was driving out from London to work on the same session more or less passed my front door. Except for a brief period when I was with Jack Harris and drove myself around in an Austin 10, I never bothered with a car. It was much more fun to be swept off by someone like Hugo Rignold who drove a very dashing red Alfa Romeo.

It's strange how people come together. One of my very dearest friends, Joe Loss, lived just across the road in Kendal Court, with his wife Mildred and their children Jennifer and David. We'd worked in the same profession although in different spheres musically, and a lifelong friendship was formed that continued right up until his very sad death in 1990. For me it was the passing of a beloved friend and colleague, and like so many of his fans I miss him enormously.

Our next-door neighbours at Hillcrest Court were a delightful young couple named Collins. Wilf Collins worked hard as a theatrical agent—and his wife was kept busy with two charming young daughters, Jackie and Joan.

In those days, you paid three months' rent in advance (the flat cost the enormous sum of three pounds a week) and you didn't pay again for another six months: three months were rent free! It was also the custom for milkmen to leave every new tenant a welcoming present of free milk, butter and eggs the day they arrived. Of course this was an exercise in public relations; it was a little embarrassing to say you didn't want him to go on delivering your daily pint after that!

In 1938 we moved down the hill again, and back into Cricklewood—into Ashford Court, a block of flats just off the Broadway. We could see the old family house in Ivy Road from the window. Although we didn't think much about the news and politics, it was becoming more and more obvious that things were getting serious as work was drying up, films were slowing down to a trickle and parties were being cancelled every week.

Every day, the crowd looking for work in Archer Street grew noticeably larger. It became a milling mass of musicians chasing fewer and fewer jobs: any dance bands that were working had the pick of the bunch in terms of talent. Those of us who had been working in film music for years and whose faces weren't known—or had been forgotten—had a raw deal.

My own situation became very bad indeed. Betty wasn't working, as she was busy looking after our young daughter. Like so many musicians, I became unemployed and was soon forced to break into my savings. By 1939 we were scraping the bottom of the barrel, penny-pinching, cutting back and doing without to make the money from any gig last as long as possible. We never knew when the next job would come my way. Eventually, we hit rock bottom, and the day came when I took my beautiful Postiglione fiddle down to the pawnshop and left it there in exchange for the magnificent sum of six pounds. And I never got it back, because I didn't have the money until it was far too late in the day to redeem the ticket. My violin was the most valuable thing I had in the world—nothing else really mattered.

Meanwhile, the family gathered together; my cousin Fay who'd become very friendly with Betty also moved into Ashford Court with her family, and my father and his new wife took a flat just around the corner in Dawson Road. We started to plan what we should do with the children if war came—by mid-1939 everyone was thinking about evacuating children from London.

We eventually decided that all the wives and children should leave for Brighton to find themselves a place away from the expected bombs. They, together with our most important possessions, were packed into cars and as they set off for the south coast, the first air-raid siren sounded. War had been declared.

I went to Brighton only once or twice as I couldn't afford the fare. It was all I could do to pay my part of the costs of this evacuation. Anyway, after a few weeks without any air raids Betty decided to come back to London and stay with her mother who had refused to leave her flat in Wigmore Street.

There was only one option left as far as I was concerned: I went to the nearest recruiting office and volunteered for service.

Why volunteer when they would have got to me sooner or later? Twenty-seven was certainly young enough to be called up to fight. But I had a secret ambition: I wanted to fly. Or at least, I wanted to have something to do with flying—and of the three services, I knew that the RAF was for me. If I couldn't be a pilot, I'd be an observer or a navigator—or even a gunner. How I knew that is another matter, as I'd never even been in an aeroplane. Naturally, I hadn't considered the fact that the RAF might have other ideas—and it was a dreadful shock to learn that they didn't want me. At twenty-seven, they said, I was far too old to start learning to fly and they sent me away. It was the first time I'd failed an audition.

It was difficult to know what to do after that. I didn't have a fiddle to play, I knew nothing except how to play the fiddle and I didn't have a home of my own any more. So there wasn't much point in hanging around London to wait for the inevitable summons for King and Country. I went to the nearest Army recruiting office and found myself joining the Royal Artillery.

Someone must have been looking after my interests that day, because I'm sure I couldn't have told the difference between one kind of soldiering and another. I was extremely lucky not to end up in the infantry. On the other hand I also missed joining what would have been an easier option for me, the RASC (the Royal Army Service Corps, known disrespectfully as 'Run Away Someone's Coming'). At no time did it cross my mind to join up as a musician. I wanted to help to win the war, not fiddle my way through it.

I had the worst time of my life in the Army. Never had I imagined that being a soldier and winning the war was all to do with folding the bedclothes properly and laying out your kit in a strict order every day. Never mind the serious business of polishing the boots, blanco-ing gaiters, brasso-ing buttons, parade-ground drill, arms drill, physical training, marching or cross-country runs—if the fold on your blankets was crooked, there was some kind of punishment in store.

The camp itself was a nightmare; rows and rows of bell-tents were laid out on a sloping field halfway up a hillside. We were squashed in eight to a tent, along with our eight full packs and rifles. There was hardly any room to move. The poor unfortunates who had the tents at the bottom of the field also had to share them with the water that flooded in off the slope every time it rained. Our bedding was straw-filled palliasses, which were quickly soaked through in the wet and damp. We were given dry straw only every third or fourth day.

However, rain was the least of our problems. It was the cold that nearly finished me off before I'd even fired a shot on the rifle range, let alone in battle. In January 1940 the temperature dropped so low that the Thames froze over, so it was no joke living outdoors in a tent with equipment the Army considered suitable.

We washed and shaved outside, at great big trestle tables set up by the single stand-pipe which provided our only running water, lining up every morning to fill tin basins. Of course the whole area was a sea of mud which seeped up through the duckboards—I could never get both ends of myself clean at the same time. They gave us a special treat once a week when we were taken off for hot baths in Uxbridge, the nearest town, but somehow we all seemed to get just as dirty again on the way back. We all swore that when it wasn't doing the bath run the transport did double duty as a coal lorry! Perhaps the powers that be thought we wouldn't notice.

Well, my family had been poor, and I'd known what it was like to count every penny—but I had no idea that life could be like this, that people could expect us to endure these kinds of conditions and not complain. The experience certainly taught me that I was built for comfort. I have never wanted to enjoy the open-air life since—give me the best hotel, a good bed and a bathroom any day!

There seemed to be no end to it—the drill, the spit and polish—but somehow along the way we were all transformed into soldiers. I think I turned out to be rather a smart soldier, clean and neat and with the best polished boots of them all though there are no photographs to prove this as none were taken. In fact, I still enjoy polishing shoes which I find therapeutic and relaxing. (I was taught to clean shoes properly—as opposed to boots—much later on and by a marvellous lady. Mr Cleverly in Cork Street, who made my shoes, employed her to clean and shine every shoe before it left the shop. She taught me how to get the high gloss with polish and a little water. Spit is simply the Army's refinement.)

The biggest surprise of the Army was to discover that I was quite good at using a rifle. They gave us Lee Enfield .303s and when we graduated to moving targets, which we practised with clay-pigeon shooting, I found I was a good shot—though I never had to use that talent for real. But the truly hilarious business was learning all the various techniques for the Lee Enfield and the system of loading and firing. You had to master the intricacies, doing each movement standing up, lying down, kneeling and goodness knows what else. But I don't think we paid the kind of attention we should have to the kneeling load; our Sergeant Gunner Instructor came from a Scottish regiment which wore the kilt—and with nothing underneath, as became obvious to us all when he leant forward to show us the correct procedures. It was an awesome sight—no wonder the Scots regiments are reckoned to have a terrifying secret weapon.

Everyone who goes through Basic Training Camp knows how much of a shock it is to the system and how interminable it seems. Yet it is amazing what the human frame will withstand. I survived (I think we all survived) and found myself given one of the cushiest jobs possible. I was posted to 303 Battery in Merton, south London, where I joined a small group working out of a couple of foxholes on Blackheath. We were manning an anti-aircraft gun and a searchlight in the defence of the capital.

This was sheer luxury in comparison with basic training. We had huts to live in—one for the men, the second for the officer and the paperwork. We had electric light and although meals came round every day from the kitchens at the HQ unit down at Merton, we had a coal fire going to heat them up. Keeping clean was no problem; if we liked we could take a bath every day at the public baths just down the road.

There were nine of us all told, including an officer and a sergeant. We all thought it was a huge joke: our 'gun' wasn't one of those serious anti-aircraft weapons, like the Bofors guns they used to move around London every day. I think the argument went that shooting at the enemy planes from different places each day might give them the impression we had hundreds of gun batteries all over the city. The Germans must have thought it curious that only a few ever went off at any one time. Ours was a Lewis machine gun which couldn't possibly have hit any aeroplane. I suppose it might just have been of some use defending ourselves if the Germans had landed down the street. The searchlight, we all knew, merely showed 'Jerry' the way into town as we criss-crossed the sky with the beams trying to catch the bombers in the light. In August when the bombings started in earnest it was dreadful to see the results the next morning; on Blackheath we were so high up that we could see right round London. The night of the great fire-bombing, the whole city seemed ringed with flames.

It was very frustrating but there was nothing much we could do, except man the searchlight as instructed and put out the odd fire. Incendiary bombs dropped anywhere, and one or two came quite close to the battery. The planes of course were flying far too high for us to shoot at as they were way above the barrage balloons. And anyway that came much later, halfway through 1940. Before that, our daily task was an undemanding routine of cleaning and polishing the searchlight and gun in the morning and hanging about the rest of the day until we came on duty at dusk, waiting for the night raid.

As soon as I got there, I wanted to leave. It might have been a cushy job but it did nothing for my morale or for my temper. Here I was, ready to win the war, and all I had to show for my efforts were blackheads all over my hands from the diesel oil we used for cleaning the gun that we never fired, and polishing the searchlight till it shone at the back. The oil got into the pores and was almost impossible to wash away. My only lasting contribution to the task was to introduce the practice of wearing gloves for this job. I was called a sissy and a nancy-boy and probably worse—but I noticed that very soon everybody had taken to wearing these gloves. I think they became standard issue.

As far as Army routine went, we had a quiet life. Being such a small unit we were more or less left to our own devices—there were no inspections, drills or endless saluting of superior officers. In fact the only time we had to smarten up was for the weekly pay parade when we polished up our kit and marched before the officer's hut.

They were a good bunch of people from solid backgrounds, most of them Londoners, though our officer, Lt McAffrey, was an Irishman. I remember one of the lads sold newspapers in civilian life, while another was a first-rate burglar turned honest for the duration; someone else kept a pub in Woolwich. There was a lot of card playing—solo and whist, and snooker too when we could get away from the site—but there wasn't a note of music. None of them had any idea of the kind of life that I had left behind.

They wouldn't have known what I meant if I'd told them about the Piccadilly Hotel, or the people I'd seen while playing for Jack Harris or Carroll Gibbons, or the film session world. Everyone knew about the Corner Houses, and I'm sure they'd all eaten or had cups of tea there at some point, but they wouldn't have paid any particular attention to the band or the people playing. At the Corner Houses, music was an accompaniment to the eating. I realised that, during the previous fifteen years, I'd travelled a long way from that little community in Langham Street and my very first ventures in the music profession.

I began to feel terribly isolated, cut off from everything I knew and valued and with no one to talk to about it. Many people must have found themselves in places totally different from their past lives. In the course of my war, I remember meeting a brilliant scientist called Jacquier/who was always miles away from the everyday world: goodness knows what he dreamt of but it had nothing to do with a life of unnecessary spit, polish and drill.

Whenever I could get away, I'd go back to town. This needed careful organisation because our main duty was at night, but we all swopped rotas from time to time to make these visits possible. Borrowing a motorbike, I'd go up to the West End to keep in touch with the feel of the city. I'd walk past some of the famous clubs, which were still playing on. They'd re-opened very quickly after war had been declared and if anything, business was better than ever. Not even the direct hit on the Café de Paris in 1941 could stop people dancing the night away. It felt very strange, looking in as an outsider, feeling bedraggled after struggling in from Blackheath on a borrowed motorbike which I never learnt how to ride properly. (I always ended up in a frightful mess with the web of tramlines at New Cross.)

I had drifted away from my wife and daughter who were leading a new life in my mother-in-law's flat. Father had gone off to do his bit in some support unit in the Army—and then dear Grandmother, who had really become my closest friend, couldn't take the strain any more and her health began to fail. It was a sad day when they took her into the Middlesex Hospital, our 'local', only a block or two away from her house in Middleton Buildings.

There was nothing they could do, and I'm only glad that I was with her when she died. I somehow knew that I had to be with her that day, May 31st 1940, a Friday, and I'd swopped duties specially. There was no one else around, just me holding her hand; and suddenly she'd gone. I felt very bleak, leaving her with the nurses and going off to tell Aunt Katie and the rest of the family. We buried her in Streatham and I believe that was the last time the Makoff side of the family got together.

Back at Blackheath, I kept myself going by thinking of how to get out—I had to find something different to do. All sorts of circulars known as ACIs (Army Council Instructions) came round asking for volunteers to do strange jobs in the Army and elsewhere. I was always willing and put my name down for anything and everything that came along as an alternative—including, most memorably, a request for recruits for the Palestine Police Force. It sounded like a marvellous opportunity to go abroad and enjoy the sun, but I suspect

159

that someone somewhere thought the idea of a Jew guarding that country at that time was a little curious. I didn't get the job.

But strange things always happen in a war. Once we were in the middle of the Battle of Britain, the RAF realised it would have to develop its strength for the future. There was a rush to build new planes and they needed the aircrew to go with them. The day came when another ACI arrived on Blackheath asking for volunteers for aircrew duties and I was fascinated to discover that having been too old for the RAF when I first joined up I was now young enough. They had raised the age limit!

Of course I filled in the forms as usual and sat back for the interminable wait, hoping against hope, considering what had happened to all my other requests for a transfer. But this time it was different; the officer in charge of our little band called me into his hut one day, telling me to pack up my gear and await 'transport' to our battery HQ in Merton where I would find further 'instructions' on my next posting.

And so it came to pass that I found myself metamorphosing from an Army gunner to an 'Aircrafthand under Training Aircrew' in the RAF. I changed from a caterpillar into a butterfly as I turned in one set of clothes and all the kit and paperwork—and picked up quite another identity. I was going to the RAF: whether as pilot, navigator, wireless operator, gunner, I had no idea, but at least I was going somewhere, doing something I wanted to do. I was quite happy to wait and see what would turn up.

CHAPTER FIFTEEN

Flying High

I was sent down to Newquay in Devon, to the Initial Training Wing, where I found myself in a group of about fifty people who had all made the great escape from the Army. It was like waking up to find yourself in another world; the RAF's approach to things was completely different. For a start we all had proper beds, a roof over our heads and hot and cold running water in our rooms. This was incredible luxury. But we didn't believe our ears on Day One when, gathered together for our first official meeting, we found that learning to fly means taking a step back into that old routine of parade-ground drill, cross-country running, keep-fit classes—with a little work on learning about aircraft thrown in for good measure.

But we were wiser men after the Army experience and did a deal with the Commanding Officer about the drill. Drill was drill whether Army or RAF fashion and we didn't want any more of it. So, if we could prove our competence to the Drill Sergeant, could we please cut it out and get on with the real business of learning about aircraft, flying and being pilots?

We were lucky that the CO was a reasonable man: drill went, and was replaced by classes with information we would normally only have learnt much later. By the end of our time at Newquay we had become a very advanced class, expert in the basic knowledge of what various planes looked like and how to tell the difference between a Hurricane and a Spitfire. And we were also pretty good at the technical details such as the various speeds for taking off and landing, what happened if you flew too slowly—and what to do if the plane stalled . . . As things turned out it was a good thing that I got those details well and truly into my head at this early stage in my flying career.

The technical side of learning to fly affected the group in different ways. While some people opted for the mechanical side, I rather enjoyed being introduced to the rules of navigating and the mysteries of flying a vector. This is the crucial business of how to plot a course to fly from A to B, taking into account how much the force of the wind speed pushes you off direction. I certainly hadn't realised that you had to fly off at an angle to compensate for the wind. I'd imagined instead that you took off, pointed the plane towards your destination and that was that.

Newquay was bursting at the seams, with every hotel turned over to housing service personnel. The RAF were running several as billets which was marvellous for us. They were comfortable, the food was good and that foxhole on Blackheath seemed a long way away. The Army was also in Newquay: a huge camp of troops, some of them reorganising themselves after Dunkirk and others just doing their basic training. We would stroll down to watch and remind ourselves of our lucky escape.

The authorities must have had a hard time to keep us all happy and occupied: our life was very leisurely once we'd given up the drill. We kept up with our lectures and that was about it. The Army people had nothing much to do as soldiers either—but they went in for dreaming up great entertainments.

One evening an Army group put on a magnificent pantomime, *Dick Whittington*, which turned out to be the traditional show spiced with great vulgarity. I sat there with my mouth open at the rude jokes, which went far beyond any I'd ever heard, even after all those years working with musicians who are a pretty robust lot. Life in the forces was an education in every sense of the word.

Then in total contrast to all the vulgarity, the star of the show turned out to be the Cat, whose dancing was absolutely spell-binding. You could easily believe this wasn't a human dancing; this really was a cat, moving as freely and gracefully as an animal. None of us could understand how a human frame could have learnt to move so beautifully through the kind of PE that was part of our daily lot. It turned out, of course, that PE had nothing to do with it. We had a star amongst us. The Cat was none other than the young Michael Soames who survived the Army and later became the leading dancer with the Royal Ballet and partner to Dame Margot Fonteyn.

We left Newquay fully trained as Leading Aircraftsmen, LACs, ready for the next stage. I had been earmarked for the pilots' training course so my next stop was No. 5, EFTS (Elementary Flying Training School) at Sywell, near Northampton. It was time to do the real thing and learn how to take a plane into the air and back down again—in one piece!

They trained us in Tiger Moths, which had twin seats, one behind the other, with the pilot sitting in the rear. When they were teaching us, we sat in front, in the observer's seat, with the instructor in the back to show us all the tricks of flying while we were up in the air. We had earphones in our flying helmets so we could hear the instructions: 'Hold the stick, the joystick, don't grip it. Now, if you move it forwards, the nose will go down, and the plane will fly like this . . .' and off it went. 'Move it backwards and the nose will go up—like this . . .' and so on. We learnt by feel, literally learning what it felt like to turn left and turn right. It seemed very simple. The big moment came in July 1942 when I was sent up to do my first solo flight. They started you off with a series of what are called 'circuits and bumps'—taking off, flying round the airfield and landing again. You went on and on doing it until the manoeuvres were right, then you would be allowed to do a series of short flights, to build up confidence and to learn how to navigate while you were in the air.

Funnily enough, I don't remember much about that first solo trip, except that it was all right. The build-up to it was much more thrilling than the event. Nobody stopped to congratulate you on a safe return down (which was what we were all worried about); they just sent you straight up again to get better at it!

On the other hand, I shall never forget the shock of flying a Spitfire for the first time—that was a nightmare by comparison. Of course, this was much later on in my career, in June 1944, when I was a fully trained pilot. I'd flown all sorts of planes by then and thought I knew what I was doing, but the Spitfire is a single-seater so there's absolutely no chance of anyone going up with you to show you how before you take the plane over yourself!

I'd studied the facts very carefully: I knew what all the knobs did, what the meters did, what the crucial speeds were for taxi-ing, take-off, climbing, for straight and level flying, for the landing approach. An error of only one or two miles per hour could make all the difference between flying safely, stalling or crashing—and as we were constantly told: 'There's no future in that!' But no amount of reading the notes and handling instructions can prepare you for the real feeling.

Even taxi-ing out to the field was a new experience. The plane was built very high in the nose, so you couldn't see over the top; it had to be yawed or zig-zagged from side to side so you could see where you were going. It took me some time to get the hang of it and make my way to the take-off point—we called it the Ice-Cream Cart—painted with huge black and white squares where there was always someone on duty to signal whether it was safe to take off and land.

I had a final chat with the instructor and prepared to set off on my first circuit and bump, exactly as any beginner would. Except that I couldn't believe the speed! It was as though I'd been knocked on the head: I had the throttle fully open—exactly as in the instruction manual—and the plane just whooshed off the grass runway. It was all I could do to remember instructions and get it flying straight and level at two thousand feet.

The take-off can only have lasted two or three minutes at most but by the time I managed to pull myself together and look around at what was going on below, I found to my horror that I was flying over Swindon, miles away from the airfield in Thame. Thank God it was Swindon and its railway yards, because otherwise I might not have recognised where I was. And it would have been difficult to find out since we were flying with no radio, no navigational aids and no contact at all with anyone on the ground.

However, having got that far and having calmed down, I thought there was no point rushing back home without using the opportunity to practise flying the plane. I was particularly keen—given the shock I'd had on take-off—to practise landing. The advice they gave you in the RAF—quite seriously—was to do some dummy runs on clouds. You could get the feel of the approach—with the right speed, the right angle of the plane—and there'd be a guaranteed soft landing. It was wonderful fun, and by the time I got back home, my technique ought to have been pretty much perfect.

An hour later, when I got back to base, the instructor was not pleased: 'Where the f—ing hell do you think you've been, you've taken a bloody long time to do a circuit of the airfield and land again by my reckoning.' Going to Swindon and landing on a few clouds was definitely not in the day's programme. Luckily he had a sense of humour when he heard the whole story—and I found out it wasn't the first time it had happened to a new Spitfire pilot. Incidentally, the landing practice seemed to have paid off because I was passed as competent to fly single-engined, single-seater planes.

But Spitfires were a long way away from the Tiger Moths we were flying in Basic Training. These were nice, friendly, easy planes which got one up in the air, good for doing a little cross-country flying and mastering some basic aerobatic tricks. In case one found oneself doing these kind of things by accident, it helped to know how to get out of the situation before something dreadful happened.

Then we were all sent abroad for more sophisticated instruction, the Advanced Flying Training, which would turn us into 'operational' pilots. Going away made sense because we would be out of the way of people doing the real flying, fighting the war. Many people went to Canada, but all of my group were posted to what was then Southern Rhodesia, each of us with the new rank of Acting Sergeant.

First there was the voyage from Greenock to Cape Town which took five and a half weeks on a troop-ship. I tried the food on the first day and just couldn't force it down. It was partly the food itself, and partly the conditions in which we had to eat our meals. A notice on one of the bulkheads stated that the ship was built to carry four hundred and fifty passengers—but there were over two thousand of us on board, crammed into every possible corner including the dining room. Hammocks were slung above the tables and mattresses laid on top of them, with mattresses on the floor as well. The resulting smell was overpowering—a mixture of crowded, unwashed humanity and stale cooking. It must have been impossible to sleep there, and eating in that stench was out of the question. For five and a half weeks I lived on cups of tea and packets of biscuits from the ship's Naafi which opened twice a day.

Being on watch was, for once, a marvellous escape; I think I volunteered for more turns of duty than anyone else on the ship. We were constantly on the lookout for enemy aircraft or submarines, or manning the Oerlikon guns—there were two or three on board, our only defence. The only other times we could get any fresh air was when we did PT and drill on deck every day. In shifts, of course; there was no way the full two thousand could be allowed out at once. It was just like being in prison.

When we eventually arrived in Cape Town, my first thought was to get off the ship and find a decent restaurant—easier said than done in a foreign city. But as the song goes, if you want to know the way ask a policeman, and as luck would have it, I met one walking down Adderley Street.

His recommendation, the Stage Door Café, was the most extraordinary sight. First of all, it was brightly lit—there was no reason to have any blackout down in South Africa—and the war had hardly affected their way of life. But secondly, at one end of the restaurant, there was this enormous, wall-to-wall, glass-fronted refrigerator crammed full of steaks, chops, pork, veal, ham and lamb—you name it, they had it. You just picked what you wanted and they cooked it.

So after five and a half weeks of biscuits I ate my way through steak and four eggs! I'll never forget it—my original order was steak and two eggs, but having demolished that lot I thought I could eat another two. Not having seen an egg for months, I'd almost forgotten what they looked like and certainly how they tasted. Looking back now you think: 'How awful, fancy pigging oneself like that!'

It seemed as though there were thousands of us training in Rhodesia. The group ended up in Bulawayo, in Camp Heany, a huge RAF city, with an airfield, maintenance units and rows and rows of wooden huts raised off the ground, where we slept two in a hut. A little further out of town there was another camp just like it. The RAF obviously meant business and I couldn't help wondering whether the Germans had any idea how many of us were coming to get them.

They did only one thing at Camp Heany: they taught us the serious business of flying properly, the operational flying that would be expected of us when we joined our squadrons. Some of us were obviously cut out to be fighter pilots, with cool heads and quick reactions—but that wasn't for me. Someone had taken a critical look at the way my skills had developed and decided that I might be better off flying bombers, so they concentrated on teaching me to fly twin-engined Oxfords.

Actually, I was surprised that they managed to teach me anything. If it hadn't been for the enormous patience and encouragement of the very first instructor I met at Northampton, it's probable that I would never have taken off at all. This man was a Sikh called Uberoi, who wore a large turban which he refused to take off, so they had to make him a special flying helmet to go on top of it. After him there was a bright young lad, much younger than me, called Shackman (a good Jewish name). He just kept on going over and over the information, and wouldn't let me get away with

Christmas Day	**Boxing Day**
BREAKFAST	
Grape Fruit Porridge	BREAKFAST
Bacon and Eggs	Grape Fruit Porridge
Bread Rolls Butter	Bacon and Eggs
Marmalade	Bread Rolls Butter
Tea or Coffee	Marmalade
	Tea or Coffee
CHRISTMAS DINNER	
Cream of Tomato Soup	DINNER
Asparagus Butter Sauce	Chicken Soup
Lemon Sole, Fried Creamed Potatoes	Crumbed Pork Chops
Roast Stuffed Turkey	Sausages
Roast Potatoes	Fried Tomatoes
Sweet Corn	Creamed Potatoes
Christmas Pudding	Peas
Brandy Sauce or Fresh Cream	Biscuits and Cheese
Ice Cream	Coffee
Apples, Oranges, Nuts, Grapes	
Muscatels, Almonds, Crackers, Sweets	
Biscuits and Cheese	TEA
Coffee	Salmon Salad
Spirits Lager Sodas Fruit Squash	Mayonnaise
	Bread Butter Jam
TEA	Mince Pies
Cold Ham	Tea or Coffee
Russian Salad	
Mayonnaise	
Christmas Cake Mince Pies	
Tea or Coffee	

RAF Heany Sergeants' Mess menu, Christmas 1942

anything. His thoroughness was phenomenal. However, Shackman later told me that he'd made a pact with himself not to give up until he'd taught me how to fly safely and properly, so that I wouldn't break an aeroplane. A plane was more expensive to replace than a pilot!

By and large the instructors in Bulawayo were an impressive lot. The one that I remember best was Squadron Leader de Belleroche (known as Rocky). He was French and a dazzling flyer as well as a good instructor; we all wondered why he was wasting his time teaching us rather than flying operationally. However, we soon found out that his true fame lay in a great party trick he used to get up to in the Mess.

Once flying had finished for the day, there was very little to do except go to the Mess, have your meal and probably get drunk. There was a good deal of alcohol around and Rocky drank more than his fair share every night. When he was ready for bed, he'd calmly bite off a large chunk from whatever glass he was drinking out of, bow a good night to the assembled company, and walk off into the night chewing thoughtfully on it!

167

Frosty Frost was another man who had the bad luck to have to teach me. He was a cockney lad, sharp as they come and a brilliant pilot who used to enjoy low-level flying around the countryside. It was an eye-opener flying with him; we'd find extraordinary stretches of open country around Bulawayo, full of wild animals who just calmly looked up at us as we zoomed over. Some people thought that it was great fun to shoot them from the air—which to me was cruel and wasteful. I much preferred just to look at them and admire them.

However, I thought low flying was splendid: the trick was to build up a tremendous speed as the plane rolled along the ground, but to keep the stick down and the wheels down for as long as possible. Once in the air you had to maintain speed, flying as fast and as low as the plane would go—which meant keeping a sharp lookout for the odd hill that would suddenly appear and get in your way. It was a tremendous sensation as you 'popped' over it. I loved it, Frosty hated it. He'd be sitting by my side in the Oxford cockpit and shouting: 'I know what I'm doing when I do this—and you don't and I'm not going to bloody well sit here and be killed . . .'

He probably had a point: I don't think I was ever a very good pilot. I can drive well, and I've never even scratched the paintwork on any car. But aeroplanes were a different matter.

The first embarrassment came after we'd got our wings, in February 1943. By now, we were fully trained flight officers and were sent up to the north of Africa for a taste of fighting the enemy. It wasn't very exciting as we were flying right at the tail end of the North African campaign and the Germans were well on the run. But we were told to buzz around a bit, just to make it look as though we were being active. By then I had graduated to flying Blenheims, with a full crew of bomb aimer and navigator, which gave one the feeling that now we were really flying seriously.

To be honest, it was dead simple; we just flew out in a straight line, turned round and came back again the same way, dropping a bomb on anything we saw below us in the desert. I think I must have dropped about four bombs in the whole of the war: there can't be many bomber pilots who can match that!

Unfortunately, trying to land after one of these 'sorties', I became a little confused about what I ought to be doing. It may have been the sun in my eyes, but much more likely it was the boredom of the run which had switched off my brain. Somehow I saw the runway coming up ahead and dropped the plane straight down on it from a height of something like twenty feet.

I remember being rather surprised at the bump—or in truth the crash—it wasn't the sort of noise or the sort of shake-up that we were expecting. Of course, it didn't do the plane any good at all and it was a sorry sight when we climbed out, with the undercarriage flattened and the wings draggled on the ground. Somehow we escaped without much personal damage. I suppose it was so unexpected that we were all very relaxed when it happened. I certainly had no idea what was coming. But I think it was at this point that they decided it was about time we stopped this training lark, and that I should return to England.

Meanwhile, Max Jaffa the musician had almost faded away. I had hardly touched a fiddle since pawning my own instrument just before the war. But there was one notable exception in Rhodesia, which came about through the kind of foolhardy gesture one makes as a result of enjoying a party too much. There was little for us to do at Camp Heany except fly, play bridge, and drink with the boys in the Mess at the end of the day, so as often as possible we would arrange parties to give us the excuse to invite guests from Bulawayo. These events frequently became very jolly indeed.

On one occasion someone, somehow, found out that I played the fiddle and introduced me to a gentleman called Chalmers Parke, the musical director and conductor of the Bulawayo Municipal Symphony Orchestra. We chatted about this and that, in the way people do at parties, but I think he must have been finding out discreetly about my fiddling because I was rather surprised when he suggested—in an off-hand way—that I might like to come and play something with the orchestra. Something like a violin concerto, perhaps even the Mendelssohn Violin Concerto which happened to be in their repertoire. I can hear myself saying airily: 'Fine, anything you like, the Mendelssohn is no problem at all. I haven't got a fiddle and I haven't got the music, but I'd love to do it.'

Then came the next morning. In the clear light of day, that morning-after feeling vanished in an instant when I got to the Mess and found waiting for me a violin, the music of the Mendelssohn Concerto and a request for a concert appearance in ten days' time. It was a sobering thought to remember that I hadn't touched the instrument for nearly three years.

But I did perform the concerto, and still have the programme to prove it: Solo violin, Acting Sergeant Max Jaffa — by kind permission of Group Captain French. When I wasn't required to fly a plane or learn about flying planes, I spent every waking minute on the fiddle. Max Mossel would have been proud of me and my devotion to scales and exercises, to get back into the feeling of playing again.

Against all odds, the concert was a great success, or so I was told. But my memory decided not to store any information on what it was like as a musical experience. I fear it was pretty awful!

Back at Camp Heany, my newly discovered skill was employed in one or two home-grown revue evenings we used to have at the RAF Association. I was quite happy to scratch away at a few tunes for them. They'd have enjoyed anything and I enjoyed the fun of performing. But that Mendelssohn Concerto was a strange return to the world of concert giving which I'd abandoned long ago: was it a last glimpse of the good old days, a final farewell to the career that might have been?

Bulawayo Municipal Orchestra

Conductor: J. F. CHALMERS PARK

20th Symphony Concert

SOLO VIOLIN: A/SGT. MAX JAFFA

(By kind permission of Group Captain T. H. French, D.F.C.)

Overture to "A Midsummer Night's Dream" .... *Mendelssohn*

Serenade for Strings: "A Little Night Music" .... *Mozart*
(i) Allegro   (ii) Romanze   (iii) Menuetto   (iv) Rondo

Symphony No. 8 in B minor (The "Unfinished") .... *Schubert*
(i) Allegro moderato   (ii) Andante con moto

INTERVAL

Two Norwegian Dances .... *Grieg*
(i) Allegro moderato alla marcia   (ii) Allegretto tranquillo

Concerto for Violin and Orchestra in E minor .... *Mendelssohn*
(i) Allegro molto appassionato   (ii) Andante
(iii) Allegretto non troppo—Allegro molto vivace
SOLO VIOLIN: MAX JAFFA

Berceuse .... *Jarnefelt*

Praeludium .... *Jarnefelt*

Four Pieces from the "Casse-Noisette Suite" .... *Tschaikowsky*
(i) Danse de la Fée Dragée   (ii) Trepak
(iii) Danse des Mirlitons   (iv) Valse des Fleurs

God Save the King

TOWN HALL,
BULAWAYO.
29th September, 1942.

Programme 3d.

The programme for the Bulawayo Municipal Orchestra concert

CHAPTER SIXTEEN

Another Kind of Pilot

There is one word which describes my war career—waiting. The next stage was always preceded by a wait, never a matter of days, but weeks and even months. Once it had been decided that Flying Officer Jaffa would be better employed back in Britain than in Africa, I was officially 'withdrawn from flying training' on March 2nd 1943—and it wasn't until the end of July that I arrived at my next RAF unit.

In the meantime I found myself passing the time—or wasting it—down in Cape Town, at the most enormous camp imaginable. It was a holding camp for all three services; there were thousands of us waiting for transport to take us somewhere else. There was nothing to do except go to the beach and play cards. And since no one had thought of how to pay us our weekly wage, or even a small allowance, we couldn't go to town in the evenings to enjoy ourselves. It was perfectly frightful: we had to lay siege to the Paymaster for the small amounts needed just to buy a beer at the Mess in the evenings. The only good part of it was that the Cape Towners couldn't have been more generous. They organised all sorts of parties and receptions for us, and opened special clubs for the Services where we didn't have to pay a penny.

But at long last, a ship came in. She was French, and so fast (we were told) that she'd be going straight back to Britain without waiting for an escort or convoy; we'd be home in a matter of ten days or so. By that stage, we would have believed anything, we were so happy to see her. Six weeks later, having stopped off at every small port you could imagine up the African coast, to gather up every size and speed of ship you could think of into a convoy, we finally staggered into Greenock.

The only casualty, as far as I was concerned, was my prize

home-coming present. I'd bought tins and tins of jam, which I knew was a scarce commodity—and bananas, an unheard-of luxury. I don't think many people saw a banana from one end of the war to the other. I'd filled one of those enormous Navy kitbags with a large 'hand' of them—a complete branch, all beautifully green, which I reckoned would be well and truly ripe in the ten days it would take to get home.

They became a very obvious reminder that you should never believe anything they tell you in a war. I don't know quite where we'd got to by the end of ten days, but I do remember watching them go ripe, over-ripe, and finally black. There was nothing else to do but throw the whole lot overboard.

The first stop after Greenock was yet another holding camp, at Eastchurch on the Isle of Sheppey—and another wait before further decisions on our futures were made. The choice they finally gave me was simple: as they had decided that I was too old for operational flying (much to my great relief), I could either stay in the RAF as an instructor on Tiger Moths or I could respond to a circular from the Air Transport Auxiliary (ATA) which was asking for volunteer pilots. There was only one option for me—I took the ATA offer. I knew I would be useless as a teacher. The few times I'd tried to teach the fiddle, none of my students made any progress; they just couldn't understand what it was I wanted them to do. Even many years later when I tried to teach my daughter Lisa, the same thing happened.

Like most people, I had no clear idea about the work of the ATA but soon found out that it was, in fact, very important. Their role was to keep the front-line squadrons supplied with newly serviced aircraft. ATA pilots spent their time collecting aircraft from squadrons and flying them to the maintenance units and back again. In some ways it was routine work but it was also certainly a challenge, with an important difference from flying in the RAF. Instead of being trained to fly just one kind of plane at a time, ATA pilots were expected to cope with any and every kind of machine that was in service.

So at the end of July 1943 I found myself back at school, at One Group, White Waltham, cramming in all the basic skills needed to fly twenty or so different aircraft, from fighters to bombers. Was I glad of all that early grounding during those weeks in Newquay! With the ATA it was a quick introduction to each plane and then they left us to our own devices. Our only lifeline was a thick cardboard looseleaf folder containing the essential details about the various planes we were likely to fly. They reckoned that a thorough look through that was all we'd need to refresh the memory.

Another and rather marked difference from the RAF was that the ATA flew these planes stripped of any kind of radio or arms and with only the basic navigational instruments, so to navigate the country pretty accurately was essential. Also we had to learn the positions of all the maintenance units and airfields. We spent much of our early training on cross-country flying, following a given course from maps which had all the names obliterated. Naturally no airfield was ever named—but the purpose of the task was to prove you'd followed instructions by landing at a selection of these unmarked airfields and having a chit signed by the officer on duty.

In many ways it was quite a dangerous job, especially when taking planes from the squadrons to the maintenance units for servicing or repairs. Sometimes they looked as though bits could fall off at any moment. Sometimes bits did! On the return trip we at least knew we were flying a machine that had been passed as in good working order. By way of encouragement, we were given special identity cards from the ATA and the Air Ministry along with papers authorising us to land anywhere at any time without first getting clearance from the ground (impossible, in any case, with no radio) and to take off whenever we liked.

The flying rules in the ATA were very simple: you flew in daylight and never at night. We started in the morning after the dawn raids and in the evening there was what was known as a 'last landing time'—so if you couldn't get home, you just landed at the nearest airfield. We all flew alone unless flying a four-engined aircraft or a Mosquito, when we had the luxury of a flight engineer on board.

Flying for the ATA turned out to be highly satisfying work. I was doing something constructive and practical, infinitely preferable to trying to teach some poor unfortunate student pilot—or worse, pushing a pen in an office.

It was a complicated business moving across to the ATA from the RAF, since the ATA was technically a civilian organisation. I had first to become a kind of civilian, even though still officially enlisted with the RAF. However, we did wear a uniform—an attractive, dark navy blue outfit with all the insignia picked out in gold, rather like the Navy. I thought it was very smart, much better than the RAF uniform, and it did wonders for our social life.

White Waltham was HQ for the ATA, and from there we were sent off to various Ferry Pools all over the country. There must have been around twenty all told, often on the same airfield as an RAF station; but we'd have our own small corner of the field with a shed and a few planes. You could say that I was stationed at Ringway, the airport at Manchester, since I seemed to spend more time there than anywhere else. ATA pilots were expected to make themselves at home wherever they finished up at the end of the day. An essential part of our flying kit was the overnight bag, which carried maps, helmet and everything needed to make ourselves look respectable for the evening.

Our official billets were always off the station, and if the billet they gave me in Manchester was anything to go by, the ATA did us proud. The Ringway Ferry Pool had quarters in one of the best pubs in the country, the Royal George at Knutsford. On my first night there, I went into the bar, met the other pilots and had started chatting and drinking when a woman came in to take our orders for dinner. As I was the new chap she came to me first with the usual rigmarole of asking what I'd like. As far as I was concerned, this was a pre-war opening gambit: choice was strictly limited wherever I'd eaten since returning to England. I thought this was an elaborate game, and in keeping with this charade I enquired what she was offering. Her suggestions were astonishing: there was smoked salmon for starters, then steak—not whale but beef—fillet, rump or sirloin.

Now I really thought she was pulling my leg and looked round to see if the other pilots were in on the joke, whether they were grinning or seemed amused . . . but no, they continued drinking and chatting. So I decided to take the 'game' further and said I'd have a fillet steak 'underdone'. Whereupon she offered more delicacies: fresh beans from the garden, grilled tomatoes and mushrooms picked that morning, to be accompanied by new potatoes or chips. However, she was very apologetic about the lack of dessert that evening—I would have to end my meal with the cheeseboard. Cheese was a rare luxury. At the time I think the ration was something like two ounces a week, and here she was offering us a full cheeseboard. That made more of an impact on my sensibilities than all that smoked salmon, steak and trimmings.

You could still have taken a five-pound bet off me that when the meal was served, it would be standard wartime fare.

After all, those were the days of the five-shilling meal, when nobody was allowed to spend more than that eating out, and most of the time all you got was Spam and other tinned food. (Actually I liked Spam, I still like Spam and even today I open a tin of it every now and then for sandwiches. It's absolutely delicious with plenty of mustard!) But the Royal George was famous for its food throughout Cheshire and beyond; people came from far and wide and the restaurant was always packed. If the menu didn't run to steak, there was always something substantial instead, such as chops or roast chicken. Goodness knows how they did it—everyone was sure there was a black market at work.

CHAPTER SEVENTEEN

Flying with the
Air Transport Auxiliary

Life in the ATA was surprisingly civilised. As we weren't really part of the Services, there was none of that spit and polish which took up an enormous amount of time in the RAF; we were a group of ordinary people who quietly went about doing a useful job. I suppose we were a kind of parcel service, picking up a plane from one place, delivering to another, where often there would be another plane to be taken on to yet another destination. Our flying rotas must have been quite complicated to set up each day.

Of the twenty-odd Ferry Pools, two, at Ratcliffe and Hamble, were women's stations. The RAF always got a terrible surprise when the women flew in with their planes; with no radios no one knew who was piloting them until we took off our flying helmets. One of the lady ATA pilots, Lettice Curtis, was a wonderful pilot. She used to race for the Schneider Cup before the war, and I think she's still flying today. I met her quite by chance when being given a lift from one station to another in a Lancaster bomber, which I'd never flown in before. (The ATA also ran a 'taxi' service taking pilots out to the right place, and collecting them and bringing them back to base at the end of the day.)

Once we'd got into the air I sauntered up to the cockpit and very casually asked, as one chap to another, where I could have a pee. I got the shock of my life when this unmistakably female voice came out from the helmet to say there was a bucket I could use somewhere in the back of the plane! I remember hoping fervently that it would be out of earshot. Of course it was my embarrassment and not hers — I doubt anything would have shocked Lettice.

She was famous for refusing to wear a skirt when she was flying and Jim Kempster, another ATA pilot, used to say that they ought to have marked the lavatory doors at the White Waltham HQ 'Gents and Lettice'. I'm not sure she would have appreciated that.

The ATA was home to some very dedicated flyers who were otherwise judged unfit by the RAF. On one occasion the pilot of my 'taxi' home had only one arm. I'd seen the plane make a perfect landing at the airfield and was fascinated to find out how on earth he would manage to take off. He was over six feet tall, so there wasn't much room in the cockpit, and while you could use one hand to trim the plane before flight, as far as I knew you needed two to operate the throttle and the stick for take-off. In the event he simply gripped the stick between his knees and off we went in one of the smoothest take-offs possible. The landing at the other end was also immaculate.

When we were up in the air he casually turned round and offered me a cigarette, which was absolutely forbidden according to the rule-book. But then my friend probably knew more about flying than whoever had written the ATA rules—he'd flown every kind of plane in the Air Force and wasn't going to let something silly like losing an arm stop him from flying.

I felt very much in awe of him: when you meet an absolute professional you become all too painfully aware of your inadequacies. Practically every time I got into a plane I had to go over the notes again, to remind myself of where the important knobs and dials were, and the critical speeds to fly it. There were several occasions when I had to fly three different kinds of planes in one day and while the principle was the same as driving different cars, in a plane the consequences were rather more severe if one forgot some small detail. In one of my more shameful moments as a pilot, I took a Hurricane in to land as though it were a Spitfire, which had a completely different set of tactics on the approach to the runway. I dropped the plane from far too high up and my small lapse of concentration might have had very expensive consequences.

With Barracudas replacing Swordfishes, you had to be extra careful about the landing gear. The Barracuda was an extraordinary plane standing ten to twelve feet off the ground and enormously heavy because it used to carry such a large load. In fact it was so heavy that the landing gear couldn't really stand up to the weight. Once the plane had landed, the ground crew would put in extra supporting bolts to lock the undercarriage when it was parked.

Obviously we all had to be careful that these bolts were removed from the undercarriage before we attempted to fly off anywhere. It was the most alarming experience if you didn't. One day, I'd got a Barracuda into the air—but I couldn't get the wheels up at all. Worse, it would hardly even fly properly. I pushed the throttle right the way through the gate into an area of the gauge where no throttle should ever be seen and still nothing happened. It was all I could do to fly the plane in a circle and land again without serious damage. The bolts had not been removed!

Landing gear got me into trouble several times; but on one occasion it was rather more bad luck than my bad flying that caused the problem. I'd been sent up to Kirkbride to ferry a Hellcat back to Lichfield. The Hellcat was a single-engine fighter made by the Americans who tended to go overboard on their use of instruments. They were gadget-mad and the cockpit was a forest of dials and switches, unlike British planes which looked simple and were absolutely ideal for pilots like me.

In British planes when the undercarriage was up, you got a red warning light that it wasn't safe to land; when it was down, the signal was green for go. But not in the Hellcat. This machine had a dial on the dashboard with a tiny silhouette of a plane on an artificial horizon which would tell you exactly what the plane was doing. There was a white line across it so you could see if it was flying straight and level. If you were, the silhouette of the plane would be dead on the line, or off it if you were flying at an angle. And when the undercarriage was down, this instrument's most refined trick was to make little wheels appear on the plane's silhouette. In keeping with the American principle that nothing should be simple, the design of this undercarriage was rather complicated: instead of tucking up straight into the fuselage, the Hellcat's wheels were turned before they folded away. It was that mechanism which caused my downfall.

I'd reached my destination, made a circuit of the airfield and prepared to land with the little silhouette showing quite clearly that the wheels were down. Unfortunately, some wires had become crossed, always a danger with too many complicated electrics. There was nothing on the picture to tell me that although the wheels were out of the fuselage, they hadn't turned forwards and locked on to the landing position. What's more, no one else had noticed either, though the duty observer at the Ice-Cream Cart should have fired a flare as I passed over him warning me not to land.

I suppose it wouldn't have made much difference if he had warned me because there was nothing I could have done about the problem but land. And my goodness, was there a horrible noise as we literally carved our way through the runway. There was a delicious piece of ATA officialese to end the story. Of course they had to hold an enquiry as I'd done considerable damage not only to the plane but also to the runway—and the verdict was: 'Pilot held responsible, but not to blame.'

Flying for the ATA certainly had its hair-raising moments and we had to take many risks. That aside, we all used our duty rosters to our best possible personal advantage, particularly when a party or a celebration was on the cards. Being free in the evenings, we found a lot of excuses to celebrate. Beer and wine were the first essentials to get organised — but so too was the food. Indeed finding good food was one of the great priorities, and where the flying rota came in so useful.

We'd all get together with our duty chits and pool our knowledge of good foraging areas. If you knew what you were doing, it was possible to find people around the country who were willing to sell you home-produced food on the quiet: eggs, mushrooms and potatoes or even some hefty slices of bacon. As far as I remember, all our parties centred around the most spectacular fry-ups. Planning the operation took some care because we had to match the aircraft to the 'destination'; flying a Tiger Moth was very useful on these occasions, as they could land in any decent field. Then all you would have to do would be to climb over a couple of fences, sort out what you wanted with the farmer or his wife and be off again very quickly. But a Spitfire was another matter, as you could only land at an airfield with a big enough runway. Then you'd have to arrange some kind of transport from the airfield to the farm.

We were relaxed about our work, happy to get on with the job—and on the whole enjoying ourselves. We'd accepted the decision taken by the powers that be, that we were too old, or too bad to be allowed to fly operationally. In all honesty, I think both descriptions applied to me: there were occasions when I'm sure I scraped through on a wing and a prayer. And certainly, there were times when my flying took a bizarre turn.

On one occasion I was taking a Swordfish across country. These were elderly machines, which the Navy used to fly with a torpedo slung beneath them—I think their last moment of glory came when they were sent in to attack the German battleship *Scharnhorst*. By the end of 1943 Swordfishes were being replaced by Barracudas so there was an endless exercise of ferrying one or other of these planes.

On this particular day, it was an extremely long flight from Sherburn in Elmet to Donnybristle, taking something like two hours and forty minutes in this lumbering old plane. By the time I was flying across the Cumberland hills I was seized with the most urgent need to have a pee. It was actually worse than urgent, it was desperate and there was no way I could land the aircraft in the middle of that mountainous country! Nor could I see any solution to my problem in the cockpit apart from the great black nozzle of the speaking tube staring at me out of the instrument panel. It was the ideal shape, the ideal container—but there was going to be a tremendous problem in getting to it. I would definitely have to get out of my seat and stand up to it.

This was possible in the Swordfish, as it was one of the last planes where the cockpit was open to the winds. However, this also meant layers and layers of extra garments to un-zip. We were wrapped up like parcels, first the uniform, and then a flying suit with a sheepskin jacket over that and everything tied on with safety straps and parachute straps. So it was an immensely tricky and acrobatic feat to unwrap myself while flying the plane, and then to stand up and get on with what I had to do. Goodness knows what it must have looked like from the ground—an elderly bi-plane, zooming around the sky in the strangest of flight paths. When I reached Donnybristle there wasn't much I could say to explain the speaking tube. I think I just parked the plane, had the chit signed and left fast!

Another time, in a Spitfire, I completely lost my way flying to White Waltham. I was flying from the north of England, following our rule-book and keeping above the cloud which was a blanket across the whole country. But when I went down through a hole in the cloud to land—after what I thought was the right amount of time flying in the right direction by the compass—I was appalled at being unable to recognise a single feature on the ground below. It was a frightening feeling since with no radio one was completely alone. Somewhere along the line I'd obviously made a serious misjudgment in my navigation.

As luck would have it, I saw the welcome colour of an RAF flying school in the distance. All their Tiger Moths were painted bright yellow, making them highly visible—they always reminded me of a swarm of bees. I knew I'd find out where I was if I landed there. The tricky part was not to lose face in front of all these trainee pilots by revealing my ignorance. Having landed, I taxied up to the Watch Office to explain myself (just as a matter of courtesy since we were allowed to land wherever we liked). 'Sorry to interfere with your flying routine, I had to land because I'm dying to go to the loo . . .' But I saw what I needed; on the inside of every Watch Office door was a large map of the United Kingdom with an arrow saying, 'You are here'. It was Leicester. Honour was saved.

The Spitfires got all the glory from the war, but there were other planes which I thought had very exciting lives too. We used to fly Mustangs down to Brenzett on Romney Marsh for the Polish squadrons. From runways that were just ordinary fields, covered with a wire mesh, they would take off to chase doodlebugs — V1s — on their way to London and try to divert them off course by tipping their wings, thereby upsetting the gyro.

Lysanders probably had the most dramatic of jobs, transporting people behind enemy lines. They could land and take off on an ordinary road; but also they could fly so slowly — at thirty miles an hour — that they didn't really need to touch down. This was meant to be secret and perhaps that was why flying a Lysander always gave me a rather special feeling.

We flew so many planes that I'm still surprised I came out in one piece. I knew I wasn't a good pilot. But my flying career ended rather abruptly, certainly much sooner than I'd expected (though in fact the war ended shortly after). I was lucky to be alive, considering that the last aeroplane I flew was deposited untidily over the airfield at Dumfries. The powers that be were not at all pleased about this, as I shouldn't have been there in the first place.

I was flying an aircraft to a maintenance unit when I noticed a definite and strong smell of burning. This had never happened to me before and there was a moment of horror when I wondered whether I could remember what I'd been taught to do in such an event. Somewhere from the back of my mind I dredged up instructions from elementary flying school: first, shut off the fuel and then dive the aeroplane sharply in an attempt to put out the fire — if you're flying at a sufficient height of course! If that fails to work, there's nothing to do except trim the aircraft so that it flies straight and level away from any built-up areas — and prepare to eject. I always thought that would be the tricky bit, making sure you undo only the harness and not the parachute. Then you jump out of the aeroplane, pushing away from the side; you pull the cord and hope that the parachute opens and you float gently down to earth. That was the theory.

I was horrified at the thought of leaping out of a plane. And of course, I couldn't do it, the whole idea was sheer lunacy—it would have killed me even if I'd got as far as opening the canopy and standing up on the seat. We had never jumped. They had told us what to do: how to jump and pull the rip-cord. They had shown us how to roll over on landing and get out of the harness. We had even watched people checking and packing parachutes, so we had some idea of what they were like. But there's a world of difference between the theory and doing the jump for real.

So I took the next option and exercised my ATA right to land the plane at the first suitable place, which happened to be the airfield at Dumfries. By this time all the correct procedures had come flooding into my head including the golden rule that in an emergency you should never land on the runway. This had nothing to do with the well-being of the pilot, but if the undercarriage was jammed or something broke off you might churn up the surface, making the runway unusable for other aircraft. As far as the rule-book went, I followed all the procedures perfectly. I did a circuit around the airfield to show them I was coming in, landed on the grass—and was out of the cockpit like a shot.

I didn't stop running until well away from the plane and I must have broken all the speed records. With a plane on fire anything could have blown up at any moment. But when I stopped to draw breath, not only was my aeroplane burning a bit but in all the landing and skidding it had banged into a Wellington bomber that happened to be parked nearby, so there was quite a blaze that afternoon. I don't think I was a popular visitor.

However, there was nothing I could do about that! Within minutes, I was in the hands of the station's own emergency services and swiftly taken off to see the Medical Officer, the MO, which was routine after any accident in an aeroplane. I remember very well being picked up off the airfield by the ambulance—or the Blood Wagon as we used to call it—and being made to lie down and stop talking. I thought this was all stuff and nonsense.

The doctor seemed to be a particularly nice chap. I told him I felt OK and didn't think there was anything broken or damaged. I felt very lucky, and very well. He said: 'Well, let me just run a rule over

182

you, take your blood pressure, pulse, temperature—all the usual sort of thing. I want you to lie down on the couch so I can feel around and see that you really haven't broken anything.' I knew I hadn't broken anything, but he insisted that I lie down just the same. His examination seemed to go on for ages—it probably took only about five or six minutes, but I remember thinking that the RAF were very conscientious about their work compared to our rather more relaxed approach in the ATA.

At last, the MO said: 'Right, good, you're OK. Let's go across to the Mess and have a cup of tea.' I thought this was an absolutely marvellous idea. I got off the bed, stood up and then fell down, flat on my face.

The MO was highly amused. He'd often seen the after-effects of crash landings and knew what was likely to happen, which is why he'd kept me in his surgery. He said he could tell from my eyes that I was suffering from shock. I don't know whether it was the shock of the crash or the shock of finding myself flat on my face after it . . . But he was right about the cure too—fifteen minutes later everything was fine.

I think the CO at my parent station was genuinely pleased to see me back in one piece, but he was also absolutely right when he welcomed me back by saying what a bloody awful pilot I had turned out to be—or words to that effect. Even if it was all down to bad luck, I'd certainly had more than my fair share of prangs in my short time with the ATA. But they do say: 'Third time lucky'—and when the CO seemed concerned about the state of my health I thought this was a wonderful chance for a couple of days' leave. It turned out to be much better than that.

The CO surprised me by saying I could have rather more than a couple of days. Having looked up my record and seen that I was due to be demobbed shortly, he'd had a chat with the station doctor and they'd come up with a plan which would give me a long stretch of leave to recover completely from the accident. It would then be about time for my demob. This was a diplomatic way of saying that he didn't want me breaking up any more of their precious aeroplanes.

Not that I minded a bit. It was 1945, the war was over and all we were doing was clearing up. On VE night I happened to be in Liverpool—and bumped into my very dear friend Joe Loss, of all people. He was staying at the Adelphi. Like everyone else, I had gone into town to celebrate—but I was on my own, away from my home station, away from people I knew. To see Joe so unexpectedly was wonderful and we celebrated together, along with all the musicians who were with him. For the first time in five years, I was talking music again. I hadn't realised how much I'd missed it all before—but I knew it was time to be getting back.

That was easier said than done and the process of getting demobbed was hilarious. The ATA couldn't do the job as I had only been seconded to them by the RAF; the whole process I'd gone through in 1943 had to be reversed. Physically I had to return to the RAF before being allowed out. It also meant going back to the waiting around and the paperwork—an immense amount of paperwork. But eventually they sent me to somewhere (Blackpool, I think) where I was given a suit of clothes, a mackintosh, a hat, a pair of shoes, a sum of money—the gratuity, they called it—and a travel voucher, which wasn't very much. And that was that. I was free to go home, a civilian again. It was November 26th 1945.

CHAPTER EIGHTEEN

A Crisis

Naturally, I wanted to get back to London as quickly as possible, back into the swing of my old life, playing the fiddle again. I'd thought about it for some time and was looking forward to restarting work. But I wasn't sure about going home: I'd been away a long time and the few visits to my family during the war hadn't been easy. The ATA had been generous over leave—we got two days for every ten flying days, taking them wherever we happened to be—but travelling to London was often difficult (because of the distances involved) and I have to admit that I made less and less effort to do so.

Home at that time was my mother-in-law's flat in Wigmore Street. Over the years, she, Betty and Elizabeth had made a life for themselves. In fact my return to them felt rather strange; their war and my war could have taken place on separate planets. There was no feeling of home-coming, no party, no welcome. I had the distinct impression that I was a nuisance, interrupting their routine.

However, I had other matters on my mind. First I needed to get myself a violin and start practising again, then find out what was happening on the musical scene. I looked at the gratuity they had given me, and worked out that there was enough for a decent instrument and a couple of weeks to get my fingers back into working order.

Finding a new fiddle was actually quite easy; I went round to Paul Voigt's shop in Monmouth Street, told him that I had about twenty-five pounds to spend and came away with a very serviceable instrument, an ivory-mounted bow and a case—which I still have. It wasn't the greatest instrument in the world but it would do for the time being, to get me back into the profession. I didn't think it would take me long to find my way back into the best of the freelance

A civilian again

jobs—then I could afford to find something better.

To have a new violin is like starting a new relationship; you have to get to know the instrument, just as you have to get to know a new person. You have to discover what makes it tick, what it does and how it behaves itself. Every musical instrument has its little quirks of character, but I think that you probably have to work hardest at a violin because each one really does have a personality of its own. A Stradivarius violin, for example, is so temperamental it can behave exactly like a prima donna.

Once I'd bought my new violin, I couldn't wait to get started. I went home, shut the door to my room, gave everything a quick polish, rosined the bow and thought: 'Right, let's start off with a few flourishes to see how it all sounds—a few scales and arpeggios, the odd passage from a concerto . . .' I like to get my balance before I start to play, to put the weight on both legs and have my back absolutely straight—this makes it much easier to move the arms freely. There's a sort of ritual before I put the fiddle under my chin and make myself comfortable holding it. Only then, when I'm properly balanced, is it right to bring the bow down on to the strings and start playing.

I got the most ghastly shock. Nothing happened. I tried to play, and I mean I tried. I couldn't play, although I tried. Everything was all wrong: the violin felt uncomfortable and unnatural to hold and the bow wouldn't stay in my fingers in the way it ought to have done. It really was impossible and very upsetting. I couldn't believe what was happening to me. Everything had been fine at Voigt's when I'd given the instrument a quick play-through. Now, nothing was working.

The violin just wouldn't stay in position. I put it under my chin in what I thought was the normal way, in the way I'd always done which was second nature to me. And it just wouldn't work. I couldn't keep the fiddle there without it slipping out if I moved my left hand, the hand that should have been putting the fingers down on the strings to make the notes. It was a strange sensation, knowing what I had to do but not being able to make it happen.

Worse still, I couldn't make the fingers work properly; they felt stiff, huge and very slow—and they all seized up together. I couldn't make them work independently. As for the bowing, I could barely keep hold of the stick, let alone move it with any kind of subtlety. It sounded as though I'd been learning the fiddle for three weeks, not playing for some twenty-five years. I had actually forgotten how to play the violin.

I put the instrument back in its case, thinking that it was all to do with being out of practice and that I'd quickly crack the problem once I decided on a plan of exercises. In the meantime, I visited some of my old haunts, met some of my good friends and had a drink with them. Forgetting the whole experience for the moment, I needed time to feel I was back in the swing of things.

London had changed tremendously: it wasn't just the aftermath of the Blitz, the bombed buildings and that grey, unkempt look of neglect. The mood had changed. The amazing escapades of the thirties had long since vanished, and there was a utilitarian feeling about the city.

It was a strange sensation to be back in London after such a long time away—and such a long time away from the music business. I felt that people had forgotten my existence. One day I bumped into an acquaintance in the street, a fellow musician, who stopped and looked at me and said in amazement: 'But it can't be Max Jaffa— you're dead!' There had been a story going around that I'd crashed an aeroplane and been killed. I was very shocked by this experience, especially as I knew that there was something terribly wrong with my fiddle playing and that I might just as well be dead. I felt that I'd killed the music, forgotten it all and been left behind by almost everyone I knew.

It was a sombre drink I had that day: I sat by myself, thinking hard and trying to work out a plan; I really had to be serious about learning to play the fiddle again, but part of me still couldn't believe what had happened and that side said: 'You can always start tomorrow.' The next day exactly the same thing happened—I couldn't play, I couldn't hold the violin securely, and I couldn't hold the bow. Nothing worked. I became extremely depressed about it and kept on thinking: 'Why won't it all work, why can't I play?'

The two sides of me were in constant disagreement: my mind told me to make a plan, but in my heart of hearts I believed everything would all be all right tomorrow. Mañana, mañana, tomorrow, tomorrow—everything would come back to me miraculously. Soon I developed a routine: I'd pick up the fiddle, try to play, fail again, and go off for a few drinks, determined that the next day I would really start the disciplined regime of practice.

This went on until my RAF gratuity, such as it was, had been practically exhausted, and I was beginning to feel desperate and frightened, almost suicidal. I couldn't think of another way of earning money apart from playing the fiddle. Of course there were in theory any number of jobs available but it never dawned on me that, for instance, I could sell socks in Selfridges. All I'd ever done was play the fiddle and I thought that's all I could ever do—or wanted to do.

But then, I had the most extraordinary piece of luck. One wonderful day, as I was walking down Oxford Street, I literally bumped into my old friend and teacher, Sasha Lasserson, who had taught me so much after I'd left the Guildhall. He was a wonderful man, and I had been, I think, one of his favourite pupils. As soon as we met, I knew that here was someone to whom I could pour out my heart, the very person who could help me sort out my problems.

Before the war, I used to consult Sasha about all kinds of difficulties and technical matters. He was one of the best teachers in the country, if not the world. He himself had been taught by the remarkable Leopold Auer, who in turn had taught all the great players. Along with Sasha Lasserson there was Mischa Elman, Toscha Seidel, a girl called Erica Morini who was a great player, Nathan Milstein (now in his eighties and still playing

Sasha Lasserson with Jascha Heifetz

marvellously)—and for me the best of them all, Jascha Heifetz.

Thank goodness Sasha was almost as pleased to see me as I was to see him. It was a great reunion. We had some coffee and talked. I told him about being demobbed, that I couldn't play the fiddle and that this was very worrying as I didn't think I could do anything about it. He was very understanding, but naturally he also thought it was all a load of nonsense. 'Once a player,' he said, 'you're always a player.'

He suggested that I should come round to his house with the fiddle and play to him and he'd try to diagnose what was wrong. But that, of course, was exactly what I couldn't do—I couldn't even play him one note. He saw at once that things were serious and that I was terribly upset. Something would have to be done very quickly.

But that meeting did the trick. I had a brainwave and said to Sasha: 'Let's try to imagine that I've come to you as a complete stranger. I've got a fiddle and a bow and I've heard what a great teacher you are. So please, I want you, the great Sasha Lasserson, to teach me how to play it.'

The problem, which he saw at once, was that I'd never before had to think about how to play the fiddle. You don't if you've an

189

aptitude or a certain amount of what people call talent for the instrument. When I found I couldn't do what had always come naturally, I panicked. And continued to panic. Sasha would have to become my psychologist, or psychoanalyst, as well as my teacher.

My own relationship to the instrument was as it had always been—a very personal thing. The fiddle becomes almost an extension of your own body, out of which you try to coax beautiful sounds. In the days when I could play the fiddle, I loved it, I loved playing, and now I was almost beginning to hate it, because the instrument wouldn't do as I asked. But it never dawned on me that this was my fault. Half the time I blamed my problems on the new fiddle—a bad workman always blames his tools!

So Sasha took me right back to the beginning; he showed me how the fiddle should be tucked under my chin, where my left arm should go and how the hand should come round the neck of the instrument. Then I learnt how to hold the bow, how to curve my fingers around the stick and get the weight balanced. He actually taught me the equivalent of learning how to walk again. I had to go right back to the basics of violin technique, where every student starts—doing long bows and scales. You practise bowing across open strings, making sure that the bow keeps in its correct position all through its length. Once you've got the bowing under control, you then find out how to put fingers down in the right place on the string to make the notes.

You have to learn the different spacing for the fingers between playing a semitone and a whole tone. You have to learn how to feel the distance from one note to another; playing scales, for instance, some notes are a tone apart and some notes only a semitone away. What's more, you have to learn how the spacing changes as you go up and down the instrument—as you go higher, the spaces are narrower, and wider as the notes go lower.

My stiff fingers were quite a problem to get working as separate digits again. I think I'd actually developed a few muscles during the war which got in the way. When I was holding a joystick in an aeroplane or clutching a rifle, I didn't move my fingers—instead my hands had to grip and tighten. I couldn't have avoided it at the time, but for a violinist it was the worst thing I could have done. A fiddle player needs flexible and well-exercised strong fingers.

To get them back, we had to start again from the beginning, doing all those exercises you are taught when you start to learn an instrument, whether it be the fiddle, the piano or anything else that needs finger movement. You have to practise each movement separately, starting slowly and doing it again and again, getting quicker and quicker at it. Gradually you build up your technique, moving from the simple scales and arpeggios and simple bowing movements to 'double stopping' (playing two notes at once) and all the other ways of using the bow.

Fortunately, I hadn't lost my ear—in fact I've never been accused of playing out of tune. That's very good for a fiddle player and a marvellous gift.

Of course Sasha's regime took time, but in the end I did it. I forced myself to do it, just as anyone would if a doctor or a specialist told them that they mustn't smoke any more cigarettes, or they must go on a diet. I would go for a lesson, practise what I'd been taught in front of the long mirror—and go back for another lesson. I saw Sasha four times a week, and the remarkable thing is that when I asked him about his fees (it could have become very expensive), he said: 'Oh, never mind about the money.' He wouldn't take a fee at all, during a period of about seven months when I must have seen him well over a hundred times.

It was a lonely struggle as I couldn't talk to my musician friends about my playing problem; in the freelance musical world, people were always desperately careful to give the impression that everything was all right with them, that they were well. Nobody ever had a problem and nobody ever wanted to hear about a problem with playing. Naturally I fought shy of going anywhere where I might bump into somebody who would ask me about my playing.

Drinking helped to pass the time. Occasionally non-musician friends joined me, but quite a lot of the time I drank by myself and I could easily have become an alcoholic. So that meeting with Sasha Lasserson was rather like seeing the Heavenly Light. He had enormous insight, which of course is why he was a great man and teacher. He obviously knew all about the taboos in the music business and he knew enough about people to understand that I had other personal problems as well. I'm sure that's why he insisted on seeing me so many times a week.

Life in my mother-in-law's flat was an empty shell. Betty and her mother had supported each other through the war, both working in the fashion world. My wife had always moved in her own circle of friends which I accepted and encouraged and I knew that she might well have developed deeper relationships when I was out of the picture. My daughter Elizabeth was no longer a small child. I felt like an intruder. There was nothing, except possibly our daughter, to hold the marriage together.

Sasha's regime of lessons helped me to come to terms with this reality: every time I went to see him he gave me so much to practise that there was nothing for it except to go home, lock myself in my room and work. I just ignored everything else, knowing that the following day I'd have to go back and satisfy him that I'd been applying myself to the violin; I'm sure that if I hadn't worked, he'd have kicked me out. After all, either I wanted to play the fiddle and would therefore put in the work—or why should he be bothering with me? So I worked very hard, practising for about four or five hours a day after each lesson, more on the days he didn't teach me.

Suddenly everything started to come together again. I began to play little pieces and found that I hadn't lost my sight-reading skills. Thank goodness for that—it's one of the most important qualifications for any musician. But there was still a great deal of hard work to be done to get back all the technical refinements of playing the fiddle and I wanted desperately to play as well as before. Knowing this, I was unwilling to return to the business until I was ready to cope with anything that anyone might offer me in the way of a job.

Getting back into the business turned out to be rather curious. It was naturally a great pleasure to be with old friends again: they seemed delighted to see me and we had a lot of catching up to do. But there were two kinds of musician after the war: those who had joined the forces to fight and those who joined up to keep on playing music in the various newly formed orchestras and dance bands. In the RAF alone, the war had created a Symphony Orchestra, an official RAF Dance Orchestra known as the Squadronaires with a second band known as the Skyrockets—and goodness knows how many small five-piece bands posted to air stations all over the country to keep the boys happy.

For those musicians—and there were a lot of them—there was absolutely no change in their lifestyle, except that they wore a uniform. In fact, the war years were a godsend for many people's careers; they got a positive boost with so much of the competition out of the way. Those musicians had a whale of a time, especially on off-duty hours when there was any amount of freelance work, playing in hotels, restaurants, film sessions, broadcasts and recordings. But I had never seriously considered spending the war playing the fiddle, or volunteering for ENSA or any of the other entertainment groups and concert parties. All I thought was: 'How can you win a war playing the fiddle?'

So, after my rehabilitation with Sasha, I had to start again right at the bottom: my first professional engagement was on the back desk of the Mantovani Orchestra. It was a radio broadcast and I was quite happy to play along in this lowly position to convince myself that I could still do the job. We had to play music that I hadn't seen before, and I remember an arrangement of some new popular tune being put in front of us to read at sight. This was quite easy and I felt reassured. In fact, it wasn't long before my confidence returned in full, and I worked my way up through the desks to become Mantovani's leader.

After I'd recovered from the trauma and gone back into the profession, I continued to go to Sasha as a paying pupil. Many professionals still have lessons because when you do a great deal of playing—whether you're giving solo performances, working in recording studios or sitting in an orchestra—it's easy to get into bad

Sasha Lasserson – a great teacher

habits. I know I did: I would look for the easy ways around technical problems, which were very rarely the most musical ways, or the ones that made the best kind of sound. So I'd go to see Sasha for a 'check-up' about once every six weeks and he would spot immediately what I was doing wrong. Once forbidden by Sasha, you'd never repeat the error.

Sasha insisted on some very important criteria. First and foremost was a singing tone and every player had to learn how to make a beautiful sound on the instrument. After all, the violin is a singing instrument, not percussive like the piano. Even if you play a virtuoso piece with a very fast stream of notes, they still have to sound like a coloratura soprano, with every note counting. Then there's the phrasing of the music; a player should have a natural feeling for the shape of a phrase, without stretching it out of proportion or getting the emphasis wrong. Of course, you can play around with the phrase in all kinds of ways, putting an extra emphasis on a note to make a point—exactly as you would when speaking.

At the same time, you have to make music with other people, listening to what they're doing to make your playing complement theirs. Every player has to know what's happening in the whole piece of music, to be aware of what the accompaniment is doing—unless of course you are playing unaccompanied Bach. But playing with a piano or an orchestra, even in the most unimportant of pieces, you have to know all the other parts.

There's a skill in making an entrance at the end of a phrase that's just been handed over to you by another player. It's absolutely vital to have that sense of time if you're playing with an orchestra, otherwise the poor conductor doesn't know what the hell you're doing.

Sasha was the most kindly of men, and at the same time he never suffered fools gladly. I remember one player (who shall be nameless) who hadn't studied with Sasha but came to him for advice. He was already giving concerts, playing concertos and recitals and had made quite a name for himself. He chose to play Sasha one of the huge and difficult pieces for the solo violin, the Wieniawski Tarantella.

He played it through and came to the end, and there was a silence. A long silence. Then Sasha said simply: 'That's perfectly dreadful—who did you study with, Schmeerienski?'

Now, 'Schmeer' is a Yiddish word for 'smear' and obviously

Sasha thought this player was smearing over the notes, not making them clear enough. So he told him to go away and start again by first practising scales to find out where the notes really were on the instrument. Only then would it be possible to begin on the showpiece, practising slowly and carefully. Sasha didn't care about this man's famous reputation or that he'd been playing it all over the place in public. (The famous player of course ignored the advice and carried on as before—he wasn't going to start again from scratch.)

That was typical of Sasha: he was absolutely plain and open about what he thought. But it didn't worry me, I knew the value of what I was getting—and if I turned out to play cleanly and in any way like the Leopold Auer school of violinists, I'd be very happy.

However, I was also reminded of the responsibilities of the performing artist. When you walk out on to a platform to give a concert, you are attempting to do much more than just play the notes and get them right. The process of getting the music under the fingers is only the first stage; making it mean something is most important.

Of course, you can't get to that stage of serious interpretation without spending hours and hours building up the technique with the music, and being single-mindedly dedicated to the task. If I hadn't been compelled to earn my living while at the Guildhall, I might have spent the time in more profitable practice and have come out with a better knowledge of violin playing. So if I'm proud that I paid my own way through my student days, I also regret occasionally that I couldn't practise as much as was needed if I wanted to become a serious concert player. Sometimes I feel that I didn't go far enough with the talent I was given, but at other times that perhaps I didn't have what it would have taken. Who knows? On the other hand, starting again with Sasha gave me a second chance. There was a goal to aim for and this time round, I could think about how I played and how it was going to work for me. I'm sure that when I came back to the music business, after all the lessons with Sasha, I was a better player than before.

CHAPTER NINETEEN

Starting Again

Mantovani had turned to conducting from playing the fiddle—like several musicians, he realised that he was better at getting others to play than playing himself. He also had the luck to be in the right place at the right time at the end of the war, and collected together a really good bunch of players from among the musicians coming out of the forces. It was a heaven-sent opportunity to start something new and right across the board people were grabbing their chances. At the serious end, Sir Thomas Beecham came back from Australia and started up the Royal Philharmonic Orchestra, while over at HMV, the recording company, there was a rival new orchestra, the Philharmonia, which boasted the cream of the country's orchestral musicians.

Entertainment of all kinds had flourished during the war: cinemas had been packed, the Promenade and National Gallery concerts had done a roaring trade and there had been full houses in theatres up and down the country whatever was on the bill. For those who couldn't get out, there was always the radio at home. The BBC broadcast music for a large part of the day. Once the fighting was over, it was simply a question of business as usual, but without the difficulties of air raids and blackouts. The public wanted it all—and more.

Popular taste always needed something new, and Mantovani cleverly saw the way things were going and provided the music that people wanted. The BBC took it seriously enough to start broadcasting the Light Programme as their second station in 1945, the succession to the Forces Programme, and Mantovani's music was exactly right for it. This was before the days of that distinctive Mantovani sound of the echoing strings—that came a little later—

but there was plenty of work to be done simply to fill the airwaves and the recording studios. People wanted sweet music and sentimental tunes, something to take their minds off the war and rationing and that dull and dreary feeling of 'austerity'.

Where there was lost time to make up was in the record business, badly hit by rationing. So there was a wide-open market and a lot of new music to learn. A new musical style had captured people's imagination when the GIs came over; Glenn Miller and the American big band sound had really opened people's ears. The recording studios were soon busy.

I got caught up in the slipstream of all this when friends got me in to play on the back desk. This quickly gave me a regular income. Playing for Mantovani—or any other popular conductor—was not a bad way of earning one's living: once he'd decided he could use your playing, you were a permanent part of the orchestra. The conductor got the dates on the strength of his name and all the players had to do was turn up and play. Obviously, the more popular the conductor, the better one's income.

Mantovani—or Monty as everyone called him—certainly had enough work for us. There were recording sessions, broadcasts and even the odd concert date. But there was also plenty of work around for musicians in theatres. They were reopening with lavish productions; Noel Coward in particular understood very well that while it was grim and grey outside, there was all the more need for escape and fantasy on stage, and this included a good orchestra. The Mantovani orchestra occupied this position for the first two of his post-war productions.

Sigh No More was a revue, the first show to go into the Piccadilly Theatre, and it starred a then unknown young actress called Joyce Grenfell. She was great fun to meet, but I only played for the last few weeks of the show before it closed. Then at the end of December 1946, we opened with *Pacific 1860* starring Mary Martin, which was the first show after the war at the Theatre Royal, Drury Lane. By this time I was leading the orchestra for Monty—and it was the first time that I had ever truly played in a theatre orchestra, down in the pit accompanying singing and dancing. I found it fascinating to see what went on and how to get the music and the stage working together.

The two halves only joined forces towards the end of rehearsals. We'd learnt the music separately, while Noel Coward had done what he had to do with his actors. It was quite some business fitting the two sides together; I think we had two or three days of stopping and starting and joining up the numbers. Sitting at the front of course gave me a good view of what was going on.

Noel Coward was always a gentleman to work with, but he was a words man and not really a musician. He would write the tunes to his songs and then Mantovani's arranger Ronald Binge did the arrangements and orchestrations. Noel didn't know a thing about musical technique. One day, when we were going through a new number, there was a terrible commotion in the theatre and Noel rushed up to us, elegant as usual with his camel-hair coat thrown nonchalantly over his shoulders but very agitated at what we were doing.

'There's a wrong note in the music,' he said. 'You're playing a wrong note! No—I mean a wrong chord. You're playing a chord that I didn't write!' So Ronald Binge came hurrying up to the front with his score, but of course Noel didn't have the first idea of where the mistake was; he couldn't see it at all in the music on the page. Nor could Ronald Binge get him to say what the right chord should be. However, the solution was very simple to Noel: 'Play them all then, until you get the right one!' That's what we did—we tried out every possible permutation until Noel heard the sound that he wanted.

Noel Coward always got what he wanted—or so it appeared. He went his own way regardless of anyone else. For example, while everyone called Mantovani 'Monty', including his wife, Noel Coward had to be different. He was the only person I know who called him 'Manty'!

The critics were almost entirely negative about *Pacific 1860*, giving what Noel Coward described as 'a blast of abuse'. The show also had the bad luck to go on in one of the coldest winters ever, when the snow stayed thick on the ground for many weeks, finally melting in May. To make matters worse, it was freezing even indoors as there were power cuts and fuel shortages. I sat in the orchestra pit trying to keep out the cold by wearing my flying boots with my evening dress. The entire audience sat shivering in their fur coats, and we could see people in the front rows covering their knees with rugs to keep out the onslaught of cold air coming at them from across the wide open stage. Even with the best of shows, it would have been difficult to enjoy yourself.

Pacific 1860 had some good tunes, but of that English, Noel

Coward gentility—the music was too 'nice'. There wasn't much humour in it and good as she was, Mary Martin seemed out of place. But the stage was beautifully furnished and the actors and actresses beautifully dressed, thanks to the designer Gladys Calthrop—who always worked for Coward. She designed the most wonderful sets: at the opening of the show, as the curtain rose, there was always a burst of applause from the audience as the lovely scene was revealed. One saw a magnificent and brilliantly lit chandelier (specially made at the most enormous cost) and the stage was filled with couples dancing. It was elegant as only Noel Coward was elegant, but that wasn't enough any more. It had closed by mid-April and was followed by *Oklahoma!* with the new kind of punch that everybody wanted. Audiences just couldn't stay away. The next show after that, producing probably even more punch, was *Annie Get Your Gun* at the Coliseum. This occupied me for nearly two years, one of them as conductor of the orchestra.

Lew Stone directed that orchestra for the start of the show and I was the leader and sub-conductor, but most of the music hardly needed direction as long as the rhythm was good. The dances were different. The music always follows what the dancer is doing and *Annie Get Your Gun* had a marvellous, show-stopping Indian Dance, devised for the whole company by a young Canadian boy called Paddy Stone. Paddy later became a very famous choreographer, and I'm sure that *Annie Get Your Gun* gave him a wonderful start. Another choreographer from that company was Irving Davies, Paddy's assistant; he also went on to great things.

After a few weeks of playing it night after night plus matinees, we all knew the show so well that we felt we could play it in our sleep. In fact Lew Stone always fell asleep in the bits where we weren't playing. He would bring his sandwiches into the pit and munch away—and then have a snooze. It was understood that someone would jog his elbow just before the next number so he could wake up to give us the downbeat. Once, we decided we wouldn't bother with this; we'd start without him and see what happened. He woke up with the most enormous jolt and I think he was half a bar behind us for a good way into the number.

Lew was one of the few pre-war fashionable band leaders who was actually a good musician. He was a pianist who knew all about arranging his own music. Lew had been with Roy Fox's band at the Monseigneur Club and took over when Fox left, giving it his own very distinctive sound. It's the arrangements which give a band a name, a unique and individual sound, that the public then recognises immediately they hear them play.

Most conductors or band leaders depended on the arrangers to make their music unique to them—and quite a few arrangers could turn their hands to anybody's style. In many recording sessions there wouldn't be a well-known 'conductor' in charge; an arranger would have music to record and they'd simply collect together a group of musicians to do it. Being Mantovani's leader certainly did my career a great deal of good as far as these other conductors and orchestral 'fixers' were concerned. I was on their books as someone suitable to hold together any scratch group of musicians.

Mantovani depended on Ronald Binge; they worked together very closely. But it was Binge who dreamed up Mantovani's absolutely individual swooping string sound. He just turned up one day with a melody called 'Charmaine', in which he'd invented a new way of playing the tune. Nobody else knew anything about it, not even Mantovani. But it's a formula which has since been built into all of Mantovani's pieces.

In simple terms, it's a built-in echo. There's no need for an echo chamber or artificial reverberation devices in the recording; it's all there in the music and done by the players themselves. Binge did it by splitting up the violins so that although they were all playing the same notes, their entries were staggered and therefore the notes overlapped. You'd have one group of violins playing the tune as it ought to sound, in time and on the beat—and another group playing the same tune, but just a split second behind them. Quite revolutionary.

As an idea it seemed extraordinary and it was quite tricky to do the first time we heard it. I tried to recreate the sound with my tiny orchestra in Scarborough; they all thought I was mad. But it worked very well with Mantovani, as everyone knows, and it gave me my great claim to fame with the orchestra. The day that 'Charmaine' was recorded, it was my job as leader to play the eight-bar violin solo in the middle of the piece. So there I am, playing on the original recording of 'Charmaine'.

Annie Get Your Gun got me my violin! After two years of such wonderful steady work (and with a bonus the second year from being in charge of the band), I was back on top financially. It was time, therefore, to find myself a decent fiddle.

Paul Voigt's instrument had served me well since the war, but the better the instrument you have, the better you play—it becomes a partnership between the two of you, rather than a battle to produce a good sound. When Max Mossel lent me his Carlo Bergonzi, my playing improved no end, thanks to the instrument which was beautifully made to 'speak' easily. There were many times when I yearned for it after I had to give it back—and when I longed for my poor Postiglione, the fiddle I'd had to pawn just before the war for the sake of a few pounds.

Portrait by Snowdon – with violins

London is well served with violin dealers, including one of the most famous of all names, W. E. Hill and Sons, known to every string player in the world as 'Hills', who used to have their premises in Bond Street. As usually happens with teachers and pupils, Max Mossel had introduced me to the firm and I knew they would be the people to advise and help me choose something that would work well for me.

The Bond Street shop was a wonderful place (they've now given it up and moved out of London) but the inner sanctum was a fiddle player's dream. It was lined with instrument cases and had an enormous safe, stretching from floor to ceiling, filled with great fiddles. By great, I mean the legendary names of Stradivarius, Amati, Guarnerius; instruments which were worth thousands of pounds, even in 1947.

Mr Phillips Hill took me through to the back and asked me a few questions to get some idea of what I wanted. But it was awful—I couldn't give him precise answers. I wanted a violin which sounded glorious but wasn't too expensive, although I had no idea what 'expensive' might mean in terms of violins. I was completely in his hands. He brought out six or seven instruments for me to play and I had a puzzling time weighing up the merits of one against the others, trying to remember what was what. It was difficult to decide between them, and yet none of them seemed quite right.

And then, Mr Hill produced yet another—and immediately I felt something special. But there was no rush to conclude the deal on Hill's part; he suggested that I took the violin away for a couple of weeks and played it every day to see how it behaved.

It was made in Cremona in 1704 by Peter Guarnerius, who came from Mantua and was known as Peter of Mantua. (He was a close relative of Joseph Guarnerius, the greatest violin-maker in the family, whose instruments are known as Guarnerius del Gesù.) The asking price for my violin was twelve hundred pounds! It was in superb condition, but I was horrified. I knew I wanted the instrument badly, but I had only six hundred pounds to spare in the bank. Phillips Hill was quite unperturbed by that; the firm would come to some arrangement with me.

All the fiddle players in the Coliseum orchestra were interested to see my violin but very dismissive; they thought it wasn't the fiddle for me, not special enough and a bit slow to 'speak'. But I'd discovered something in just those few hours of playing it: the more

I played, the more the sound seemed to grow. Every day, it became more and more alive, and responsive, and glorious.

After a fortnight, there was no going back. It was just like falling in love and I had to have the instrument. The more I got to know it, the more it responded to my playing. Phillips Hill was delighted. Apparently the instrument hadn't been played for about ninety years—it had belonged to a couple of collectors, not players, so it was what is called 'asleep' and needed to be awakened. Apparently in the official book about the Guarnerius family of makers they explain the phenomenon in terms of young people and old people. Youngsters can jump out of bed and are ready to go, while old people stagger about a bit and have to loosen up before they're good for anything.

Even now, each day when I first pick up my fiddle, it's very sleepy and I have to give it a couple of hours' hard playing to wake it up (which wakes me up too, thank goodness!). We start enjoying ourselves when it sounds vibrant and alive. In a strange way it seems to be something to do with tuning up the wood: the really great fiddles have a very straight grain in the wood, but my Guarnerius has a notch in the straight grain and it curves round. I've never ever regretted buying it and it has never let me down. I must say, it's treated like royalty; no one apart from me is allowed to touch it except Jean—and when we have a break during a rehearsal, I remind people to be careful by sticking a large notice on top of the case:

Das machine is nicht fur gerfingerpoken und mittengraben. Is easy schnappen der springenweek, blowenfusen und poppencorken mit spitzensparken. Ist nicht fur gewerken by das dumkopfen, das rubbernecken sightseeren keepen hands in der pockets, relaxen und watch der blinkenlights.

You need notices like that with some of the people who come backstage to see you and ask about the music and the instrument. 'So it dates from 1704!' said one fan. 'Did you get it when it was new?'

CHAPTER TWENTY

Back in the Swim

It took me probably a couple of years to get back into that top group of musicians with whom I'd worked before the war. None of us was taken back just for the sake of old times; we had to prove again that we were up to the job—which basically meant showing that we could play anything that was put in front of us. The music business is highly competitive and it takes only a short break away from the studios for everyone to forget who you are and what you can do. There are always plenty of people, especially younger players, waiting for their chance to take your place.

Working for Mantovani gave me a foot on the ladder—but when I made my way up to the front desk and started to lead the orchestra for him, it reminded everyone about Max Jaffa. Very soon I found myself right in the middle of the post-war boom in music-making; when Monty didn't need me, I was off leading all sorts of orchestras for recording sessions and broadcasts. I even joined the BBC's Studio Players—but more of that later.

Some years afterwards, when I was listening to the record request programme *Housewives' Choice*, I suddenly realised that on every record they played which had an orchestra, I was the leader and I was playing the fiddle solos. It was a nice contrast to those months of struggle which only Sasha and I knew about: you could say it proved how successful his treatment had been.

Successful players could be kept very busy indeed in the light music world. There was work available seven days a week from nine o'clock in the morning until ten at night and we would play for at least two sessions a day, often three and sometimes even four. Once you were on the books of the top fixers, you were practically guaranteed non-stop work; the difficulty was in turning it down. I

With Norrie Paramor and George Elrick at the Abbey Road studios

was playing for the likes of Ray Martin, Norrie Paramor, Sidney Torch and many others who were making records at HMV and Columbia—there was a group of us working for them who were almost 'house' musicians. The record companies were busy changing over from 78 rpm to LPs, so everyone was busy re-recording all their popular hits.

We also worked all over London, moving from the HMV studios in Abbey Road to Decca in West Hampstead, to Philips at Marble Arch and to and fro between the BBC studios in Broadcasting House, Bond Street and Maida Vale. Film sessions were held out of London at the various studios in Beaconsfield, Denham or Elstree. Film music was very lucrative and relatively relaxed in terms of the hours worked; it usually took three or four days to record the complete score but we often packed in two and a half or even three sessions' worth of music, starting at nine thirty and finishing between four and five thirty in the afternoon. That gave us time to get back to London and cram in a fourth session at the end of the day, which I often did. It does no end of good to your self-confidence to be in demand—but it also helped to keep me away from a home which was far from happy.

In fact, it was hardly a home at all. As soon as I began playing again, I decided it was necessary to look for larger premises. I found the ideal solution in Bickenhall Mansions, an Edwardian block of flats in Marylebone, which seemed to be twice the size of anything I'd ever lived in before.

Just inside the front door were a couple of rooms probably once used by maids, then a long corridor stretched away to the main part of the flat. For four pounds and fifteen shillings a week inclusive of rates, my wife and daughter could live their lives at one end of the flat and I could have an almost separate existence in those two rooms by the front door. I could come and go and practise without disturbing them, and they could entertain their friends without having to worry about me.

By that time, my wife had a very good job working in the showrooms for Worth, the dress designer. She was petite, good-looking and always well turned out—and naturally, she had her own circle of friends and business acquaintances. She didn't need me any more and we had nothing in common. However, in the early fifties, divorce was out of the question—it was just not done in those days, even with so many people changed beyond all recognition by their experiences in the war. It was certainly not done in Jewish families. You kept up a front, a pretence, and got on with your lives as far as was possible.

Of course, we were both civil to each other when we met in the mornings or during the day. We sent Elizabeth to Merstham Grange, a boarding school in Surrey, where there was a charming headmistress who we knew would give her the best possible support. I'd promised my wife that I would stay with them both until Elizabeth was married.

In the meantime, there was work. The life of a session musician is a world apart from that of the musicians you see playing at public concerts. Hardly ever did I play in public to an audience—very few of us did. Our world was the recording studio, playing to a microphone and the red light; our job was to play whatever music was put in front of us as quickly and efficiently as possible. Very little of it was 'great' music. We were professional back-room boys playing whatever was needed for a special purpose, and we knew we could play anything.

In the best sessions, we recorded light music or dance music for well-known conductors such as Mantovani; that was a pleasure, because the melodies were good and decently arranged. At the end of three hours you felt you'd achieved something worthwhile. We'd also work for people like Ray Martin, Bob Farnon, Ron Goodwin, Sidney Torch and Wally Stott who were recording the same kind of tunes—similar music but with different arrangements.

Then there was background music for films, which helped

provide the atmosphere and excitement. Those were often stop-start sessions recording nothing more than a few phrases at a time which would later be 'mixed' together with sound effects and the dialogue. We also did a similar job for what is known as 'library' music: several publishers had collections of recorded music to fit a variety of moods and styles and they added to them regularly as fashions changed.

These provided useful music for people making short films or commercials. We would go into the studio to record several tracks which might be sweetly romantic, or busy sounds which were possibly suitable for a film about factories, chase music, spooky music, period music. All of it was written in a familiar style, very close to a well-known tune or piece but just slightly different. In fact, it wouldn't do to be too recognisable, because the point of library music is that it can be used again and again. So we were recording pale imitations of the real thing—and we could do that on a 'read-through' and a 'take'.

To be honest, money was the only reason we worked at this end of the business. It was quick, you didn't have to think very hard and there was an enormous demand for it. In fact, if you wanted to make a decent living as a musician—as an ordinary musician, not an international soloist—you had to work in the commercial business. Even Dennis Brain, who was the best horn player in the country and famous all over Europe, played sessions to boost his symphony orchestra income.

On one occasion he was actually doing three recording sessions at once for the BBC in their Maida Vale studios. You could only do this if you played a solo instrument like a horn or a trumpet that wasn't needed in every piece; fiddle players were usually kept busy in every single number of the session. Dennis had done a deal with each of the conductors so that they'd do the pieces with horn parts at a specific time during the three hours—and he just went from one studio to the next.

Poor Dennis eventually came to a tragic end. He'd been playing in a concert up in Edinburgh at the Festival and had a booking for a session the next morning in London, but rather than take the sleeper he decided that he would drive back overnight. Nobody knows how his car crashed—we could only imagine that he fell asleep at the wheel. Everyone was deeply shocked; it was a huge loss to music. I was very sad at losing a greatly admired and respected friend.

There were two requirements for playing as leader on sessions: first, that you could play your instrument to the highest of standards, and second, that you could sight-read to perfection. There was never any time to work at getting the notes right or find clever ways of avoiding the tricky bits; you saw the music on the music stand and you performed it. The next time you played it through would probably be the actual recording.

On one session for the BBC, I had a last-minute call to come in and replace the leader of the orchestra, Michael Spivakovsky, who had been taken ill. This was a recording with the big Light Music Orchestra (now the BBC Concert Orchestra) conducted by Michael Krein, a member of a famous musical family. He went in for rather up-market music, including proper concert pieces like the suites from Tchaikovsky's ballets.

When I eventually arrived at the studio, the music to *Swan Lake* was on the desk, including the famous violin solo which is quite a difficult piece to play. I'd never played it before in my life and we would shortly be broadcasting it live. I had the luxury of about half an hour to practise. (That's actually not easy in a building jam-packed with musicians. I found myself retreating to the gents' lavatory, where at least I'd be guaranteed good acoustics!)

Much later on, I discovered that in the theatre, when you're playing this solo to accompany the ballet, the solo violinist is in a slightly raised position, so the dancers can be seen and all the swoops and runs in the music adjusted to match their aerial leaps. So it's played much more slowly and is therefore not nearly so difficult.

But this versatility was not recognised financially, nor did the Musicians' Union help to get leaders paid more. I should perhaps explain that the only professional musicians who can play in public without joining the Musicians' Union are soloists; the union is tightly run in that respect. You have to join if you want to play.

However, there are extraordinary inconsistencies about the MU. They look after you when you're at the rough end of the rank and file players, but the better known you get, the less they're interested—even though the battles probably get tougher the higher you climb up the tree, because there's more at stake. Once I'd got to leading orchestras, they lost all interest.

In the fifties there were about half a dozen session leaders in London. Between us we seemed to do every orchestral recording, film recording and orchestral broadcast, as well as being linked to some 'permanent' group, as I was to Mantovani's.

One day four or five of us happened to meet and start talking about our lot as leaders. We were paid no more than the players in the first violins; yet we would often find waiting for us the most enormously complicated cadenza to play note perfect, giving it the kind of panache needed for part of a great violin concerto. There might also be several huge solos, all to be learnt in only a few minutes' huddled practice in a corner while the others were having coffee before the session started.

This time, instead of just moaning, we decided to ask the union to try to do something about it. I was elected spokesman—heaven only knows why, as I had never negotiated with anyone in my life. However, it wouldn't have mattered who had gone to the union, because they weren't impressed with our argument. As far as they were concerned, they negotiated only the basic fee. If we thought that we could—and should—be paid more for the work we were expected to do, then it was up to us to negotiate for ourselves.

In which case, I said, we didn't see the point of being in the union. I reasoned that paying our subscriptions entitled us to some kind of return. That didn't worry them either, if we wanted to resign. We could resign—it was entirely up to us. I resigned.

Forty-eight hours later I found out what I'd done when I walked into the Decca Studios in West Hampstead for a recording session with the Mantovani Orchestra. I said hello to everyone, they all said hello back; but when I took my fiddle out of its case, all fifty of them immediately put their instruments away. 'Sorry, Max,' they said, 'we can't work with you. You're not in the union any more, and you have to be a member of the union in order to play with this unionised orchestra.' The word had got round fast, spread by the union officials whose job was to go to all the recording studios checking up on people's memberships. The directive was that if Max Jaffa turned up, they weren't to play with me as I'd left the fold.

It wasn't so bad on the first day, but by the eighth or ninth I could see I was going to starve very quickly. So I had to swallow my pride and apply to rejoin the union. To this day my membership card carries the date of my rejoining, not the date when I originally became a member. The Musicians' Union was not very interested in my decision to return. 'You know,' they said, 'that there is a fifteen-guinea premium to pay on top of your membership dues. Welcome back!'

There were times when I had some very distinguished players sitting behind me in the section; leaders of famous symphony orchestras, and even Sasha Lasserson, but I was never aware of any envy or jealousy. I think they accepted me as a leader because I was good at my job. The job of the leader is to mark up the parts, put in the bowings, and generally to make all the music sound good.

In a session we hardly ever knew what music we'd be playing or who else would be involved, which of course sometimes led to the most marvellous surprises. I shall never forget the day we all piled into EMI's Abbey Road studios. I was leading and playing solos and we were being taken through the music by an American conductor no one had met before. We were still sizing him up when a young lady arrived to join us for some vocal solos.

It was only when she started singing that we realised this was Judy Garland. Somehow, you never think that the stars you see in the movies are actually real—but here she was, working with us. I had a wonderful bonus from that occasion: she'd done her numbers and we thought she'd left the studio, when she suddenly reappeared, came up to me, went down on one knee, threw her arms round me and kissed me—to thank me for the solos I'd played for her! I'd thought they were fairly ordinarily schmaltzy numbers but she thought they were beautiful. It just shows that one's never the best judge of one's own work.

The next time we met was in 1960, when we were on the same bill at a Gala Variety Performance at the London Palladium for the St John Ambulance Brigade, honoured by the presence of the Queen Mother. The artists included the Trio, Bruce Forsyth, Cliff Richard, David Kossoff, Billy Dainty, Des O'Connor, Russ Conway and Norrie Paramor. I'm certain Judy sang 'Somewhere Over the Rainbow'.

In 1953 I was engaged to play the violin solos in a weekly series of twenty-six broadcasts called *The Forces Show*. These were recorded at the Garrick Theatre and presented by Jack Buchanan, complete with pearl-grey trilby hat. He owned the theatre and lived in a flat 'above the shop'. Also on the show was a regular singer called Diana Dors, plus the Geraldo Orchestra and a famous artist each week.

The best-known guest was undoubtedly Bob Hope, who arrived with no fewer than four scriptwriters who were feeding him his jokes while he waited to go on. The series was fun to do, Jack Buchanan

Jack Buchanan

was a charming person to work for, and the BBC producer, Bill Worsley, knew exactly how to make life easy and enjoyable for everyone.

Session playing could at times be awful, with badly arranged music and some arrogant and rude conductors, but I always tried to keep my temper. As the leader I was a buffer between the conductor and the rest of the players. Sometimes it was very difficult. There was one occasion when I was leading for a well-known conductor who was driving us all round the bend with his anxieties about the music. He was particularly annoying to me with his constant questions: 'Max, how do you think this should go? Should we play it like this or like that, should it be an up bow or a down bow?' Every five minutes he would stop to ask about another detail—which was hardly important, given that we weren't playing anything more than some fairly routine arrangements. It was just stopping us from getting to the end of a particularly dreadful session. Suddenly, I could stand it no longer: 'For me,' I said, 'I'll play it sideways . . .' and scraped my bow up and down the strings so that it made the most appalling noise. The whole orchestra collapsed in uncontrollable laughter. It broke the tension, but this conductor never asked me to lead his orchestra again!

In any orchestra there'd always be someone who'd interrupt the

211

play-through to announce: 'I've got a wrong note.' It was Phil Green who put a stop to that question by saying, 'So, if you know it's wrong, play a right one.' Phil Green was a composer and arranger for whom we had a lot of time. He was a great character, a good conductor and a fine musician. He would if necessary rearrange music on the spot: 'Violas, at bar fifteen play such-and-such instead of what's written,' and he would hum a few notes to give the rhythm. 'Cellos, bar twenty-three, do so-and-so, clarinets do such-and-such.' And that was that.

As players, we considered ourselves at the top of the tree, professionally speaking; we were always in work, always in demand. Inevitably some people began to give themselves airs about how good they were. A very good friend, Louis Stevens, with whom I'd often shared the leading of an orchestra, turned that way. Louis was a lovely player and produced the most marvellous sound from his instrument. However, he did become rather grand and used to make disparaging remarks about other players in the section. On one occasion, he made an ostentatious gesture by presenting me with a cigarette lighter as a gift for no special reason that I could think of.

Louis made himself the butt of a lot of ribald comments but of course it helped pass the time in sessions to dream up ways of playing tricks on him. The best of these was the work of another fiddle player, Maurice Taylor, a great friend of mine with whom I often worked, playing on the same desk. Maurice lived in the country, near Thorpe Bay, and he found out that Louis Stevens hated anything to do with bugs or creepy-crawlies. One day when working on a BBC session (which he knew Louis would be leading) Maurice brought up some snails which he planned to put into Louis's cup during the coffee break. Word had somehow spread to all the five studios, which were full of musicians. We all organised our breaks to coincide so the canteen was packed for the classic moment.

It was absolutely wonderful; Louis took a sip of coffee and suddenly saw four antennae waving around in his cup. Of course he couldn't see the joke and was absolutely appalled. It kept us laughing for a good hour until the end of the session.

Strange things happened to my mind during these sessions. I could sometimes switch off almost completely, thinking, 'Well, this isn't Brahms or this isn't Beethoven.' And yet, when it came to the solo that seemed to be in every piece, instinctively I would give it my best—just as though it were Beethoven or Brahms. It was like eating junk food all the time, and pretending that it was a decent and really satisfying meal.

Proper concerts were where I found real pleasure: hearing 'proper' violin playing, from the likes of Milstein or Isaac Stern or, best of all of course, Jascha Heifetz. Then I'd say to myself: 'That is what music is really all about'—and wake up next morning to the reality of a three-hour session of library music or whatever was in the diary for the day.

Very occasionally, there was an opportunity to do some 'real' playing, in a concert. Reg Kilbey used to conduct an amateur orchestra in his spare time, called the Edgware Symphony Orchestra. (I took to calling him 'Sir' Reginald Kilbey, since all conductors seemed to get knighted.) Many of us went off to play concertos with them—Jack Byfield did several and 'Sir' Reg asked me to play the Mendelssohn and then the Tchaikovsky Concerto, for a public concert at Wembley Town Hall.

Since the Tchaikovsky is one of the most difficult concertos in the repertoire that was quite a task. I had to learn how to play the piece again mid-sessions—and to snatch every odd moment I could to practise. In fact, when Brodsky, who was the soloist for the first performance, saw the score he had an absolute fit and asked Tchaikovsky to make several passages easier. (Later, Leopold Auer decided to put back some of the virtuosity, and made an even harder version than Tchaikovsky's own original.)

I had the most terrible shock when I walked out on stage to find that a large number of my friends and colleagues had made their way out to Wembley. I hoped they had come to lend moral support, rather than to enjoy the mess I might be about to make of the piece. Right in the front row I was horrified to see the familiar face of Daniel Melsa, a marvellous fiddle player who made quite a career as a soloist as well as a session player. He used to sit way behind me—in the third or fourth desks—but he could play absolutely anything. 'Go on, Danny, play something,' we used to say when we were bored, and he would rattle off something like Paganini's *Moto Perpetuo* — which is non-stop virtuosity and high-speed violin technique from beginning to end. He would just play it without a mistake in sight.

The concert went well—but it convinced me that I was psychologically unsuited to the solo player's life. There's nothing so lonely as standing in front of a large orchestra, about to launch oneself into some of the greatest music ever written.

CHAPTER TWENTY-ONE

In the Bosom of the BBC

The BBC welcomed me into their fold early in 1947, booking me for a broadcast from their studios in Maida Vale. This was a complex of five music studios of all sizes which had been built from an old skating rink. It was a great crossroads, a meeting place for musicians of all kinds: at any one time you might find there the Symphony Orchestra playing with a top soloist and conductor, a light music session, some chamber music and a couple of small popular groups. It was absolutely buzzing with music and musicians.

That first day, Tom Jenkins was leading the orchestra for that famous programme *Grand Hotel*. Tom and I hadn't met for ages—probably not since before the war—but he immediately said: 'Oh, good, Max. We need a violinist.' In fact, if I remember rightly, he might even have said, 'We need a *good* violinist . . . Why don't you come and join us in the Studio Players?' Of course I said I'd love to. The BBC had started the group which became the Studio Players during the war and they were the backbone of BBC light music. They must have done hundreds of broadcasts. The group had a nucleus of about fifteen players who were augmented as necessary by other ad-hoc players to form all sorts of different groups and orchestras. That's how I had come to be called in for the day.

There was the London Concert Orchestra, about thirty strong (which I eventually found myself leading); and the London Theatre Orchestra which played music from the shows, and became the BBC Variety Orchestra for broadcasting in the variety programmes. It wasn't necessarily a question of the same bus with different drivers—some of the orchestras were made up of different players—but it meant that the BBC was employing a vast number of musicians, both freelance and on contract. It was a valuable source of work.

A solemn BBC photograph

A lot of my pre-war chums had found a haven in the Studio Players, for example the oboist Leon Goossens. One of his sisters, Marie, played the harp (while another sister, Sidonie, was the harpist with the BBC Symphony Orchestra). The flautist was Geoffrey Gilbert (one of James Galway's early teachers), Reginald Kell played the clarinet, Archie Camden played the bassoon and Dennis Brain the horn. My fellow violinists were Albert Sandler, Jean Pougnet, Reginald Leopold and Tom Jenkins, and Michael Krein conducted. (He also played the soprano saxophone.) Reginald Kilbey played the cello, Aloysius Beers—'Wishy' Beers, we called him—was on the double bass, and Jack Byfield was the pianist. All of these musicians were household names.

As the BBC Salon Orchestra they'd kept playing all through the war. Evacuated to Evesham they'd be playing one broadcast during the day, another one in the middle of the night and probably three the next day. They performed a really vital task, maintaining a stream of music and bolstering morale—good reasons for keeping them out of the Services. Their broadcasts became extraordinarily popular; the programmes were wonderful and musically in a different class from the dance band shows also popular at the time.

(But I don't think people listening could have realised quite how famous the musicians were!)

The BBC offered to put me on a programme contract to the Players. I would have to make myself available to them for a minimum of four broadcasts a week, in whatever combination of orchestra or ensemble they wanted me to play in. In return, they would pay me a regular fee. If I did any more, then they would pay the going rate for each extra session.

When we weren't working for the BBC there was nothing to stop us taking on work outside—which I was doing anyway, with Mantovani and other orchestras. But it was a great help to know a guaranteed sum of money was coming into the coffers each week.

It was an education for me. In any one week we could be asked to play popular hits from the shows, brand new scores for films or the great classics of the repertoire. We played overtures such as *Poet and Peasant, Morning, Noon and Night, The Silken Ladder*; excerpts from famous operas such as *Orpheus in the Underworld*; *Swan Lake* and *The Sleeping Beauty* ballet suites; Strauss waltzes and polkas and even some of the smaller symphonies by Haydn and Mozart. Almost all the great composers have written lovely pieces of what we think of as 'light' music—tunes everyone can whistle or hum. Most people would probably recognise Beethoven's Minuet in G or the *Humoresque* by Dvořák or Mendelssohn's *Midsummer Night's Dream* music.

Four sessions a week sounds like quite easy work—but you could be asked to play at any time of the day or night, and in the fifties an early morning broadcast probably meant a rehearsal that started at 6 a.m. Goodness knows how anybody could work out which end of the instrument to play at that hour, considering that we'd probably been working until midnight the night before. But we felt we were on a kind of production line: they wanted the music, we could play it and there was no point in being a prima donna about it. The BBC, after all, was—and is—the biggest employer of musicians in the world.

The BBC were also pretty good as talent scouts with their ears to the ground for the most promising newcomers. I can remember the most extraordinary morning, when a young guitarist came to make his broadcast debut with us. We were quite shocked by his appearance: longish hair combed back in a greasy quiff, drain-pipe trousers and thick-soled shoes—he looked exactly like the teddy-boys of the time. But he took his guitar out of the case, tuned up, and launched into some Bach or something. He turned out to be the young Julian Bream, one of the most glorious guitarists and lutenists in the world.

Mostly, we were happy-go-lucky at work and had a good laugh whenever we could. Often that happened at the expense of the other BBC people who came across our paths, particularly the producers and the announcers. Poor old Freddy Grisewood couldn't understand the snorts of laughter he used to inspire, but we all remembered the wartime despatch which he began with the wonderful words: 'The troops spent last night in olive *groves* . . . I'm sorry, that should have been *olive* groves'. As far as we were concerned, Olive Groves was a dignified concert soprano, much in demand on the oratorio stage.

Bill (Wallace) Greenslade perpetrated another of our favourite howlers. We were playing a mixed programme: I'd just finished my solo and was tiptoeing across the stage while the announcement was going on for the next piece. And in mid tiptoe I heard him say: 'Now we're going to hear a piece for harp, played by Gwendolen Mason. "Love's Fascination" arranged by John Thomas.' Well, there was no mistaking the fact that the entire orchestra was 'corpsing' with laughter. Dear old Gwendolen all innocent and unknowing carried on playing while we dirty-minded musicians stifled our ribald giggles.

Another amusing story again concerns an announcer. Henry Krein (brother of Michael), a virtuoso accordionist, was mad keen on French-sounding popular music, and found a group of like-minded enthusiasts to broadcast with him. He has gone down in studio folklore too, for demolishing an announcer who mispronounced the word 'chameleon'—giving it as 'ch' as in church, rather than a hard 'c' as in cat. Everyone in the studio heard—and it might have been picked up by the microphone—as Henry stage-whispered in disgust: 'Chunt!'

My great joy was to meet up again with Jack Byfield and Reg Kilbey. They were very dear colleagues whom I'd enjoyed working with before the war, but working together with them in the BBC developed that friendship into something quite new, thanks to those little groups that came out of the Players. At the end of our broadcasts the announcement went something like: 'That was the *Casino Orchestra*, conducted by Reginald Kilbey. The pianist was

Jack Byfield and the leader was Max Jaffa'. Then there was: '*Melody Mixture*. That was directed from the piano by Jack Byfield, the leader was Max Jaffa and the principal cello was Reginald Kilbey.'

Later I formed an ensemble of my own for a programme called *Melody on Strings*. It was a double string quartet with piano and double bass as well; we played a mixture of fairly high-class music with bits of chamber music, some of the popular pieces and a few special arrangements. Strangely enough, the announcement at the end went: '*Melody on Strings* with Max Jaffa. The pianist was Jack Byfield and the cellist was Reginald Kilbey.'

Each group sounded different from the others: we chose many types of music, and a considerable number of pieces were specially arranged for our various combinations of instruments. As with any dance band, we never simply played off ready-printed sheet music.

Everyone had to liaise with the other groups and we planned our programmes three to four weeks in advance. The BBC Music Library kept a list of what everyone was performing so we could check that nobody had chosen the same piece at lunchtime which we wanted to play that evening. The BBC has a wonderful library of music which they've acquired over the years, and it is continually updated.

Very quickly it became a routine that Jack, Reg and I would work together for three of our four contracted sessions a week. We agreed that this round of *Casino Orchestra*, *Melody on Strings* and

Playing with Jack and Reg to accompany the Hastings Girls' Choir on the Sunday evening programme Nocturne

218

Melody Mixture was getting a little much. But one day, as the three of us were sitting having a cup of coffee in one of the BBC canteens, we thought it was time for a change. Jack suggested that we resuscitate the 'old Trio'.

Jack, Reg and Albert had been the famous Albert Sandler Trio, which was very popular both on the radio and in concerts before the war. I remember going to hear them at the Dominion Theatre, Tottenham Court Road, when they topped the bill in a variety show. Albert Sandler was an enormously talented player, one of the very first people to broadcast regularly for the BBC. He started at the Grand Hotel in Eastbourne, moved up to the Park Lane Hotel in London—and then played in the music halls, which is where Jack and Reg had met and joined him. He was an absolute sensation there. During the war, he moved back to the BBC and continued the Sunday night performance *Grand Hotel*, from the studio—but sadly he became very ill. Albert made a slight recovery from his illness, enough to lead the Palm Court Orchestra for a *Grand Hotel* broadcast—but I nearly cried hearing the deterioration in his playing. He never came back after that. I will always have a fond memory of playing beside him in one of our sessions.

But nothing had taken the place of the Trio on the radio, leaving a mass of good music that wasn't being heard. Jack's suggestion came as a surprise, but none of us could think of any good reason why we shouldn't start another trio and the three of us decided there and then to put the idea to the Head of Light Music. In those days the BBC was much more informal, without the red tape of having to make appointments and present programme proposals in writing. If you wanted to see someone, you went directly to his office to discuss your business.

The boss, Douglas Lawrence, was there, so we put forward our suggestion: 'What about a trio? How would you like the three of us to do some broadcasts?' He made up his mind immediately: 'Splendid, marvellous. How about doing one next week?' We did— and that's how it started. We began as the New BBC Trio with all of our names being credited—but that took too long to say, especially when we moved to TV in 1954. Then we became known as the 'Max Jaffa Trio'.

It meant, however, that I had one week to learn a completely new repertoire. I hadn't played in this kind of ensemble since my very early days working with the two ladies at the Station Hotel,

Richmond. But I had excellent teachers in Jack and Reg, who took me through most of the music from scratch.

There is a wealth of music published for piano trio, but the way Jack and Reg had worked with Albert Sandler meant that very little of what they had played survived as actual music on paper. Most of their music was specially arranged (a lot of it by Jack)—but after all those years of concerts, both he and Reg knew them all by heart and had long ago lost the manuscripts. There were other arrangements in the BBC library but none with that famous Albert Sandler touch.

So they gave me a crash course on the fiddle parts. For that first broadcast, they decided that all the tunes we played should be tunes that I already knew—which was lovely. This meant I had the easy bits, while Jack played the harmony and Reg exquisitely expanded the melodies.

Making music with Jack and Reg was absolutely marvellous. We played together more or less seven days a week for something like thirty years, and we never had a cross word. Never. Obviously there was a certain amount of discussion about what we were going to do with a piece of music—but most often we simply worked out new

Making music with Jack (centre) and Reg

arrangements on the spot. Jack would say: 'We'll play this there,' and he'd play the phrase and I'd learn it. Then somewhere else Reg would want to play one part and give me another and we would probably argue the toss for about three minutes. And then Jack would perhaps say: 'Never mind, I'll play it and you two play something else.'

Once I had got into the swing of things and learnt the repertoire, we found that we played together so well that we hardly needed to rehearse our concerts. In fact, the only time we were forced to rehearse was for the TV shows when we did it for the benefit of the cameramen, the sound people, and I suppose, the director.

We played from memory, feeling that music stands cluttered up the stage and came between us and the audience. And from an eventual repertoire of hundreds of items, most of the tunes soon became second nature to us. Nevertheless I do remember the day we had to improvise an invisible stand. Jack always wrote some new arrangements of old tunes for the television programmes. Television really eats up material; millions see your act during the broadcast so you have to find something new for each show.

Jack would bring the newly arranged parts to the TV studio on the day of the broadcast. We would then memorise them as we played our way through the camera rehearsals, and work out who was to play what, when and where. It wasn't difficult because we usually knew how the piece went. Poor Reg had all the hardest bits to do because Jack always gave him the kind of musical detail which made the arrangement special to the Trio and distinguished us from anyone else. So Reg had to do the real memorising every time. When Jack arranged 'The Flight of the Bumble-bee' with a very difficult cello part, Reg found it hard to memorise, and as time moved on towards the broadcast he became more and more worried.

Our solution was wonderful. Luckily, I always stood slightly in front of Reg when we played, so I sellotaped the music to the back of my dinner jacket. This enabled him to see it quite clearly. I had to be careful not to turn my back to the camera—but as far as I know, no one was any the wiser.

Sometimes, work got a little on top of Jack; he was such a good musician that everyone wanted him to arrange music for them. There was one famous day when he was working on an arrangement for the Trio of what he called 'Waltzes from the Operas', but he'd left it till the last minute. He was writing out the parts on the train coming from Brighton (where he lived) to Victoria. He knew the piano part and had managed to finish the fiddle part but there just wasn't time to do the whole of the cello part before the train arrived and he had to get into a taxi and dash to Broadcasting House. I've kept the original manuscript of the unfinished cello part because it was an absolute Jack classic: the music peters out with the immortal words: 'Reg, for Christ's sake, busk *Faust*!'

CHAPTER TWENTY-TWO

A Serious Relationship: Jack and Reg

Our weekly radio broadcasts laid the foundations for the Trio's success; they gave us the time to become really comfortable together as an ensemble. It was a great privilege for me to work with two such wonderful musicians. You often read about the rapport between players in the top string quartets where they play as one; I think we made music like that—the three of us working as one.

Meanwhile, as we were getting into shape, somewhere out there over the ether we were building up an audience for our music. After the war, while there was certainly a change of mood, there was also a hunger for something new and different in entertainment and a sense of nostalgia. The world had changed beyond recognition and people wanted to be reminded of the tunes and songs they had grown up with, and would always love. We were lucky in that we played the kind of music that lasts, that has an appeal for each generation as they discover it. You can't go far wrong with pieces by Haydn and Mozart, Schubert, Tchaikovsky, Beethoven; Viennese waltzes, medleys of Gilbert and Sullivan, gypsy music, entr'acte pieces and the tunes from operetta and musical comedy.

Jack arranged them all for us, and he was certainly our central point of reference. He was the most brilliant musician. He could play anything from sight that you put in front of him, put the music into any key—which he was always doing for singers who felt uncomfortable with the pitch of their music—and he could remember practically any piece of music you cared to mention, for whatever instrument.

Jack became a great friend, and we shared an abiding passion:

Jascha Heifetz. If the great Russian violinist was playing within easy travelling distance, we would be there. We would always go to hear Jascha Heifetz recitals together and discuss the music and how he played—and the next day Jack would stop playing in the middle of something and say: 'You know, Max, you should go to a Heifetz concert every day because you always play so much better after you've heard what he can do on the violin.' I'm still wondering what kind of a compliment that was.

We knew everything about his playing and his repertoire—we had all his records, playing them so often that we went through several copies of our favourites. When Roy Plomley asked me to cast myself away on his Desert Island, he was more than a little irritated to discover that I intended to pass the time with no one but Heifetz; indeed, with nine Heifetz performances on the eight records, because I included his version of Bach's D Minor Concerto for two violins, where he plays both parts. He must have felt that I was seriously obsessed.

Plomley and his producer thought I should show an interest in other recordings, not realising that I was pulling their legs and had a mixed selection of records ready. But the only records that I have ever seriously collected are by Heifetz. There will always be Kreisler of course, and these days brilliant younger violinists like Itzhak Perlman, Kyung-Wha Chung, Anne-Sophie Mutter and others. For me, the playing of Heifetz has never been bettered: his sound is so glorious, strong, lyrical and rich—and always appropriate to the music he plays. Nothing is too difficult for him. It sounds effortless.

Yet, having said that, I remember a famous occasion when we simply could not believe our ears as he played a very obvious wrong note in the Mendelssohn Violin Concerto. Sir Malcolm Sargent was conducting, and even he looked quite shocked. Jack and I gasped in astonishment, and some delight—Heifetz was human!

A couple of days later, we were both having a drink at the Savage Club, when the superb Russian pianist Benno Moiseiwitsch walked in with Heifetz as his guest—which, of course, sent us into the most tremendous flutter. The Savage Club boasted many fine musicians among its artistic membership, but as far as we were concerned, Heifetz was in a class by himself. Benno had known him for ages; they often played sonatas together and had indeed recorded Beethoven's 'Kreutzer' Sonata.

We all gathered round to talk to the great man—and Benno did the unmentionable by asking about violin players who play the wrong notes in the middle of the Mendelssohn Concerto. For the second time in two days, Jack and I gasped in horror. But Heifetz wasn't at all upset; he knew exactly what Benno was talking about. He had been playing two concertos in that concert, the Mendelssohn in the first half and a modern work in the second—the concerto he'd commissioned from Sir William Walton in 1939. It's a lovely piece but very difficult to play, and to memorise. He turned to me and said: 'I know exactly what wrong note I played, and where in the concerto. I was thinking of the Walton. Wouldn't you?'

I learnt of a visit Heifetz made to the great violinist and teacher of the day, Carl Flesch. During this visit Carl Flesch, who was a superb technician and wrote many studies on fingering difficult passages in the classic violin concertos, said to Heifetz: 'I think I have found a fingering for a certain passage in the Brahms Violin Concerto. I would like very much to have your opinion on this fingering.' He showed the music to Heifetz who immediately said: 'I must try it.' He took Flesch's Stradivarius and played the passage with the Flesch fingering. It came off beautifully. 'I must play it again,' he said—and again it came off perfectly. Heifetz seemed to be delighted, saying: 'I must play it a third time.' Which he did. But this time it was not so perfect. He put down the fiddle and said to Carl Flesch: 'I don't like it. It's not safe.' This just goes to show the perfection that Heifetz demanded of himself.

When Jack was a student at the Royal College of Music, he had had a very promising career in front of him as a composer. He studied with the Grand Old Man of the College, Sir Charles Villiers Stanford, who taught many of our best composers, so they had obviously recognised his talent. But I think Jack and Stanford had an uneasy relationship: Stanford thought a lot of him, but they had rather different ideas on what music was all about.

The very first composition that Jack took to Stanford had a strange reception. He played it through—but Stanford didn't say much; he just put his arm around him and said, with a twinkle: 'Jack me bhoy' (he was an Irishman), 'thank you, I think you need a holiday!' It wasn't quite the comment that Jack had expected. Several years later, he played this composition to a publisher—who immediately accepted the tune—and of course asked what the title was. For the College, Jack had called it something like 'Prelude to Romance'; but he could never resist finding a ruder alternative and told the publisher it was 'The Barmaid's Lament'.

I don't think he expected that the title would be taken seriously for a moment; no genteel piano player could possibly be tempted by 'The Barmaid's Lament'. The publisher decided that it would do much better as 'Adoration'. The next problem was more serious; the name Jack Byfield was not going to be a romantic attraction. But publishers are given to flashes of inspiration, and Jack suddenly found himself transformed into 'Nino Tirani'. As it turned out, it was quite a winning combination; Nino Tirani's 'Adoration' became a popular piece which I played a great deal, and indeed recorded. I wonder whether Stanford ever knew how wrong he'd been.

Jack's attitude to life probably stopped him from making the most of his talent; good musician that he was, he could never put up with the prima donna attitudes that he'd have had to endure in the concert world. He was much too interested in all kinds of music to devote himself day after day to all that practising and rehearsing. He had an affectionate irreverence for all music and musicians. And he kept Reg and me constantly amused with his sense of the ridiculous, especially when he gave the Byfield treatment to favourite tunes and songs. These all got alternative words and titles—for example, 'The Maid of the Mountains' became 'Hag o' the Hills' . . . but I'm afraid the words were always unprintable.

Jack was a tall man, quietly spoken and rather shy. He had a stammer which made him slightly reticent with strangers. It also made him very wary of speaking in public—which is why he let me do all the talking. It took years for him to brave a few words, in fact not until he started introducing his own piano solos at Scarborough. By the time he realised what he was doing, it had become perfectly natural.

He was a wonderful and kind man. Old ladies were charmed by him—one even left her house to him in her will. It was Jack who put me up for the Savage Club; the membership there is mainly confined to people in the arts, with a few scientists who were belatedly admitted when they decided science could also be a suitable occupation. Every second Friday, there is an entertainment put on by the members.

Jack's great friend and pianistic idol was, as I've said, Benno Moiseiwitsch—and if Jack thought highly of Benno, the compliment was certainly returned. They would spend endless evenings together, talking about pianists and piano music. I had the most wonderful

Jack Byfield at the piano

Benno Moiseiwitsch: a Savage Club menu

time with both of them, because they talked about a completely different world from that of our everyday session life. Benno was an international concert artist, and he worked with the best orchestras and the world's greatest conductors.

Benno Moiseiwitsch often played the piano along with another pianist, Mark Hambourg. They'd joke endlessly about what they were going to play, along the lines of: 'I'm going to play Beethoven.' 'Oh yes; and who's going to play the piano?' It was a friendly but quite fierce rivalry. Joe Davis, the snooker virtuoso, was once a guest when Benno and Mark were enjoying another little pianistic competition—and his wry comment was that he could have given the first one 'seven blacks'.

I enjoyed the Savage Club. I'd long wanted to be part of it, ever since I used to wait for Max Mossel when he took me home from the Guildhall. It became a home from home for me, a place where there was a strong tradition of friendliness. If your guest happened to arrive before you, it was an unspoken rule that anyone who was around in the bar would look after them, buy them a drink, make them feel at home.

The senior male of the royal family is always an honorary

member—but when the Duke of Edinburgh came for a visit just after he was given his membership in 1953, there was nothing extra special about the arrangements. This was in the days when the club was in Carlton House Terrace (it now shares premises with the Lansdowne). Benno took Prince Philip across to the window which overlooked the Mall and said: 'You'll get a very fine view of the Coronation procession from here—why don't you join us on the day?'

Jack was one of the untidiest men I've ever known: he always had cigarette ash down the front of his jacket and he could never sit down to a rehearsal or a recording session without first laying out all his smoking paraphernalia on the top of the piano, with a tin of thirty or forty roll-ups ready to get him through. I don't think he was really happy unless he had a cigarette stuck to his lip! He wouldn't survive in today's no-smoking climate.

Eating was another great interest. He was a gourmand rather than a gourmet; his diet seemed to consist entirely of eggs and bacon, fish and chips, pork pies and particularly whisky. He rarely asked for anything else, even at home!

Above all, he absolutely lived for his music: day and night he was either playing it or making arrangements of it for other people. His great musical idol was Brahms—sooner or later you'd hear a phrase or a harmony that came straight out of Brahms, so much so that I dubbed him Johannes Byfield. His musicianship was wonderful, and a great source of security to me because he had an infallible memory. If I couldn't quite remember how a piece went he'd quickly scribble it out on a scrap of manuscript paper—and I knew he would cover on the piano anything that went wrong.

And then, he always loved to play games with the music. When the mood took him, he would start quoting snippets from other pieces, weaving them into the accompaniment. He knew exactly how far these musical jokes could go before they interfered with the main piece—and he knew exactly how they would make their effect. I loved trying to match his musicianly wit.

On one occasion Jack and I had been engaged to give a short after-dinner recital to about 150 men, in a private room at what was then the Martinez Restaurant in Swallow Street, off Regent Street. Jack and I had arranged to meet at the Savage Club before this recital. What a mistake this turned out to be.

As always, there were a number of Brother Savages in the bar, and without thinking we had a few drinks, but suddenly realised that we ought to hurry to get to the restaurant in time. Arriving at the Martinez we were met by Clarence Wright, the man who had engaged us. He came down the stairs to tell us that they were not quite ready—and we were to have a bottle of champagne. Whilst we were enjoying our champagne another man came down the stairs, stopped dead and called my name. I looked up and recognised him; his name was Vairo, and he had been the manager of the restaurant on board the *Avelona Star*. We hadn't met for thirty years. He was now the manager of the Spanish restaurant, and insisted that he, Jack and I should remember the *Avelona Star* by drinking some of his own special sherry.

Clarence Wright then appeared, saying that the gentlemen were ready for the music, and took us to the room in which we were to play. (Now please remember that we'd had drinks at the Savage Club, and the champagne and sherry.) We entered the room and saw that there was a concert grand piano on a dais facing our audience. We looked at the audience—all men in dinner jackets and black ties—and it was obvious that they were rather the worse for drink. We didn't quite realise that so were Jack and I.

I unpacked my fiddle and bow, walked out on to the dais, Jack to the piano, and I into the curve of the piano, to a smattering of applause. I asked Jack to sound the 'A', the note for tuning. It was only then that I realised how drunk *we* were, for Jack with both forearms (fingertips touching) played the full length and every note on the piano, looked up at me and said: 'Take one out of that lot!' Our audience laughed, and I couldn't quite find a chin under which to put the fiddle. I knew then that it would be impossible to play.

Addressing the assembled company I told them that because of their kind hospitality (the champagne), we were not fit to play—and looking at them, added that they were not fit to listen. Would they mind very much if I told them some stories instead? They seemed to come to life and applauded the suggestion vigorously. I was told later on that for some forty-five minutes I told many risqué stories, and a number which were more than risqué. Our audience all seemed ecstatic, applauding furiously and laughing uproariously.

What a recital! We hadn't played a note.

Never again did Jack and I drink before a concert.

We might well have needed a few drinks to deal with one of the most curious requests I ever received. At the lovely Lees Cliff Theatre in Southend, Jack and I were playing what we liked to call 'a recital of encores', the sort of short, charming, popular and amusing pieces that other violinists bring out at the end of classical recitals. Sir Thomas Beecham used to call them 'lollipops' and he was absolutely right; they were sheer, sweet pleasure. As often happened, we found a written request waiting for us before the concert. This one I can remember verbatim: 'If it is in his repertoire, would Max Jaffa please play the Resurrection Symphony.' I even filed the piece of paper so that it would never be lost.

We liked very much the phrase—'If it is in his repertoire'. It might have been possible, but only if given the hundred or so other musicians needed to play the work. Mahler's Second Symphony has soprano and contralto soloists, chorus and organ, as well as the orchestra which is itself swollen with lots of extra horns and trumpets, and the piece goes on for about eighty-five minutes. I don't think it was quite our style—certainly no 'lollipop'.

Reg Kilbey was more serious about playing the cello—and he and Jack had a special rapport which came from playing together in the Trio long before I'd joined them. They were very close personally, and spent a lot of time together with their families. But he too enjoyed a good joke, and told his own brand of funny stories— laughing at them himself, which endeared him to me enormously. Reg always started a conversation with 'I say . . .' and always finished off a story with 'By Jove!'

When he wasn't playing the cello, Reg was a conductor, and a very good one; he eventually gave up the cello to concentrate on it. He was also a good-tempered conductor, which was rare, but then Reg was one of the kindest of men as well as one of the most professional. Players really liked him and they still talk about him with admiration today.

He was of medium height, plumpish and gave the impression of being very cuddly—perhaps that was something to do with being a family man. He was unpretentious and unsophisticated. His favourite meal was spaghetti, baked beans and chips, and he would be pissed as a newt on one gin and four tonics.

But how deceptive first impressions are: you would see Reg come into the studio, looking very unassuming, sucking away at his pipe—but when he sat down to play the cello, you knew he was in love with the instrument. He made the most beautiful sound you could imagine; I've never heard anyone (not even Casals) play Saint-

Saëns's *Swan* like him. His treasured and adored cello was a Grancino.

It was this precious instrument which gave Eric Sykes a dreadful idea. He asked us to play on his TV show. On stage there was the grand piano for Jack, and room for me to stand slightly in front as I always did. But for Reg, there was a chair and a music stand right on top of a huge pillar—in fact he had to climb a ladder to reach them. Of course, the suspense was awful. Would he make it? How about his vertigo? What on earth was he doing on top of the pillar? Once up there, he turned round, someone handed his cello up to him—and he dropped it. There was the most enormous gasp from the studio audience at the thought of Reg's beloved cello smashed to matchsticks. But of course it wasn't—they'd replaced his beautiful Grancino with some old box instead.

If I had the easiest task, playing the tunes, as the cellist Reg worked very closely with the piano. Part of the time he might be reinforcing the bass, giving the tunes a good solid foundation, or he'd be filling in the harmony with his own figurations and maybe a countertune to mine. Then he might even play a duet with me—playing the same tune in unison or a third or a sixth away. We were playing chamber music together; listening hard to each other's playing just as any piano trio would do.

One of our best reviews came in *Punch* when Henry Turton described us as 'three first-rate musicians who play with style and ease and that mutual understanding which is always a pleasure to watch in an accomplished chamber group'. And Philip Hope-Wallace, the music critic of the *Guardian*, gave us enormous pleasure because he touched on what we felt was really important (though we didn't play his kind of music); he recommended everyone to watch and listen to us for the marvellous ensemble which, he said, 'ought to be the envy of many'.

CHAPTER TWENTY-THREE

On the Road

As we did more and more broadcasts, the three of us found that we built up a concert life to match. Goodness knows how we managed to fit everything into diaries already crammed with BBC work and recording sessions. Our working day could stretch from nine in the morning to ten o'clock at night and much later if we were driving back to London after a concert.

In the early days, none of us liked to give up a morning's work, so we generally drove to concerts independently. We would arrive in the afternoon early enough to have a look at the hall, try out the acoustics and hang up our dress clothes. Neither Reg nor I ever elected to travel with Jack if he were driving, though we did sometimes give him a lift. Jack at the wheel was a hair-raising experience; as Reg put it: 'He scares me rigid, because he wrestles with his car.'

That was absolutely true. Being a chain-smoker who rolled his own, Jack never had enough cigarettes to hand and he had the alarming habit of rolling the next one while driving. I didn't think it was possible to do both at once. Jack even gave himself an extra handicap: he always drove with huge thick gloves, and would never take them off as he tried to roll these thin little cigarettes. It was terrifying to watch as it became a double wrestling match: one huge hand fighting with the wheel, the other scrabbling about with tobacco and cigarette papers. There was a horrible fascination in the contortions involved.

Of course, the car was covered in ash and tobacco: Jack smoked so much that no normal ashtray could possibly be big enough for him, so his car had an extra one bolted to the dashboard. It was a huge solid rubber thing, with a glass interior, which looked rather

Smokers all!

like a motor car tyre. But it was open to the winds and more ash flew
out than stayed in as he drove along.

I sound terribly self-righteous about smoking—but am reminded
of my own cigarette-smoking days, which nearly ended in tragedy.
Some of the sessions we played had such undemanding music that we
became more and more blasé and casual about the performance. If I
was smoking a cigarette, I wouldn't bother to put it out when the red
light went on to record. It was quite easy to hold the cigarette and the
fiddle bow at the same time.

But one day the piece went on longer than I'd bargained for and
the cigarette burnt down to my fingers before we ended the music;
there was nothing I could do but grin and bear it. I ended up with a
terrible burn right on and above the nail.

That kind of burn is the very devil to heal. This one just
wouldn't get better, and inevitably it became poisoned. I was in a
dreadful state, with a swollen hand, feeling rotten, and we had an
important concert to play that same evening. I felt I had to go on—I
simply couldn't let everyone down. However, other people were far
more concerned and insisted I went to see a doctor. It wasn't merely
a question of missing one little concert; if I didn't do something
about the finger quickly, it might have to come off, and then there
might never be another concert at all.

As it was a Saturday morning, most specialists were away.
Fortunately my doctor was at his consulting rooms in Harley Street
and he managed to find a surgeon who agreed to see me. I raced

233

round but to my horror, I realised as he examined this sick finger of mine that his hands were shaking like a leaf. They weren't little shakes, they were enormous trembling shakes—two or three inches in all directions. He knew what I was thinking and told me that I'd have to trust him: so far, he'd never had the shakes once the knife was in his hand. It was an awful moment of indecision but I had to tell him to go ahead. He lanced my finger and tidied it up beautifully —and I carried on playing, in that night's concert and after.

Travelling by train didn't really appeal to us, unless we knew that there was a late service which would give us time to unwind a bit after the performance and still get us back to London to have a decent night's sleep. It was always good fun to chat to the people who had booked you and to some of the audience. But we liked to be in control of our own destinies. I certainly did, after the most extraordinary fiasco with transport in Eastbourne one evening.

I well remember being booked by Harold Fielding to play solos at a Sunday concert there. Since it was a one-off show and there were good train services to Eastbourne, I decided for once to abandon my car. Ted Ray had also been booked for this concert but at the last minute had to cancel. Instead Harold Fielding sent in a young unknown by the name of Tony Hancock who had come down from London by car. Tony suggested that it would be much more fun if I drove back with him after the show; I wouldn't have to hang around for a train, and we'd be back home by midnight.

Unfortunately, none of us realised that there had been the most tremendous downpour during the show. It was an absolute deluge which had badly affected Tony's car. When we all piled in to start the journey home, we found it had been completely flooded out. All the electrics were sopping wet and nothing was working at all. Of course Tony was quite calm about it: the car would dry out in a matter of minutes—there really wasn't any problem and we would all get home in good time.

So off we went to a restaurant to have a meal together while we waited; we had a wonderful time and it was a great pleasure to get to know this young man a little more. We all recognised him as a talent that would go far, and here he was—a very unassuming and friendly person. And of course, very funny too. But alas, when we'd finished the meal and returned to the car, there was still not a spark of life to be had from it. The rain had well and truly soaked into every nook and cranny. By that time, there was also no chance of getting to the last train; even if we had been able to catch it, I don't think I'd have wanted to leave Tony stranded there by himself. So all we could do was to trail around the town trying to find a garage open, or a mechanic who might still be up and about, to get the car dried out with some kind of heater. I wouldn't have believed what a difficult proposition that would turn out to be in Eastbourne—the whole town seemed soundly asleep.

We went round garage after garage, ringing bells, knocking on doors, shouting. But no one was prepared to do anything for us and the car wouldn't dry out on its own. Eventually at three o'clock in the morning I gave up the struggle and took a taxi back to London. I had to be in a BBC studio at eight. After that I resolved always to be responsible for my own transport and never to depend on anyone else if I could avoid it. Poor Tony never forgot it—and it became a running joke between us for years.

As a trio, we loved playing for people. Our concerts were a lot of fun and we had some very amusing moments. When you are constantly dealing with new people, there's ample scope for mistakes in the travel arrangements—and, I might add, by all parties involved. The Free Trade Hall in Manchester provided one of our funniest memories. The three of us turned up there one winter afternoon, when it was pouring with rain and freezing cold. We arrived at the stage door and were very surprised to find the hall bolted and barred. Surely, as they were expecting us that night, there ought to be lights on, a general bustle or at least some signs of activity? It was also a little disconcerting not to see any posters publicising the concert. We were playing for Toc H which we'd often done before and we knew the organisation well. They were always efficient and, as far as I knew, there had been nothing odd about the arrangements this time. We just assumed that there must have been a change of management at the hall or that they had decided to go about their business differently. So we banged on the door, rang the bell—and banged and rang again and again, until eventually the door opened a crack.

Then it was flung open, and there was the friendly face of the stage doorkeeper, someone we'd known for years. Naturally we were very pleased to see him. 'Can we come in out of the rain?' we said. Of course we could, but he was also a little puzzled: 'Tell me, Max, what brings you to the Free Trade Hall today?'—which I thought was a bit odd since the doorkeeper always knows everything that's going on in the hall. 'What do you mean, what brings us to the Free

Trade Hall? We've got a concert here tonight!' 'Oh no you haven't,' he said, with a broad grin. 'You've got the time right and the date right. But you're a whole year early. Come back again this time in twelve months!' Jack's only comment was that I was as dim as a Toc H lamp.

An annual event for the Trio was to play for the Barnsley Co-op's Education Department after their Annual General Meeting which they held at the Arcadia Hall above their store. After several years we knew everyone very well indeed and became extremely friendly with the organisers. It was a date we really looked forward to. So I don't know what came over me one year when I packed my bag before the drive up to Yorkshire, but when we arrived, I discovered to my horror that I'd left my evening dress trousers at home.

This had never happened before—or since—and I was absolutely appalled as I considered myself a well-dressed musician who took a great deal of trouble with his clothes. There was consternation all round and the concert organisers despatched people here and there to see whether they could find me dress trousers that would fit. I think I must have tried on every single pair in the Co-op store (and probably every single pair in Barnsley) but none of them would do. If they weren't too long in the leg, they were too wide in the waist and I felt it was impossible to play with dress trousers rolled up or hanging loosely from braces.

We decided to compromise. Since we were all wearing rather tidy dark grey flannel trousers with white shirts, it was agreed that we should play dressed like that and abandon our dinner jackets.

We were sure the Co-op wouldn't mind but we felt an explanation and apology were needed before the concert, so the audience wouldn't feel they'd been let down on their special occasion. The secretary decided that this was the sort of message that could go into her introductory speech before we came on stage. While we were waiting to go on I heard the electrifying words: 'Owing to an accident with his trousers, Mr Jaffa . . .' and the rest was drowned in a great wave of laughter. I can honestly say that it took great strength of character after all that to go on stage and face the audience.

Most of our entrances were better than that. We rather enjoyed doing something out of the ordinary when we walked on stage; not just walking on, bowing and starting to play like most people. I think our best surprise was when we did a police concert in Nottingham. As we were heading for the stage, we passed a dressing room containing a long row of police helmets and overcoats—this was irresistible.

We each picked the coat and helmet that would look the most ridiculous. Jack's helmet perched on top of his head, and his coat was too small, Reg was absolutely swimming in his and mine trailed right down to the ground: I'm far too short ever to have joined the police force. On we went, looking like a sub-section of the policemen's chorus from *The Pirates of Penzance*—and everyone loved it.

Whatever the concert or occasion, in some way I've always tried to involve the audience. I enjoy talking about the music, introducing it and trying to create a relaxed atmosphere. Sometimes I'll talk about a piece quite straightforwardly—but telling an anecdote or even a joke about a piece is much more fun. With the Trio concerts my little chats became a feature, since more often than not we went on to the stage truly not knowing what we were going to play. We never had printed programmes but knew the concert would be a mixture of trio music and solo spots from the three of us. The recipe depended on the audience and how we felt at the time.

My chats to audiences came about quite by chance. In the very early days of the Trio we were playing a Sunday concert in the old Winter Gardens at Eastbourne. The hall was absolutely packed with a very welcoming audience, so it looked as though we were in for a good evening. As we started to play, I became aware that my feet were freezing cold while my head and the upper part of my body were rather hot. I couldn't work it out at all—my feet were getting colder and colder by the minute, but Jack and Reg didn't seem to be bothered. However, they were sitting down.

On stage, there was an unusually large bank of lights blazing at us, far more than we'd ever had before at a concert. When it came to the interval I discovered the reason for both the lights and the cold. During the week the theatre was showing a spectacle on ice—one of those extravaganzas like *Holiday on Ice*—and here we were doing *Melodies on Ice*! They'd covered the stage with rush matting but this didn't stop the chill rising. It was such an extraordinary feeling, and such an extraordinary idea, I felt I had to share it with the audience. It caused considerable amusement and laughter—but Jack and Reg were frozen with horror, never mind the ice underfoot. In their minds, you didn't mix music with chat.

Afterwards Jack and Reg realised that talking to the audience had actually improved people's enjoyment of the concert—and they agreed that the music hadn't suffered either. So after that Eastbourne concert, I persuaded Jack and Reg that chat could be included if suitable. Anyway, whatever we might have planned to play in advance, audiences frequently sent us requests for special tunes, so spontaneous conversation developed as the concert proceeded.

I'd walk across to Jack at the piano to tune up: 'What's the local "A" like, Jack?' So he would hit the 'A' and I would tune, giving us time for a quick word. Then I'd say to the audience: 'I'm so sorry, you must forgive me, but you know I use this tuning-up process so I can ask Jack what it is we've just played and what we are going to play next. So now I can tell you.'

Quite often Jack didn't even tell *me*, he'd just start a piece—which was taking a bit of a risk. But that was Jack all over; he knew the music was so deeply ingrained that responding to the tunes was second nature. We once worked out that from memory we could play something like fifteen and a half hours of music at a moment's notice. So it seemed only natural to plan our concerts on the spot.

Talking over a score

Having fun was a great part of performing. I remember once turning to Jack and asking him sotto voce: 'What shall I play?' and he replied in a stage whisper: 'Play "The Burnt Bottom".' Well, I was stumped; I'd heard of the Black Bottom but not the Burnt Bottom, and had no idea what he was talking about. Without waiting for me to work anything out, off he went with the introduction to Monti's *Czardas*. Then it dawned on me. Of course!

It was lovely explaining it to the audience: 'Ladies and gentlemen, we have just played Jack Byfield's arrangement—of "The Burnt Bottom"!' I gave the title extra weight and emphasis, and enjoyed the deathly hush as people wondered what on earth I was talking about. They, like me, knew the piece very well but couldn't imagine why I'd introduced it as 'The Burnt Bottom'. Of course there was a wonderful laugh when I made the connection: 'Charred arse—"Czardas"—a Hungarian dance.' But I'm afraid to say it's been 'The Burnt Bottom' ever since. This was one of my favourite moments in any concert and I still enjoy it.

They say you can tell a good audience because it is absolutely quiet, though I've always thought it's equally likely that they're asleep as much as listening. I've always been lucky in having audiences which at least look as though they're paying attention. The most telling test is to play a piece which ends on a long quiet note. With a good audience, when you get to the end of that long note there should be a complete silence before the applause, as though everyone is still spellbound. Of course it's a trick that all concert violinists use regularly; and even when this note has ended they still leave the bow on the string, waiting. The applause can't start until they lift the bow. Then it feels as though everyone can begin to breathe again.

Occasionally the chemistry works in reverse, and the audience applauds before you finish playing. Then you start to wonder if they're applauding because they want the music to finish and it hasn't or because they are so excited. It used to happen when we played a ridiculous medley which ended with the last part of the overture to *William Tell*. Just imagine, three people on piano, fiddle and cello playing 'tiddle-um tiddle-um tiddle-um tum tum' and so on, with the fingers and bows flying like mad. It was so exciting and out of hand that audiences always applauded well before we reached the final chord.

Once, quite spontaneously, while the audience were applauding and cheering, we all stopped playing—even though we hadn't finished the piece. I turned to Jack and Reg and whispered: 'Just play the last chord, nothing else.' When the applause died down, we smiled, bowed and got ourselves together as if to begin another piece, but all we did was play the last chord: 'Chung!'—just like that. Of course everyone applauded all over again. All I said was: 'You must wait, you see, you must wait. We hadn't quite finished.'

In some halls, we'd find ourselves with the audience filling not only the auditorium but the space behind us on the stage—which gave those people a very strange perspective of the concert. After thinking about this for some time I had a sudden brainwave as we were about to play an encore.

Turning to the people behind us I said: 'I've just realised that we are very rude—or at least I am. I've been playing with my back to you, completely ignoring you . . .' And then I told the audience in the front that they'd have to enjoy my back view while I played the next piece specially for the neglected audience sitting behind us. It was a simple thing to do, but went down particularly well—which, of course, was marvellous for us, because there's nothing more satisfying than coming away from a concert feeling that everyone has had a good time.

There have been times when the audience has given us something to laugh about. I remember going down to give a concert in Portsmouth, another of our annual events. As far as we were concerned, we always played in the same large church hall—but for some reason, this particular year, it seemed to be absolutely freezing. It was the coldest hall that any of us had ever experienced—even during the war—despite being filled with people.

I became colder and colder. My fingers felt like lumps of solid ice and I wondered whether I would be able to play the solos we always included in the programme. In Trio concerts we'd start off together, then we'd break and play some solos or duets, then the Trio would come back together to finish. If we had a guest artist there'd be a spot for their solos too. On this particular evening, whenever I wasn't playing I could feel my fingers completely seizing up.

At the interval I desperately needed something to warm me up, so I put on my coat, tied a scarf round my neck, and said I was off to get a drop of whisky. This was absolutely unheard-of; my usual rule is never to drink, either before or during a concert. But this was a dire emergency, I just had to have something 'medicinal' or I wouldn't be able to play at all. Whisky, I knew, would give me that little glow inside. Jack and Reg didn't want to join me because they had come ready provided with hip flasks. A fine bunch they were not to have alerted me before we left London.

Off I went in the interval to the pub, which was immediately opposite the stage door. There were a lot of people at the bar, but I pushed through to the front and found myself standing next door to a man who was ordering a large round of drinks, crisps and so on.

As he made room for me he looked my way and said: 'I know you. I've seen you before. Now where could we have met?' This is the kind of routine that everyone knows and all I could say was: 'I'm terribly sorry, but I don't think I know you. I was in the RAF during the war, could we have met there?' 'No.' 'Could we have met . . .' and so on. We went through a whole list of possibilities without any success. Eventually he said: 'Well I'm sorry, do forgive me, I hope I haven't been rude. I do know you, I know I know you, but I've got to get back to the concert.'

So that's what being on the stage is all about, I thought, decidedly humbled. He'd been looking at me while I'd been playing to him all through the first half and he didn't recognise me. Funnily enough, the concert was the one possibility that hadn't occurred to either of us. I thought this was absolutely wonderful and worth developing further, so when we returned to the stage I told the audience what had happened and asked the man to stand up so we could introduce ourselves properly. 'Well, now you know where we've met, and how we met!'

In between, if there was an in-between in our playing dates, I enjoyed myself. Betty, my wife, had long ago given up trying to take part. I think the final straw had come when Jack, Reg and I did an eight-week summer season in 1954 at the Villa Marina in Douglas, on the Isle of Man. There were five others with us in a kind of 'Palm Court' ensemble which played in the open air, every day, between one and three o'clock in the afternoon, after which we were free. The Trio's fee for this hardly arduous workload was a hundred pounds a week each.

Jack and his wife Jill had rented a cottage, Reg and Gladys took a flat in Douglas and I'd rented a furnished cottage at Laxey, a short distance from Douglas, for Betty and our daughter Elizabeth. I remember it very well; Nurse Rhodes' Cottage, which had four bedrooms and all the usual facilities, cost the huge sum of four pounds a week inclusive of all running expenses.

Playing a summer season gave everyone the chance to relax and let their hair down; no one had to rush to the next session, no one had to be up early the next morning. So there were some magnificent celebrations. Joe Loss was also on the island—his band was playing at the Dance Hall—and he was renowned for his parties. But they weren't the kind that Betty enjoyed very much and she and Elizabeth went back to London almost as soon as we'd started work. We didn't amuse her, she didn't understand our work, and she certainly didn't understand our sense of humour, which, I suppose, is particular to musicians. We should never have tried to have that kind of a holiday together. Betty had her own world just as I had mine, and we got along very civilly as long as we kept ourselves and our two worlds quite separate.

I can't say that I was desperately unhappy. There were jokes, silly stories and fun with the audience—and I was constantly stopped in the street for a chat and asked for my autograph. There were always people around to talk to, and some very nice girls to get to know rather better. One evening Joe Loss gave a party and I met a glorious girl called Sheila who made the rest of the summer terrific fun.

I came away from that summer season with one of the most wonderful cars in the world, an Austin Ruby 7 saloon, number plate FLO—hence Flossie. She cost me sixty-five pounds, and she never went wrong in all the time I had her. I loved her dearly and swore that we would never be parted but in fact the dreadful day came when I was driving with Ann Meo, a great friend of mine, and we passed a showroom with two Rolls-Royces for sale. She insisted that I stop and look at them. I bought one and traded Flossie in for ninety pounds. The Rolls, a Sedanca de Ville, cost me £375.

(Ann was like that, impulsive, imperious and absolutely right in whatever she decided to do. For years she worked in the BBC's Sound Archives—but when they appeared not to be taking her work seriously, she moved over to ITV and put her phenomenal brain to much better financial use. She was totally uninhibited. I remember we first met during lunch one day in the BBC's lower-ground-floor restaurant in Broadcasting House; following a session in the Concert Hall we were queuing up at the counter for our food when I suddenly saw this rather remarkable-looking girl giving me the most blatant wink! We immediately became the closest of friends.)

Ann always had a wonderful sense of style. Sometimes, rounding off a 'merry' and enjoyable evening together, we'd call in at Ciro's for a late supper. I would sign her in as 'Lady Bracknell', a role she carried off to perfection, and of course the waiters, not knowing any better, saw the 'title' and fawned all over her.

Years later, she rang me up out of the blue, and asked if she could borrow my Rolls-Royce—she needed it to make a certain kind of impression to get a job. She was adamant: the new Jaguar, which I had just bought and offered instead, wouldn't do at all, it was all wrong in terms of social style. Whatever the job was, she got it.

There was a sequel several years later to the tale of my first Rolls-Royce. I came out of a broadcast from the Paris Studio in Lower Regent Street—and there was Flossie! She was shining bright, her bodywork polished to a T; one of the studio attendants had bought her and lavished tender loving care on her, even to the extent of putting up curtains. I was thrilled.

However, that first Rolls gave me a taste for these cars. She was called Agnes—again from the number plate, AGN—and we had a fond relationship. In 1959, some years after we parted company, I saw her sailing down Wimpole Street, and I swear that she gave me a smile as she passed by. But I suppose my most memorable car was the silver Rolls-Royce convertible I had years later, which featured in the opening shots of a TV programme we did from the Spa at Scarborough. There I was, in close-up, grandly driving on to the Spa and waving rather regally at the camera—which then pulled back to show that this awfully grand machine was being towed by a donkey.

CHAPTER TWENTY-FOUR

From Radio to TV

The lovely thing that happens when you broadcast regularly is that you start to 'belong' to your listeners. They take you into their homes and feel you've become one of the family. People get very passionate about what they hear—or see. And we were soon to find out quite how passionate a British audience could be.

We knew that we were a success on radio because the BBC continued the Trio broadcasts—even in those days, audience response meant a great deal to the powers that be. But we honestly didn't know quite how successful we were until some years later, when one of the radio announcers, Michael Brooke (known to his friends as 'Reggie'), asked whether we would be interested in appearing on that new medium, the television.

Of course we were game for anything, we enjoyed playing and were quite happy performing wherever asked. So we found ourselves, late one evening in 1954, doing a television broadcast 'from the radio studio', with Reggie Brooke opening the programme sitting in a mock-up of a radio announcer's booth as though starting a normal radio broadcast.

It went something along the lines of: 'Ladies and Gentlemen, many of you will have enjoyed hearing the Max Jaffa Trio on radio, where they are regular broadcasters. We thought that for a change you might like to see the Max Jaffa Trio—so here they are.' The camera then pulled back from a close-up on Reggie, and focused on what looked like a radio studio where for half an hour we played away in our usual style. And that was that.

Two days later, an emotional phone call came from Lionel Salter, who was then in charge of the music broadcasts on television. All I could understand was that something wonderful had happened and would we urgently find a time when the three of us could come to see him. Any morning we liked, as soon as possible—we only had to phone his secretary to confirm the time and he'd be waiting for us.

When we arrived, there was no coffee but instead Lionel immediately asked his secretary to show us something. In fact she couldn't do it by herself and a number of ladies had to help her carry in armfuls of letters, all asking for more broadcasts of the Trio. Apparently the BBC had also been inundated with phone calls. In their experience no single programme had ever generated such a response.

We were stunned; unless we could see our audience—and of course we couldn't when we were playing in a studio—we rarely thought about them, so this response was quite astounding. A nice surprise, of course, but it was unnerving to know that a programme planned so casually had made such a hit. 'Would you like to do some more?' asked Lionel Salter. In fact he was most insistent, excited and raring to set up an immediate series of Trio broadcasts. Of course we agreed.

Music at Ten

245

In true BBC fashion, it was two years before the planners managed to find a spot for our second television appearance. On May 13th 1956, we started *Music at Ten*. So much for instant success! Never mind, it was the first of what was to become a widely acclaimed and highly successful television series.

Music at Ten was practically always live, opening with a camera close-up of a clock on the mantelpiece in an elegant drawing room. It wasn't a real room, but a clever set designed to look like the comfortable drawing room of a great English house; the TV audience were guests at the house party who would settle down for a little after-dinner music. There was one snag, that the clock was actually set to real time and the television programmes which we followed nearly always overran so I often found myself introducing *Music at Ten* at five past or seven past or even ten past ten.

Since I always introduced the music we played at concerts, everyone thought it was natural that I should introduce the television programmes too. I was asked to provide a script, but in a lifetime of broadcasting I have never used a script. The BBC did of course need some persuading. 'Please trust me,' I said. 'I promise I won't use any words ending in 'unt, 'uck or 'uggery.' They smiled and eventually let me have my own way.

On *Music at Ten* we regularly had a small choir made up of young and talented singers just out of the Royal Academy of Music. Their beautiful singing and charming personalities contributed greatly to the success of our programmes. They were called The Linden Singers. We also invited a guest to appear on each programme, and were fortunate enough to have such great artists as Alicia Markova, Beryl Grey and Svetlana Beriosova; we had the Scottish solo dancer, Bobby Watson; Kenneth McKellar, Ian Wallace, Geraint Evans, Owen Brannigan . . . the list goes on and on. Needless to say they helped enormously to enhance the quality of the programme.

I believe the show's success lay in its simplicity. We didn't give it the showbiz treatment, but were just there to make music or perform for the audience's pleasure. A great deal of the atmosphere created was thanks to the skills of our director, Christian Simpson, who worked hard to maintain the illusion of spontaneity. Spontaneity it wasn't; we rehearsed a great deal before the transmission to make it look natural. There was always a detailed camera script which took hours to plan and get right. Even then, with a live show everything could change while we were on the air, if a camera suddenly stopped working or if there was some other kind of technical hitch. The floor manager would somehow signal to us and then we would improvise. It was often rather exciting when that happened—but only because we were confident that everyone in the studio knew exactly what was coming next.

The effect of the show was quite extraordinary; it became something of a cult, and we were told stories about whole streets of people walking their dogs early so that they could get back home in time to watch us. We became public property and topics of general conversation. People would stop us in the street asking for autographs and fan mail poured in to the BBC requesting signed photographs. Someone even wrote to me asking for the name and address of my tailor! Strangely, most of the fan mail came to me rather than Jack and Reg, but then I suppose that I was the 'front man'—the one standing up to play—and we were called the Max Jaffa Trio. It might have looked as though they were there to support me—which I can assure you was very far from the truth. We supported each other.

However, Jack was still embarrassed by his stammer, which seemed to affect him at unpredictable moments. He was fine when among friends, but any public occasion or meeting someone new would bring it on. He told us that it was hereditary; his father also stammered, even though he had been a very successful Regimental Sergeant Major in the First World War. He'd once had a dreadful experience when on parade to greet a new commanding officer, who turned out to be even more badly afflicted. The CO eventually managed to get out: 'Hhhhhhhow do you do, Sssssssssergeant Major Bbbbbbbbbbbyfield.' Jack's father was horrified; he felt sure that if he stammered his reply, the new CO would think he was taking the mickey. On the other hand, he had to say something; he couldn't stay silent for ever because that would have had an equally unfortunate interpretation. Apparently the silence was agonising until he had a brainwave and found a piece of paper to write: 'I stutter too!' No one wanted to put Jack through that kind of public ordeal.

There was one wonderful occasion when recognition wasn't quite what it could have been and Reg and Jack got their own back on my 'fame'. The Trio had been playing at the lovely Queen's Hotel in Leeds, at a large private dinner with two or three hundred guests. We'd been a great success but they hadn't thought to feed us—either before playing or after, by which time it was all too late and the kitchens had shut up for the evening.

We were hungry, so having left our bags at the station before the late train back to London (it was one of those rare occasions when for some reason we didn't drive up) off we went on our quest for food. After about 9 p.m. in the fifties, it was always fish and chips—nothing else. The advantage was that you could hunt your supper with your nose. That evening in Leeds we soon smelt supper walking towards us—the couple eating out of a newspaper must have been startled out of their wits as we buttonholed them to find out where they'd bought it.

It was just as well they gave us precise directions, because even with the smell of frying I'm sure we'd have missed what I can only describe as a hole in the wall, dug out from what was otherwise a blank face. There was the smallest glass front and hardly room inside for more than about four people. Running it were two women, one serving at the counter, facing the audience so to speak, and the other one doing the frying.

We squeezed in with Reg and Jack taking up positions either side of me at the counter. The woman serving definitely did a double-take: 'Cor, you look like Max Jaffa,' she said. 'Did you know that you look like Max Jaffa?' What could I say to that? She turned to Jack and said: ''Ere, have a look at this chap, doesn't he look like Max Jaffa?' and Jack looked and said: 'No, not a bit, he doesn't look like any photographs that I've ever seen of Max Jaffa.' So she turned to Reg, and said: 'Doesn't he look like Max Jaffa?' Reg made the classic reply and said: 'Max Jaffa, who's Max Jaffa?'

With typical Trio empathy we immediately pretended that we didn't know each other, collected our fish and chips, and walked away holding our separate packets until out of sight around the corner when we could collapse with laughter. (But I had a word with Reg: 'That was a bit much, saying you've never heard of Max Jaffa.' I thought that really took the biscuit.)

With each season, we became more and more daring. I've always tried to find new ways of keeping everyone's interest, so we filmed out of the studio to vary the visual surroundings. For instance, we played from some genuine period drawing rooms in stately homes which gave us an excuse to programme music that was different from our usual light classics.

The day we went down to the Brighton Pavilion, we made it to

On the Radio Times *cover*

the front cover of the *Radio Times*. We played eighteenth-century pieces, Mozart and Haydn as well as some English popular tunes of the day, with suitably Chinese-sounding music to blend with the Chinese decor. The Linden Singers dressed up in Regency costume and serenaded us from the kitchens, amongst the pots and pans. It would have looked wonderful in colour but of course in those days, at the end of the fifties, colour television was still a long way off.

Gilbert Harding was supposed to have been our guest that day; with his rather acid wit and sharp tongue he was a popular television personality on quiz shows and talks programmes. He'd become Brighton's most famous resident and would have given us a guided tour around the Brighton Pavilion. Sadly, he was taken ill just before filming and rushed off to hospital. I was flung in at the deep end and had to assimilate a wealth of information about the beautiful building, as Chris Simpson decided that I should introduce the programme.

My mind used to work overtime, dreaming up new ideas for the sequences we filmed. I would often phone poor Chris late at night with suggestions that we should do this or that . . . Sometimes they were crazy ideas, but he was such a brilliant producer and director and so far ahead of his time in terms of television techniques, that he managed to make them all work.

One of our most successful ideas was for the Trio to play the 'Ride of the Valkyries' — the symphonic interlude from Wagner's huge *Ring* cycle, which needs an enormous orchestra, including masses of brass instruments and funny things like Wagner tubas. On film, you'd see just the three of us unleashing all this sound. I thought it could be done using mirrors but it took Chris Simpson ages to work out precisely how. Remember, in those days there were none of the technical facilities that we have today, such as computers, videotape recording and split screens.

Eventually Chris devised a way to do it using trick visual techniques with mirrors reflecting back on themselves until it looked like an enormous orchestra playing the 'Ride of the Valkyries'. All the violins and violas were Max Jaffas, all the cellos and basses were Reginald Kilbeys and all the other instruments were either Jack, Reg or myself miming to an orchestral recording. We three made up the entire symphony orchestra. It was a lot of fun and a huge success.

One of our gentler ideas was to do Walton's *Façade* and make Reg appear to play the saxophone very convincingly. You would never have known he was miming to a recording. Later on I wanted to repeat the Valkyrie trick with Tchaikovsky's *1812* overture, and this time Chris's team was even more clever with the mirrors. There we were as ourselves as well as making up this huge orchestra: I remember playing the timpani and the tam-tam while the cannons were firing and smoke billowing. We all three ended up dressed as French soldiers marching and pushing cannons.

One day the Prom queue outside the Albert Hall had some

Reg, Jack and myself busking outside the Albert Hall

unexpected entertainment. We arrived in tatters and rags (provided by BBC Television's costume department) pushing a small upright piano on a fruit barrow which we took right up to the artists' entrance, where the Prom queue more or less ended. We busked away at a selection of pieces for the camera—and the queue—and went down the line with a hat to collect money. There were some wonderful double-takes of surprise as people didn't believe their eyes.

What we hadn't bargained on was a great commotion from the artists' entrance when the orchestral manager came rushing out saying: 'The concert's about to begin. Where's my orchestra—they ought to be on stage by now!' It turned out that half the BBC Symphony Orchestra had come out of the hall to listen and watch us. I think the word had got around that the Trio had fallen on hard times.

The camera went on rolling as we collected the money, picked up the instruments and pushed the piano along to where all the cars were parked. There we stopped to count and share out the takings. (I think we collected something like thirteen old pence, which was a pretty poor night's work with a three-way split—we'd have to do better than that if we ever considered taking it up for real.) But we'd stopped, naturally enough, by our own cars: Reg had an Austin Sheerline, which looked rather like a Rolls-Royce and was about the same size; Jack had an enormous Wolseley and I had a very old Rolls-Royce (which I wish I had today!). It made a wonderful sight, these dreadful and disreputable-looking buskers getting into three such immaculate cars and driving away.

One of my favourite moments came from the large number of letters which regularly arrived asking how the Trio started. We thought we'd show everyone. We dressed up in Victorian clothes with the appropriate wigs and had a photograph taken as a trio, with Jack, Reg and myself in a stiff Victorian pose. Jack was sitting at a harpsichord; although historically inaccurate, this gave the feeling of antiquity we wanted to create.

During the programme this photograph stood on our usual piano — but suddenly, the three figures came to life, stepped out of the frame, walked across to another part of the room and played the Boccherini Minuet. Then they walked back into the picture frame and became the still photograph once more. 'So,' I said to the audience, 'in answer to all your letters, we "inherited" the Trio from

Out of the picture frame

our fathers . . .'—which of course everyone could see was a black lie and not to be taken seriously.

New ideas came from all kinds of places, and in 1958 when *Woman* magazine published an article about the Trio they suggested that we should make a programme around viewers' requests. We asked people to send postcards telling us their favourite tunes which we then gathered into a list of the top hundred most requested pieces. This produced another shock. So many people wrote that there were tables piled high with letters and Chris Simpson had to take on extra staff in order to cope. Thirteen thousand letters had arrived almost by return of post after the broadcast. One old lady had even written to say that she would be prepared to wait ten years to hear her choice played.

Incidentally, that list still lives on. Once the story of the list appeared in the press, a Light Programme music producer rang up television and asked to borrow it for a new series he was planning. That programme was inevitably called *Your Hundred Best Tunes*. By now it must be one of Radio 2's longest-running shows.

CHAPTER TWENTY-FIVE

Off the Screen

In 1958, the BBC received so many requests for the Trio that six extra programmes had to be made. They called them *A Little Music*, featuring only the Trio. The Linden Singers, who were our TV partners, had also become so popular that they were busy on a concert tour. The public even wanted us on Christmas Day—so we had a special set for that occasion, with a table laden with goodies and a cherubic choirboy as the soloist. We may have been sentimental and easy listening, but for a long while we were in the top ten television shows and that was lovely!

Meanwhile, during all this TV success, we were still contracted to do four broadcast sessions a week for the London Studio Players. Mind you, they were rather good, and every now and again I had my own programme on the Home Service. *Max Jaffa and his Orchestra* was rather a super change from the endless rounds of *Melody Hours*, *String Songs* and that perennial *Melody on Strings*. They even let me loose on *Grand Hotel*.

Once people associate you with something particular, for years afterwards you're always linked together regardless. *Grand Hotel* has haunted me—in more ways than one. It intermittently returns to radio and immediately people start talking to me about it and the time when I used to lead that orchestra.

I'm sure I have the distinction of being the shortest-serving leader of the Palm Court Orchestra. I was on the programme regularly for only about a year, though I had done the occasional broadcast before. Indeed, I remember doing a *Grand Hotel* from the Royal Festival Hall as part of the 1951 Festival of Britain, when we were one of the first concerts in the building (before it had officially opened). I believe we did the very first broadcast from the hall.

A BBC photograph at the time I was leading the Palm Court Orchestra

Grand Hotel was started by Albert Sandler. The first broadcast was in 1925 from the Grand Hotel in Eastbourne with Jack Byfield playing the piano. The broadcasts went on from there right up until the war, when the programme was moved into a BBC studio. My old friend Tom Jenkins was then in charge, until he became seriously ill, when Jean Pougnet took his place. Jean had to retire because of trouble with his arm and that was when I took over. After me, Reginald Leopold led the orchestra.

For some reason, listeners to the programme all over the world connect Max Jaffa with *Grand Hotel*. When I look through the press cutting book, I see that newspapers were always talking about my 'Palm Court' music or '*Grand Hotel* style'. This has a strange influence on the way stages are decorated when I play.

It has long been a Jaffa family joke that when I walk out on to a concert platform, we can almost guarantee that palm trees will be present. Nine times out of ten, they'll be there and no matter what I say, I can't escape them. Even at Scarborough, for all the twenty-seven years I played there, the stage was cluttered with beautiful palms supplied by the parks department. Now I'm not complaining, because they were really very gracious palms and we also had huge flower arrangements, a sort of herbaceous border all along the bottom of the stage, instead of footlights. But I never managed to persuade the council that we were playing in the Spa Grand Hall, not *Grand Hotel*. I wonder whether the palms ever disorientated the audience?

There was one occasion when I managed to get my own back on the set designer. Jack and I went up to Tyne Tees Television in Newcastle to do a guest spot on a programme being hosted by that great bass and dear friend, Owen Brannigan—who had often appeared with us in concerts and on our programmes. Inevitably, what should we find in the studio but those palms again, dotted all over the place. I hope I laughed; but I certainly objected slightly. 'Must we, do I have to? Can't I ever play the fiddle without a palm tree in sight?'

I think people saw the point, but it was too late to change the set. So Jack and I decided that the best response was to be positive and instead to have a bit of fun with the palms. I persuaded them to put all these palms together in one spot—there must have been about six or eight bushy plants—to form a great jungle. Then without saying what we were going to do, Jack and I went off to wardrobe and poked around in their tropical section to see what we could find in the way of props.

When it was time for our entrance on the show, we made a great performance of fighting through the undergrowth while Owen Brannigan was doing the introductions. Poor chap, the audience ignored him and was completely distracted by this mass of waving branches. At the appointed moment, we finally emerged from the jungle as weary tropical explorers, wearing the most marvellous pith helmets. The audience was wonderful—they literally shrieked with laughter, making all the effort worthwhile. Of course this did nothing to stop the plague of palms.

It was just as well that we stayed in radio as television hardly provided a regular income. We might have been offered something like six programmes a season, but when I look back through the diary I see that there were four- to six-week gaps between them and I remember how we had to juggle our diaries every time they arranged the next programme.

At that time the great battle between ITV and BBC was already fierce, and the ITV companies were interested in finding programmes that would persuade an audience to move over to their network. STV (Southern Television) sent a questionnaire to viewers asking which artists they'd most like to see and the Trio came near the top.

That was how we came to be offered a twenty-six-week series on STV, an offer which we really couldn't refuse. But the BBC was aghast: they felt it was a betrayal, a lowering of the standards. I was sent a personal letter by Kenneth Adam, the then Head of Television (who lived in the same block of flats as I did), begging me to reconsider our decision to defect—pointing out, quite justifiably, that the BBC had looked after our interests pretty well over the years.

That was certainly true, but it wasn't BBC TV but BBC Radio which had given us the good times and an enormous amount of work in various ways. There was no reason for any of us to abandon that. Above all, radio offered the opportunities to promote our individual talents quite separately from the Trio: Jack was in great demand as an arranger, and Reg appeared all over the place as a soloist as well as a conductor.

I too was busy; particularly in the recording world, where I was still leading many orchestras. Most of the sessions were for Columbia, where an old friend, Norrie Paramor, was in charge of artists and repertoire recording. I found myself booked for all the big sessions. Strangely enough, the Trio itself did very little recording, even when we were so popular on television. But then we never pushed for recordings—I suppose it suited us better working for other people.

Radio was and is always looking for new ideas and new ways of presenting music. Some years after I'd joined the London Studio Players, it dawned on me that there was something missing in the music we played. There was really very little chance to hear what I call the 'Evergreens', those lovely tunes by Jerome Kern, Gershwin, Cole Porter, Ivor Novello and Irving Berlin. We were all too busy trying to keep up with the new songs and show tunes. Moreover, I thought that 'Evergreen' music would be very interesting to conduct.

I went to Frank Wade, the then Head of BBC Light Music, to suggest that this was such a good idea that we should start up a new orchestra. I put it to him that we would need lots of strings, some woodwind, a harp and a rhythm section; plus some new and modern arrangements for some of these absolutely beautiful tunes. Then we would have a new programme which both kept the old tunes fresh in people's minds and yet was up to date with the popular new sounds and rhythms.

It wasn't as extravagant an idea as it sounds; the players were around and already contracted to the BBC. Frank Wade could see that it would be filling a gap, and told me to go ahead. All I had to do was to organise some willing players, corner a producer who wasn't too busy to do the paperwork for us and find some arrangers who could start work.

It was a wonderful and completely absorbing task. Before long I'd gathered together a collection of some hundred and fifty tunes, arranged by people like Wally Stott, Eric Jupp and Frank Barber; and of course Jack Byfield did some for me. Their arrangements were first rate, classics of their time, and I was still using them years after the days of the Studio Players. I've also recorded most of them on LP.

This new orchestra was about twenty-five strong, and though I say so myself, we made a lovely sound, new and different. It was very much a string sound, with a little woodwind, a horn, a harp and a rhythm section. My solo fiddle played the part of the vocalist, crooning away all those wonderful tunes. The word for it is probably 'romantic'—at least, that was how I described what I wanted to the arrangers.

Since every orchestra had to have a name, Frank Wade found the right name for us. He came to listen to us one day and decided we should be called 'The Orchestra Elegante'. It was difficult to believe we were that different from other orchestras of the time, especially when I looked round and saw exactly the same faces who turned up to play for *Melody on Strings*, the Casino Orchestra and even the Palm Court Orchestra.

Well, I was lucky with the idea; the audience enjoyed what we were doing and many broadcasts later, in 1957, we were sent off to Venice to represent the BBC at an International Festival of Light Music. This was a competition where seven orchestras played in the great Piazza San Marco, each one giving a short concert which was broadcast and televised. We were all given separate platforms on which we played our own particular repertoire. It was the most extraordinary concert; the weather was perfect and we began playing at around midnight, each orchestra trying to outdo the ones that went before. We had a huge audience. The Piazza San Marco was filled with seats, and there must have been many thousands of people present with goodness knows how many more hanging out of windows and balconies. Although it was supposed to be a serious competition, it was great fun for the players and audience. At one point the Orchestra Elegante stopped the show, when I played a

At the Light Music Festival in the Piazza San Marco, Venice

flamboyant piece of gypsy music and we had to encore the whole piece. We could see the TV people agitating furiously about their timing arrangements but we just ignored them and carried on regardless.

We didn't win the Golden Gondola—strangely enough, that prize went to the Italian orchestra—but we came home with a lovely silver gondola, which is still around somewhere in the BBC (at one time it was on display outside Frank Wade's office). We also had an unexpected bonus, namely a *Grand Hotel* broadcast from the Excelsior Hotel on the Lido. It makes a world of difference when you're playing in the right kind of ambience, and the hotels on the Lido couldn't be more 'grand'. Ever since this broadcast, I've had an ambition to do a whole series of *Grand Hotel*s from all the most famous and elegant hotels in the world.

Before I left England, I had been asked to buy an Italian basket. I decided to take the Rapido from Venice to Milan, which would give me enough time to carry out my task in a leisurely manner before being reunited with the orchestra at Milan airport. When I reached Milan I walked round the city centre, and to my great delight discovered a marvellous little shop with the most beautiful baskets in every possible size and shape. They spilled out from the shop on to the pavement outside, and inside they were so packed from floor to ceiling that there was hardly room for two people to squeeze past each other.

Some customers were there when I walked in, but as soon as the man saw me he threw up his hands: 'Ah, maestro, maestro . . .' He'd seen the television show from Venice the night before—and there I was, the next day, in his shop! 'Madonna . . . what a coincidence!' I felt just like a film star, basking in his compliments. People never became quite that effusive in England.

CHAPTER TWENTY-SIX

Meeting Jean

All in all, professionally speaking, life couldn't have been better. By the mid-fifties I was part of a very successful radio series, television had started, I was making records, both as leader of the orchestra for several conductors and in my own right as a soloist—and the Trio had more than enough concert work. I was busy playing from first thing in the morning till late at night.

That's how I kept going. If I'd stopped to think about where my personal life was heading, it would have looked fairly bleak. Going 'home' meant little more than walking ten paces inside the front door to the two rooms which were my bedroom and study/office. If I met Betty in the morning before either of us left for work, we had a polite exchange of pleasantries, no more than that. I saw more of Elizabeth as I'd asked her to work for me, to sort out my bookings and expenses and to help me to answer the mailbag, which was becoming considerable. At the height of the television programmes, I was getting some four hundred letters a week. Finally printed replies had to be prepared because we just couldn't cope with the sheer volume of the correspondence.

It was better not to think about the private life of Max Jaffa— better rather to concentrate on being a musician and playing for people who enjoyed music, who enjoyed us. That gave me pleasure.

It was also very easy to do: perhaps even too easy, to smile and be polite to the fans, jolly with the backstage people and support one's colleagues on the evening's programmes. It became a routine— and, like most routines, it was one day surprisingly and totally overturned. It was the most extraordinary and marvellous shock, and it really changed my life.

The year was 1956, and the Trio had gone down to play in

GUEST ARTISTES

JEAN GRAYSTON, *Contralto*	MAX JAFFA *Solo Violin*
REGINALD KILBEY *Solo 'Cello*	JACK BYFIELD *Solo Piano*
HAROLD HALL *Hon. Conductor*	STANLEY MATHEWS *Organist*

PROGRAMME

PART I

HYMN FOR CHRISTMAS DAY
"O Come all ye Faithful" · · · · · · · · · · · · · · · · *Adeste Fideles*
CHOIR AND AUDIENCE

ANCIENT CAROL (15th Century)
"Welcome Yule" · · · · · · · · · · · · · · · · · *Parry*
CHOIR

TRIO
"La Bohème" Selection · · · · · · · · · · · · · *Puccini*
"El Relicario" · · · · · · · · · · · · · · · · *Padilla*
Old English Airs · · · · · · · · · · · · *arr. Jack Byfield*
MAX JAFFA, REGINALD KILBEY, JACK BYFIELD

SONGS
"O Thou that Tellest" (Messiah) · · · · · · · · · · · *Handel*
"The Monkey's Carol" · · · · · · · · · · · · · *Stanford*
"Ave Maria" · · · · · · · · · · · · · · · · *Gounod*
JEAN GRAYSTON (Accompanist : Stanley Mathews)

FESTIVAL CAROL
"Ring Out, Wild Bells" · · · · · · · · · · · *Percy Fletcher*
CHOIR

'CELLO SOLOS
"The Broken Melody" · · · · · · · · · · · · · *Van Biene*
"Arlequin" · · · · · · · · · · · · · · · · *Popper*
REGINALD KILBEY

CHORAL FANTASY ON OLD CAROLS
"Christmas Day" · · · · · · · · · · · · · *Gustav Holst*
CHOIR

CAROLS
"Good King Wenceslas" (Spring Carol of the 13th Century)
CHOIR AND AUDIENCE
"Silent Night" · · · · · · · · · · · *Trad. : arr. Henry Geehl*
CHOIR

SHORT INTERVAL

PART II

CAROL FOR LADIES' VOICES
"Gesu Bambino" · · · · · · · · · · · · · *Pietro A Yon*
(Chinese melody arranged as a Carol introduced by two members of the Club recently returned from China).
Part Song—"Bethlehem Night" · · · · · · · · · *Arthur Warrell*
Old Rhyme "Christmas is Coming" · · · · · *arr. Walford Davies*
CHOIR

TRIO
Meditation from "Thaïs" · · · · · · · · · · · *Massenet*
Selection from "Countess Maritza" · · · · · · · *Kalman*
MAX JAFFA, REGINALD KILBEY, JACK BYFIELD

SONGS
"Dream o' Day Jill" (Tom Jones) · · · · · · · · *Ed. German*
"Songs my Mother Taught Me" · · · · · · · · · *Dvorak*
"Softly Awakes my Heart" (Samson and Delilah) · · *Saint-Saens*
JEAN GRAYSTON (Accompanist : Stanley Mathews)

PIANOFORTE SOLOS
Nocturne in D Flat
Waltz Brilliante in A Flat · · · · · · · · · · · *Chopin*
JACK BYFIELD

Chorale "Jesu, Joy of Man's Desiring" · · · · · · *J. S. Bach*
JACK BYFIELD AND CHOIR
Tyrolean Carol "Greetings" · · · · · · *arr. Desmond Ratcliffe*
CHOIR

CHRISTMAS HYMN
"Hark ! The Herald Angels Sing" · · · · · · · *Mendelssohn*
CHOIR AND AUDIENCE

VIOLIN SOLOS Selections from his Repertoire
MAX JAFFA

TRIO
Selection from "Samson and Delilah" · · · · · · *Saint-Saens*
MAX JAFFA, REGINALD KILBEY, JACK BYFIELD

FINALE
"The Holy City" · · · · · *Stephen Adams, arr. Doris Arnold*
ARTISTES AND CHORUS

GOD SAVE THE QUEEN

The programme of the concert at which I met Jean

Portsmouth as guest artists for the Milton Glee Club. There was another performer on the evening's programme, so just before the concert started I went round to the guest's dressing room to say hello, and to wish 'all the best' . . . I remember opening the door to the singer who was appearing with us . . . to find myself absolutely swept away. There she was, already dressed for the concert, all in white and looking almost like a bride. She took my breath away!

We didn't say much to each other, just 'Hello, I'm Max Jaffa, how nice to meet you' and so on, then I began the concert. I heard myself introducing the music; we played for a bit, then she came on to sing, and I knew that something absolutely wonderful had happened to me. I wanted to know a great deal more about this Jean Grayston. I remember listening to her with my heart pounding, hoping that she was going to be good, that I would enjoy her singing, for I knew I was going to spend a lot of time with her! And, thank God, she was good. (Actually she was more than good, but I have to tone it down as I don't want her to get a swelled head at this time of her life.)

Jean calls our meeting love at first sight—because that's what she felt. There was an instant chemistry, a terrific spark between us. She laughs about it because when she turned up for that concert, she

261

was a little upset to find herself lower down on the billing than the Max Jaffa Trio. At the time, she was rather a grand young lady, singing on the Third Programme and performing with the Glyndebourne Festival Opera. She'd actually made a mental note to take her agents to task for booking her for a concert with such low-brow musicians.

We were both aching for the concert to end, so that we could find out more about each other—and as luck would have it, neither of us had travelled down to Portsmouth by car so there would be plenty of time to talk on the train without the distractions of driving. Then we found that Reg had come by train too so it meant the three of us sharing a carriage. (Jack didn't come back to London—I think he spent the night in Portsmouth treating himself to whisky and fish and chips.)

However, Reg was always tactful and he settled himself in one corner and looked to be fast asleep while Jean and I got to know each other in the other corner. We were soon very relaxed with each other and more than a bit affectionate, and I'm sure the half of Reg that wasn't really asleep put two and two together about our meeting and realised we were more than a little enamoured. By the time we arrived at Waterloo, we were about to embark on a relationship which has now lasted over thirty years. (As I've always said, she looked good, she felt good—and by golly she did me good!)

Needless to say, it all became rather ridiculous just before we arrived at Waterloo. I said to Jean, hopefully: 'I've got my car here— have you got transport?' but she was being met. All I could do was take her telephone number and promise to be in touch.

I phoned immediately, first thing in the morning, and we arranged to have dinner together. I would take an evening off, collect her from her flat and take her to some special restaurant where we could talk without being bothered. Of course taking a night off was extremely rare for me; it meant a serious rearrangement of schedules and finding someone else to do the work for which I had been booked. As far as I was concerned Jean was the one to be booked—by me!

I arrived to collect her at her flat, complete with a box of what I hoped might please her—marrons glacés. It was a large presentation box, beautifully wrapped, but more, it was something to break the ice, to help me get over the first awkward moment. For some extraordinary reason, I felt rather shy at seeing her again. But she greeted me very affectionately and said: 'Ah, marrons glacés, marvellous, thank you.' Wonderful; nothing had changed and we felt exactly as we had done when we left each other at Waterloo. And so we went to dinner.

Now let's skip about four or five years, just for the sake of this story. After we got married and were about to move house from Jean's flat to where we now live and I was helping Jean pack all her things—lo and behold, suddenly there appeared this very same box of marrons glacés. Unopened! She said, 'Well, I couldn't tell you at the time! I hate them, I couldn't possibly eat them. Since tasting one, I've never eaten another.' (But on the other hand, she had kept the box . . .)

In fact it was a difficult courtship. Our first dinner together was to be the last one for a long time. An evening out was a rare luxury. Jean would say: 'Well, can we at least have dinner together? How about tomorrow or the next day?' and I'd say: 'No, I can't manage that. I've got a Trio concert, or a BBC broadcast, or a recording session for so-and-so,' and I'd get my diary out. All too often all I could offer was 'If you've got twenty minutes to spare tomorrow morning, we could meet at the BBC's Maida Vale Studios during the orchestral break and have a cup of coffee.' Sometimes even this was impossible because Jean had many singing engagements. I travelled everywhere with my diary; it was the oracle which ruled my life and without it I would have been in serious trouble. Nearly every day I was booked to work in three different studios for three different sessions in three different places. And sessions were often the place to pick up more work for the coming weeks.

But there was one compensation: at least we could meet in private. Jean had her own flat in Great Cumberland Place and I'd go round there to relax once the last session was over. There was no doubt that we were deeply in love, and we had a great deal of catching up to do to find out about each other, who we were, what we liked, what we wanted. It was a strange experience in some ways; for the first time in years, there was someone special who really cared about me and what I was doing. Very soon, going to Great Cumberland Place felt like going home.

But even that was fraught with difficulties. I had promised Betty that I'd keep up appearances until our daughter Elizabeth was married. We had agreed that only then could we both be free to follow our own destinies. So for the time being, life with Jean had to be kept as discreet as possible.

As time went on that was easier said than done. Television had made the Trio famous and turned me into public property. It was extraordinary how complete strangers would come up and chat to me in the street as though they'd known me for years. People also felt free to ask the most personal questions; one of them even queried whether my hair was real, or did I wear a toupee. That enquiry wasn't addressed to me but was printed in the letters page of the *Radio Times* and then taken up by the press. I had become good copy for gossip writers.

Unfortunately, I was pretty easy to spot. The places where musicians worked were well known and people in the business are notorious gossips. What's more, I was then driving a lovely old Rolls-Royce which wasn't the most unostentatious car I could have chosen. People in the business all knew the car, neighbours knew her and many passers-by recognised me when I drove by. So for each visit to Jean, there was quite a business of parking the car around the corner and dodging in and out of the back entrance.

There was another reason for keeping the Rolls out of sight, which I discovered a few weeks later. Jean's family was rather touchy about matters of public appearance and how one behaved. All of them abided by a strict code which regulated what they might or might not do, even down to the cars that were suitable for the various levels of seniority in the family. Parking the Rolls outside Jean's flat would clearly not be in the proper scheme of things. But I didn't know anything about that until one Sunday, fairly soon after we'd met, when for the first time Jean took me to have lunch with her parents.

They had realised that there was someone pretty serious, even though Jean hadn't told them who I was. She might have had a flat of her own and wanted to run her own life and been forever away doing a concert or a performance—but they still kept a watchful eye on her. An invitation to lunch was their way of signalling that they wanted to have a look at me.

There we were, on our way to lunch and to meet Jean's parents, when she asked me to stop the car in Cavendish Avenue, just around the corner from their house (and indeed from where we now live). But we didn't get out; instead she turned to me and became both business-like and a little mysterious. 'Now, there are one or two things that I think I ought to tell you,' she said. I'm not sure whether I was terrified or not by what she might be going to say, but I certainly felt I'd better listen.

'In the first place,' she said, 'my family's name is not Grayston, it's Gluckstein.' Well, that was all right; years ago when I'd played at the Corner Houses, the 'Pop' and the Trocadero I'd been well looked after by a Major Monty Gluckstein who was in charge of all the entertainment side of the business. 'Oh,' I said, 'any relation to the Gluckstein of Salmon and Gluckstein?'

'Yes, that's my family. I changed my name because I wanted to make it by myself. If people found out I was a Gluckstein, they might think I had pulled strings to get work.'

They would have been formidable strings indeed, as Salmon and Gluckstein was really a dynasty ruling a small empire. They owned restaurants and hotels (J. Lyons was only one of their companies) while other members of the family went into the law and politics. It was and still is one of the leading Jewish families in Britain.

'And there's another thing,' Jean went on. 'Perhaps I'd better add that my father and mother are Sir Louis and Lady G.' It was only much later that I discovered that Sir Louis was a most distinguished man and renowned for all the work he did to help others. He had fought and been decorated in both world wars, rising to the rank of colonel; had served as MP for Nottingham East for fourteen years and been knighted for services to politics; had been a barrister, and later a QC; President of the Royal Albert Hall for fifteen years;

The first photograph of the two of us together

Treasurer, then Chairman, of the GLC; and Treasurer of Lincoln's Inn, and of countless other organisations too numerous for me to mention.

All I could think was, 'Oh God, now what does that mean? Am I dressed properly for Sunday lunch? Shall I know what to say? What will they expect me to do?' But having got her confession out of the way, Jean didn't have a care in the world. I looked fine, she thought; there was nothing to worry about, nobody expected me to do or be anything in particular and I'd find that lunch was a perfectly normal one.

When we arrived, I got another shock. I was introduced to Sir Louis and Lady Gluckstein, who couldn't have greeted me more warmly, making me feel at home and asking me what I'd like to drink. But I was rooted to the spot, transfixed by Sir Louis.

As anybody who knows me knows, I'm not very tall. There's a curious thing about many fiddle players, indeed, nearly all fiddle players: we tend to be short and stocky—and, of course, Jewish! But Sir Louis Gluckstein stood six feet, seven and a half inches in his stockinged feet. I felt dwarfed—I was sure that I only came up to his knees.

Thankfully Jean's mother was a normal woman's height, just a shade shorter than I am, so that was all right. But Sir Louis' stature was a bit tricky to manage at first. Nevertheless, we became very good friends; not just father-in-law and son-in-law, but very close, dear friends, even though it was difficult for us to communicate walking along the street together. Once we sat down with a drink and a cigar we really got talking and there was no problem.

Sir Louis is dead now, alas, but he used to tell his friends an apocryphal story of the day I came round to ask him a rather important question. 'Max arrived and said he wanted to see me. We went into the sitting room, where he said: "Sir Louis, would you please lie down—I wish to talk to you!"' If he lay down on the floor and I stood up, for once I'd be taller than him!

That first lunch turned out to be a very pleasant occasion. The Gluoksteins were both unassuming and friendly. Once they saw that Jean and I were really serious about each other, we quickly became friends. And after we were married that friendship turned into a deep love.

Of course, when we married I used to laugh about 'marrying the Boss's daughter', remembering my early days in the Corner House.

However, I came to understand very quickly that I'd not only found Jean, but I had been welcomed into a very warm and supportive family. They stood by us and helped us through the four years or so when I was unable to leave my first wife and daughter, and when the worst happened over our eventual divorce, the Glucksteins closed ranks and stayed with us to weather the storm.

CHAPTER TWENTY-SEVEN

A New Life

The very first time Jean came to sing with the Trio proved absolutely that there was a magic about her. She'd told me she was rather nervous about working with us, and was very anxious to do well. (So was I, I wanted her to have a perfect evening!) The concert was in Weymouth—another Sunday evening affair—and we planned to make the best of the day, driving down in the Rolls, slowly and peacefully, to arrive relaxed and looking forward to the concert.

I thought Jean would be tempting fate when she said she had prepared a rather special picnic lunch—but it was a perfect day, and we set off in high spirits. Then that well-known problem started to interfere: where should we stop to have the picnic? I was getting rather hungry—in fact very hungry—as lunchtime came nearer and nearer, but Jean wasn't satisfied with any of the possible stopping places I suggested.

We drove on and on. I'd slow down at a likely spot but she always said no. Finally I became more than a little irritated by this— after all, we were only going to eat lunch! What kind of a place did Jean have in mind for her lunch party? She was very particular: 'A lovely lawn, leading down to a stretch of river, with nobody about to spoil the peace and quiet.' 'And with swans too,' I said, a little sharply. That, she thought, would make the place perfect.

'Right,' I said, 'I'm turning off here, and if we don't find it in the next mile—that's it, we'll stop anyway.' And around the next corner, there it was: the lawn, the perfect quiet stretch of river with no one about. We couldn't believe our eyes. Neither of us had ever travelled that road before. So we stopped and settled ourselves on the bank, enjoying the glorious day. And then the swans floated into the picture. Jean couldn't have organised it better if she'd planned it for weeks.

Jean quickly became a regular guest on our concerts and broadcasts, on both radio and TV—when she could fit us in, I should say, because she was highly successful as a singer in her own sphere of music. Her diary was filled with engagements to sing all over the country: Handel's *Messiah*, Mendelssohn's *Elijah*, the Verdi *Requiem*, Brahms's *Alto Rhapsody*, Elgar's *Dream of Gerontius*, Beethoven's *Missa Solemnis* and a host of smaller works. She starred in concert performances of various operas—*Carmen* was her favourite—then there were song recitals, concerts, broadcasts.

I absolutely refused to push her cause, especially with the people with whom the Trio worked, but I did suggest her name as a good singer to producers at the BBC and left it to them to make up their minds. I knew that she had such a good voice and a marvellous stage personality that when they heard her sing, they would naturally want to book her; concert organisers were very happy for her to sing with us and the Trio's concert performances became more like a quartet.

I realised then what good friends my musical colleagues were. They all saw the two of us together whenever we could be, they must have known we were very serious about each other and they all knew about the state of my marriage. The scandal value to the press would have been considerable, yet no one breathed a word.

The break-up of marriages was a well-known hazard in the music business, so that covering for good friends was all part of working together. I remember an occasion some years before I met Jean when Jack, Reg and I were emerging from Broadcasting House to go our separate ways and enjoy an evening off. I saw to my horror that not only was my evening date waiting for me outside, but also my wife and another woman with whom I was having a mild flirtation, all unknown to each other!

There was absolute consternation on my part at this serious breakdown in my diary arrangements—and I dived back into the building to hide in the gents' lavatory until the coast was clear. Jack and Reg were rock solid: one of them took my wife off while the other went to the second young lady, each saying that it was no good waiting for me, I wouldn't be out for ages as there was some extra work that I'd been asked to do which was prolonging the session. My real date was left waiting for me, blissfully unaware that there had nearly been a disaster.

I became a different man when I met Jean. There was no one else I wanted to be with—and there were never enough opportunities to see her.

There are good and bad sides to being a freelance musician. Certainly, taking on a long-term contract gives you some idea of your income in the foreseeable future, but with freelance work you know from the start that there's no security in it. There is never any pension or superannuation scheme as part of the job—and the saying goes: 'No play, no pay.' That's how it's always been. The other side of the coin is that if you don't like what you are doing, you don't have to go back to it. At least that was the theory. In practice nobody ever turned down a job they were offered—unless they were otherwise busy. In fact, it was Jean who taught me to say no, in the nicest possible way.

She'd been through many months of seeing me at odd times, of our snatching meetings together between sessions, of waiting up late for me to come home at the end of the day. Even though the Trio was rapidly becoming very successful through the television programmes, I still couldn't give up the old habit of saying yes to every job offer. But Jean was concerned about the long-term prospects for our relationship, and she knew that our lifestyle was a recipe for disaster. We couldn't hope to build a future together living like this; before long it would stop working on the personal level, and then the work would suffer too.

She challenged me one day, saying: 'The time has come when you must decide if you are going to continue playing in all these various orchestras and doing all these session dates, or if you are going to take yourself seriously as a performing artist and concentrate on what you do best—doing more concerts with the Trio and playing the violin as a soloist.'

By this time, late 1956, the Trio was being invited to play all over the country and even abroad; we could have given a concert every day of the week. 'How long is it since you had a holiday?' she asked. And I had to say I couldn't really remember. I was pretty sure it had been several years ago, though I had a dim memory of a weekend at Brighton once with a 'Mrs Smith'. Jean said, quite tartly, that if I went on like that, I'd simply collapse.

It was the first time I'd really stopped to think about what I was doing, and it was quite a shock. On the one hand, I had become well known as a television personality—the programmes were very popular—and yet I was still following the same old routines of the session world, playing any date that I was free to do.

Jean was right and I made up my mind to be more choosy about work. I started by taking on dates only when I was asked to lead the orchestras—there would be no more 'co-leader' work for me, sharing the job with another player. I agreed to maintain a permanent association with certain orchestras and broadcast programmes. I enjoyed playing for *Grand Hotel* and would be happy to lead and play solos for old friends like Wally Stott, Mantovani, Ray Martin and Norrie Paramor . . . I felt I owed them some loyalty, since they'd stuck by me through all the years.

But after a while, it became apparent that I really didn't have the time to accept even that kind of work. Jean brought it home to me that I used to play the fiddle well enough to be a soloist and I also liked conducting—and I should be doing more of that. To my surprise, I found more and more people wanted me to do just this when I wasn't playing with the Trio. That's when I took over *Grand Hotel*, and introduced my own shows on the Home Service where if it wasn't *Max Jaffa and his Orchestra*, it was *Melody on Strings* again. Goodness knows how many people were tuning in to the programmes every week.

Eventually I realised that I could give up the security of the contract with the BBC's Studio Players. I found myself doing so much work outside the BBC that it was very difficult being tied down to a regular series of weekly engagements. Furthermore, if they wanted me to appear regularly as a conductor and as a soloist, it was about time I got the appropriate fees.

Jack, Reg and I took the plunge together: we all resigned from the BBC and asked them to engage us separately for each broadcast. We felt like free men.

But for the time being we were busy with our old-style TV show, *Music at Ten*, which was soon to be joined by another called *Look Here*. This was a mixture of the Trio evening and another show I'd done called *Max Jaffa Presents*, a magazine programme with many different parts which forced us to spend a great deal of time in television studios preparing for it. There was also much more work for me doing the introductions because we planned more guest artists, a quiz show and a lot of filming outside the studio.

The very first programme sent Derek Bond out and about in Scarborough—which turned out to be rather prophetic for me—but

I found myself required to look at Blackpool with him, filming up the tower, as well as interviewing the local ballroom dance champions. In Glasgow we went to Pollok House, where we decided that the Trio should arrive from across the lake by boat, an idea which was nearly ruined because the city was shrouded in mist the day we filmed. Luckily it lifted just in time for the cameras to catch us rowing furiously.

In the new series, I'm not sure that the audience was unanimously happy about the ideas—but there was certainly some reassurance from one of them when we went to Bristol Zoo. Young Jacky decided that I was just the right person to give him a ride and climbed up into my arms. Apparently, being cuddled by an orang-utan is a great compliment.

On *Music at Ten* we had become such an institution that some guests began to enjoy disrupting our supposedly stately routine. We billed Ted Ray in the *Radio Times* as a guest instrumentalist—as 'Ted Ray (violin)'—though I'm not sure that his fiddle playing was quite up to making a proper quartet with us, whatever he threatened.

Ted Ray as guest violinist

But Ted enjoyed making the most awful jokes and puns about me and the Trio and it all came very naturally to him since his signature tune was 'Tangerine'—he would play a few bars of that and then launch into a set of Jaffa jokes. 'Jaffa has a-peel' was probably his worst but most frequently used. I preferred: 'He's the guy who sounds the six pips!'

Vic Oliver, another musician entertainer, would also say things like: 'My violin playing makes Max Jaffa look like an orange', while Max Bygraves' version went: 'I knew him when he was a tangerine', and Jimmy Wheeler used to call me 'Orange bonce'. Even in 1937, when David Burnaby (who was in the original show) returned to do a revival of *The Co-Optimists*, he often used to come to the front of the stage and greet me in the pit (where I was conducting the orchestra) with 'Evening. Jaffa good time?' or: 'Evening, Mr Jaffa, how's the fruit salad?'—pointing to the orchestra. I began to wonder how much more I would have to put up with, when the Jaffa Orange Growers wrote to ask if I'd judge a competition for a set of musical variations on 'Oranges and Lemons'.

I became fair game for a lot of people: Jimmy Edwards, the trombone-playing comedian, offered me up as the first prize in his show *Music for Jim* in a competition to guess an orchestral chord. Thank goodness nobody won: they all forgot or wouldn't or couldn't send in a crucial part of the reply which was to enclose a five-pound note along with the answer. Some viewers were bold enough to ask for a substitute, saying they preferred Sheila Buxton to me—but a thirteen-year-old said if she wasn't sent Max Jaffa she'd stop being one of Jimmy's fans. I think my favourite was Morecambe and Wise having a set-to on fees, when the punch line came out as 'I could buy Max Jaffa AND his Trio for twenty-five pounds'.

I often made guest appearances on other people's shows, where I'd invariably be the butt of some terrible humour before being allowed to play. But whatever the invitation, you had to do what your host wanted—everyone's programme had some special slant to it. On his *Saturday Spectacular*, Arthur Askey made a joke of treading on a violin—not mine, thank goodness—and threatened to accompany me on the piano. This occasion was actually very tense because Arthur's mind was only half on the programme as he expected to be told he was a grandfather at any minute. I was extremely worried that he'd remember only some of the stream of instructions we were being given by the floor manager. Poor Arthur seemed to have one eye permanently glued on the control room, waiting for a signal to come to the phone.

In all the concerts I've played, I think there was only one occasion when I had to see the music. Val Parnell asked me to appear on his very popular programme *Sunday Night at the London Palladium*, one of the top TV shows—live of course in those days—and with an enormous audience. Val Parnell asked me to play Rimsky-Korsakov's 'Flight of the Bumble-bee'. This is a difficult little piece, tricky to memorise because the notes buzz about and around themselves so much that it's easy to take a wrong turning and end up in a completely different place from everyone else.

It wasn't that I didn't know the piece—I'd played it often enough, but always with Jack and Reg, who I knew would follow me wherever I went and cover whatever mistakes I made. Playing with an orchestra is a very different matter; furthermore, all the familiar cues come on different instruments, which is quite unnerving if you're used to the piano sound. By the time you've registered what is happening, the piece has raced by so fast that you've probably gone wrong anyway. On the day, the rehearsal went rather well; I got through all the tricky corners and felt very confident. It was in the hours stretching away to the performance that the rot set in. Doubts crept into my mind from every side; what if I didn't hear the cues, what would happen if I turned back on myself—could I trust the entire orchestra to follow me?

There was only one way round the problem, and that was to have the music somewhere near so that I could look at it—just in case. It was out of the question to play from a music stand and there wasn't any room to prop the music up in the footlights; anyway, everyone would have seen it. However, the ideal solution was to put it down in the orchestra pit. There was an upright piano, the back of which fortunately was facing the stage, to which I could pin the music. I could see it quite clearly if I stood almost in the footlights.

As soon as I knew it was there, all my troubles rolled away. I was safe! With 'The Flight of the Bumble-bee', it isn't a question of reading the notes—they flash past too fast anyway. You actually follow the shape of the music on the page, you know what the notes are doing simply by the way their line curves up and down. Lucky old me—the orchestra was most amused.

Taking a wrong turning is every musician's nightmare: one of our favourite horror stories happened to Eugene Pini during a

Workers' Playtime, which always was broadcast live from a real workplace or factory. He took the wrong turning in Massenet's 'Méditation' from his opera *Thaïs*, a fairly long piece of about five and a half minutes. The way Eugene Pini went about it, it took nearer seven; everyone held their breath when he got to the critical junction for the second time, in case he did it again. It must have been their combined will-power which forced him through, but it was a close thing. Everyone swore that he wavered dangerously—but luckily chose to come down on the right sequence of notes.

The only other really difficult moment that I can remember was the occasion when the producer Francis Essex invited me to play the finale of the Mendelssohn Violin Concerto on one of his shows, with the orchestra conducted by Jack Parnell. That sounded a lovely date and I was looking forward to it, but after playing it through in the rehearsal there was consternation from Francis. We'd taken far too long, given the timing he'd allowed. When he told me he wanted the movement in about four minutes, I knew that he'd been listening to Heifetz's recording, which I thought was a practically impossible speed for anyone to match. But I had to do it for the sake of the show, and I did. It was a most alarming experience.

Luckily for me, most of these guest appearances couldn't have been more pleasant. I also worked with Vera Lynn, Jimmy Wheeler, Max Bygraves, Alan Bennett and Jonathan Miller, Eric Robinson— and dear old Harry Worth who asked me to act rather than play the fiddle. We'd met on several occasions and he thought it would be great fun if he was to play the violin in his show, while I gave him some lessons. So there I was on *Here's Harry*, appearing as the Honorary President of the Woodbridge Orchestra. Those lessons

With Harry Worth on Here's Harry

turned out to be more dialogue than lesson—but I found that I could remember the dialogue almost as easily as I could memorise new music and when we got to the first rehearsal, I was word perfect while Harry was still using a script. Of course he remarked on it and we had a bit of a giggle over my being such a clever so-and-so.

But when the show went out live, I fed Harry a line and got nothing back but a blank look of something like panic. He wasn't even ad-libbing to cover his memory lapse, so I did it for him: 'I think you might want to say something to me about . . .!' and we romped home to the end of the sketch. Once it was all over he suggested that I ought really to give up this fiddle-playing lark and turn to acting, since I'd made such a good job of it that evening. We became very good friends, and had great times together in Scarborough when he came up for a season at the Floral Hall—where, incidentally, he broke all records for attendance.

Alan Bennett and Jonathan Miller also wanted me to act: they dressed me up as the Emperor Nero fiddling away while Rome burnt—which made everybody laugh. It was an interesting sensation, playing the fiddle in a toga/sheet. It added another meaning to sheet music.

It was all fun, and made a change from radio work and straight concerts; the two sides definitely helped each other and I found my professional work nicely balanced. But my real pleasure came in the Trio concerts, when Jean was with us as a legitimate soloist, part of the evening's music. I became ever more impatient to marry Jean.

CHAPTER TWENTY-EIGHT

A Way Out

In March 1957 my daughter Elizabeth married a young man named Gerald Kingsley, also in the music business, who I felt would look after her well. (They now have two daughters, Emma and Kate, both grown up now. Kate even plays the fiddle.)

I then felt free (as Betty and I had agreed) to leave home for good and follow my own destiny. After all, I'd stayed with the two of them for twenty-two years, most of them as a stranger in my own home. I wasn't worried about Betty's ability to look after herself. She had joined her mother's dress business during the war, then worked for Selfridges before becoming a vendeuse at Worth. Someone who knew the business as she did was a valuable asset to any top-class shop.

However, moving out of Bickenhall Mansions and starting divorce proceedings was easier said than done. As soon as I left the flat, Betty decided the marriage was worth fighting for. She followed me around checking up on my movements and would regularly turn up on my front doorstep. Naturally I had to leave a forwarding address for my mail and she'd bring it round personally in a suitcase—which also contained her clothes. It was altogether a very difficult situation.

Her visits stopped only when I managed to find myself a one-roomed service flat at the White House in Albany Street. I was safe there, with a porter on the door instructed not to let her in. I felt outraged: as we had made an agreement to divorce once Elizabeth was married, I continued to pay all the bills at Bickenhall Mansions, and since Betty wasn't working, I also gave her a regular allowance.

The divorce proceedings were a nightmare. On the one hand there was the certainty of happiness with Jean, but on the other, the price I was being asked to pay made divorce impossible. There was no way I could find the kind of money being demanded as well as look after Jean. I tried every possible compromise but Betty was adamant and there seemed no answer to the problem. I therefore rang Jean to call the whole thing off, knowing that if I couldn't get a divorce, we had no future together.

After my sad phone call, Jean and I met in a dreary little café where I told her the whole sorry story, and explained that the only decent thing I could do was to say goodbye, and for us to go our separate ways.

However, I hadn't taken into consideration the Gluckstein family temperament. Jean would have none of this defeatism and nor would her parents. They'd seen us together for four years and difficult years at that, and it was plain to them that we ought to be married. Jean's father offered his help over this final hurdle, and I went to see a leading solicitor, Stanley Rubinstein, already a very good friend, who happened to be the honorary solicitor to the Savage Club. Stanley was the senior partner of a fine, long-established firm but didn't deal in divorce himself. However, he said he knew the very person I needed.

Down some old steps and around the corner, we found his

Jean – a Snowdon portrait

daughter Joan. Stanley said: 'She is the finest divorce lawyer in the country and will tell you exactly how to go about this.' Miss Rubinstein took one look at the demands Betty was making and commented sardonically on their extent.

She was completely unmoved by the obstacles put in our path. She was calm and confident and stuck to her arguments. At the same time, the Glucksteins gave us every kind of backing they could: the whole family would stand by Jean and me until a reasonable agreement was reached. It took some time.

Eventually the terms of the divorce were formally settled, but despite the legal agreements, everything became petty and sad. A neighbour in Bickenhall Mansions, who acted as a kind of go-between whilst Betty and I were talking through our solicitors, phoned to say: 'You can't take the piano—otherwise the divorce is off!' I had bought a piano for Elizabeth when she was in her teens, but now she was married and had left home without it. Betty didn't need it, but as a professional musician I often did. By the end of our divorce, the piano turned out to be a trivial matter. Betty kept everything, since I eventually left with only my clothes, my music, some documents, personal mementoes—and of course my violin. I left behind all the paintings and pieces of furniture which I had collected, or which had been given to me over the years by friends in thanks for my music. I can honestly say that the financial value of these presents was irrelevant—but to this day I miss these things because of the memories they hold for me.

As soon as the divorce was finalised, it was spotted by the press and I became good headline material. The day after, I remember going for a haircut, at the Cumberland Hotel as usual, where there was a marvellous barber who had been working in the same premises since well before the war. Outside the hotel entrance I saw this placard screaming the news: 'Max Jaffa divorced.'

Every newspaper carried the story. They continually asked me for comments, and whilst I knew that they were only 'doing their job', reading headlines like 'Max Jaffa's Marriage is on the Rocks' was a very painful experience, despite my total relief at finally being divorced.

Once the press discovered my new romance, and further that the lady in question was not only Jean Grayston but Jean Gluckstein, they pursued us relentlessly. Fortunately for us, most of the press mixed Jean up with a cousin, another Gluckstein, and they spent their time on a wild-goose chase, hounding her day and night. We felt terrible about this invasion of her privacy—but it did give us a chance to get organised.

We planned to marry as soon as it was legally possible, on June 24th 1959—but after four long and difficult years since our first meeting we wanted a private, simple day, without the press. Jean didn't even have an engagement ring because if we'd been seen going into a jeweller's together, it would have alerted everyone to a wedding. (I actually gave her one on our first wedding anniversary.) In the meantime I carried on as normal, doing broadcasts, sessions and concerts, giving the impression of 'business as usual'. We managed most successfully to keep our marriage plans secret, despite having to give two days' notice at Marylebone Register Office. The only people attending the ceremony were Jean's parents, her two brothers Roy and David and my agent George Elrick and his wife. It was a very quiet affair indeed.

I suspect I was especially subdued because George had arranged what turned out to be a rather eventful Stag Night—ending in a narrow escape from death! George, Mantovani and Billy Butlin had taken me off for a splendid evening which started with a slap-up dinner at the Café Royal, a black-tie occasion, joining about two hundred other guests from the National Sporting Club. After the meal, there was boxing.

This all took place in a private room upstairs; there were six or eight to each table, surrounding a boxing ring where a series of young hopefuls boxed a few rounds. They were still amateurs, but after every bout, the guests threw money into the ring for each pair to share out. It was an extraordinary occasion, and of course the boxing was accompanied by a lot of drinking and smoking—a completely male affair, and a rather good idea for a Stag Night.

When we left the boxing, the stairs down to the ground floor seemed too steep for us, so we decided to take the lift—which took us far further than we intended. Something in the lift's mechanism broke, sending the whole thing crashing down into the well. We could all have been killed, but the only casualty was George who cut his chin. The rest of us emerged covered in dirt and broken glass—but we were much too 'relaxed' to care. In the cold light of day, we realised how lucky we'd been.

I had a second narrow escape only a few days later when we arrived for our honeymoon at the Excelsior Hotel on the Lido in

Venice. There was a huge mahogany wardrobe in our rooms, which when the door was open looked likely to topple over. That is exactly what happened, but with me underneath. Thank goodness it was so huge, because when the entire monster started to tip, I scrambled inside it, clutching on to the clothes as the enormous wardrobe crashed down on top of me. (For once I was genuinely glad to be a small man.)

Of course Jean feared the worst. She had heard me shouting and rushed into the room. It looked as though I must have been squashed. But then she became aware of muffled cries of 'Get me out of here'—and managed to heave the thing upright again. When we'd recovered from shock she suggested that this was obviously a warning against cupboard love! But it had proved to me (as if I didn't know before) that there was more to Jean than her beautiful singing, phenomenal skills as a cook, secretarial abilities, love of life and overwhelming generosity to friends and strangers alike.

We hardly had a wedding reception as such, but celebrated with a group of very close friends followed by dinner with Jean's family. The plan was then to leave quietly for our honeymoon the next morning. But by the time we returned to Jean's flat, the word had got out and we found the press at the front door of the building.

We sneaked in through the back door, and bypassed them, but by 1 a.m. the phone and front door bell were constantly ringing. There was no escape and only one way to stop this—to open the door

Wedding-day telephone call

and face the crowd of reporters and photographers from the *Daily Express*, the *Daily Mail*, news agencies, and goodness knows who else.

They knew we were 'Just Married'—and wanted the story and pictures. I was pretty cross but Jean was absolutely true to form. 'Oh well, you've spoilt everything anyway,' she said. 'Come in and have a cup of tea.' She never changed from being, as our family say, 'The hostess with the mostest'! Visitors are immediately welcomed, watered and fed.

We certainly had the oddest wedding night, sharing it with journalists and photographers who all piled into the flat to take pictures and ask silly questions before I pointedly said that not only was it very late, but it was our wedding night . . .

'Where are you going in the morning?' they asked, and we said: 'We're not quite sure.' We were sure of course, and went to Venice.

CHAPTER TWENTY-NINE

A Troubled Start

Venice is one of the most magical cities in the world, and has become an absolute favourite of ours. Jean had never been there before, but I'd fallen in love with the city on that BBC light music jaunt several years earlier. We both agreed that it was the only possible choice for our honeymoon, and were looking forward to three weeks at the Excelsior Hotel on the Lido, a well-deserved break. There'd be not a note of music, and no rushing around London or across half the country. We planned an idle life of swimming and enjoying ourselves in the sun and wandering around the city. It was my first holiday in something like seven years.

Our four years of strange meetings had brought us closer together, and the more time we shared the more confident I became in myself. Those were the years when the television programmes really blossomed. Apparently the Trio was reaching audiences of three and a half million people—and many other TV shows wanted me on as a solo fiddle player!

When I read the reviews now, time and again the comments are about easy, unforced, relaxed programmes. Yet when I think of the strain my private relationships put me under, living a double life, it's hard to understand how this didn't show. Indeed I thrived on it. The answer was simple—happiness. Jean made me feel that at last I belonged somewhere and with someone. I was forty-three years old, and life was beginning again.

The worst feeling in the world is having happiness knocked out of your grasp. The sun goes in, a bitter taste fills your mouth, you feel helpless, sick, and in despair at the unfairness of it all.

There was no warning. It was the fourth day of our honeymoon: Jean had gone off to buy herself a sun hat and I was on the beach soaking up the sun, when I was approached by an old friend of Jean's (now Lady Philippa Phillips) who happened to be staying at the hotel. She asked whether we'd seen the *Daily Mail* that morning—and said that if we hadn't, we ought to. Well, of course we hadn't bothered with newspapers, we had other things to do. Besides, we wanted to forget London and everything about it.

There was a banner headline: 'Max Jaffa's father says: Yes, I feel ashamed when I draw my National Assistance'—followed by a story designed to stir up spiteful gossip. My father was complaining that success had taken me away from him, hinting that while I was on an expensive honeymoon in Venice, he was living on two pounds and four shillings a week. There was also a picture of my daughter, who, like my father, had been shocked to read of my marriage: 'A daughter does expect an invitation to her own father's wedding . . .' she was quoted as saying.

I went absolutely cold when I saw it. If my father was drawing National Assistance (which I genuinely didn't know) then it was on top of the weekly pension I had been giving him for years. It was paid in cash through my solicitors, so there were records to prove this. And if he thought we'd drifted away from each other in recent years, it wasn't success that did this, but the divorce. As far as he was concerned a marriage was a marriage for life, and I should stick with Betty, however miserable or difficult it was.

My father may have been many things, but he was certainly not a liar. It was obvious that no one had checked the facts properly. I thought that the article was a deliberate smear, and the comments from my daughter gave away her part in it.

We couldn't allow this kind of story to rest; left unchecked and undefended, it could escalate out of all proportion. Everyone would jump on the band-wagon to smear my name, Jean's name, the Glucksteins'. Who knew where it might end? Our names were big enough for the press to have a field day. Print and be damned was already a well-known way to sell newspapers, even in 1959; they were quite happy to print first and pay for the damage later.

So it was goodbye to Venice and our longed-for three weeks of bliss. Within two hours we were on the first train to Milan, from where I flew straight to London. Meanwhile, Jean waited for me at a quiet hotel, safe from the journalists we discovered were already swarming out to Venice. What a great honeymoon!

Back in London, the Glucksteins had already alerted my

solicitor and the barrister Gerald Gardiner was then consulted. He advised immediate legal action against the *Daily Mail*. My entire career was at stake as audiences expected their artists to be decent and honourable. Television was also unforgiving about scandals, real or fabricated. It was seriously on the cards that my current success could be swept away instantly and I would find myself returning to the anonymous grind of the session world.

Once we'd started the legal process, there was no more that I could do, so I returned to Milan and found that Jean had been well looked after by two cousins she happened to have met in an art gallery. (The Salmon and Gluckstein clan stretches far and wide.) We decided to try to forget the horror of the previous few days and start our honeymoon all over again.

We wanted to stay in Italy and still thought the Adriatic coast was a good idea. Rimini was one possibility, or even Ravenna, but we ended up at a hotel in Riccione, a small town I'd heard was quiet and pleasant. However, neither of us had reckoned on the ubiquitous Vespas on which the young whizzed up and down, giving us a sleepless night. The next morning we checked out of the hotel. Our honeymoon was proving a great success story!

The tourist office promised that we'd find peace and quiet at Milano Marittima—and it was perfect. It was right on the beach, set among pine trees, and we had a big light room. There was sun, sea, pasta, wine—and peace as had been promised. We had a wonderful time.

The hotel owner was a very friendly chap who encouraged us to enjoy ourselves like a pair of teenagers. He even took us waterskiing in his wonderful shiny new motor launch, which was reputed to be the fastest boat on the Adriatic. Jean proved an absolute natural from the word go, while I sank to the bottom like a stone. It was all very galling—and I argued that she had the unfair advantage of having skied in Switzerland. It was also easier for me to say that I didn't enjoy the experience (rather than to be shown up in front of her).

The owner was very sad when we told him that we wanted to spend our last few days in Venice but being a romantic soul, he suggested that the best way to travel to Venice was by water. If we could bear to stay one more day, he'd take us there in his famous launch in return for lunch on arrival! Neither of us had ever approached Venice by sea—and it now seemed the only way to arrive.

But in the morning, the weather had broken: after days and days without a cloud in the sky or a breath of wind, suddenly it was grey and decidedly breezy. Neither Jean nor I said anything, but we were both acutely aware that this was not going to be the promised idyll across the water. Nevertheless we set out, but after ten minutes of an increasingly bumpy journey we both began to turn a paler shade of green, and asked to be put ashore to catch the bus. Sadly, we have never seen our hotel owner again, so I don't know if he made it to Venice, because *he* was going on regardless. To this day Jean swears that he must have sunk, and that if we hadn't got off when we did, we'd surely have gone down with him.

The bus was another adventure; we stood by the side of the road and flagged down the first one with Venice on its destination board. Of course, we had no idea that there were several categories and that we'd chosen an elderly and scruffy country bus, absolutely packed with local people and produce including live chickens and which stopped at every village en route! Having lugged the suitcases on board neither Jean nor I could be bothered to get off again when we found out our mistake. As a result we had tremendous fun. Every time the bus stopped, people talked to us and gave us endless cups of coffee. By the time we reached Venice, the passengers knew our complete life history.

I paid the price in another way too. When we got to our hotel, I found I'd given my life-blood to the experience: the Adriatic mosquitoes had also been fellow passengers—and I'd become the dish of the day.

Once in Venice, we went straight to the famous Hotel Danieli, which is right on the Grand Canal. With only a few days left before our return to England, we made the most of every minute. It was mid-July, but still possible to go exploring if you started early enough in the day. Since Jean had never been before, we walked and walked, enjoying ourselves discovering this enchanting city. We went to art galleries and churches (there must be one on every corner in Venice) and we saw glass-making at Murano, where we bought the most beautiful red and white striped dish, which is still in our bathroom today.

I found a marvellous shirt-maker who made me a wonderful collection of shirts—all white—and in just forty-eight hours. They were so well made that I've still got some of them thirty years later. We ate and drank, and spent hours sitting watching the world go by on the Grand Canal—or listening to the music at Florian's Café in the Piazza San Marco. It was rather nice, for once, to have someone else playing the tunes.

Neither of us was looking forward to going back to London, the court case, the gossip and general innuendo. But we knew we'd have to face up to it—and had been warned that the case would take a long time to get to court. In fact it took nearly two years, but the *Daily Mail* finally retracted on the very day that Jean gave birth to our first daughter, Naomi, on 21st April 1961.

It's impossible to describe the relief of knowing that at last it was all over, and coupled with this was the joy of Naomi's birth. What a day.

(Incidentally, we made a much better job of going to Venice on our twenty-fifth wedding anniversary, when Jean gave me a present of a holiday at the Cipriani, one of the world's great hotels, set in the most beautiful gardens with its own swimming pool. It's on the Giudecca, just across the Grand Canal from the Piazza San Marco, and there's always a motor launch to take one across in just a few minutes. We were taken by the manager to our magnificent rooms and there we found that the hotel had given us a 'welcoming' bottle of champagne and a single red rose for La Signora—a rose three foot tall at least. I immediately asked for another glass so the manager could join us with some champagne—and he gave us a toast: 'To a very happy *Golden* Wedding Anniversary!' I hadn't realised my grey hair had made me look quite that distinguished!)

It was an ordeal to come back to England after the honeymoon, to face the public and find out how they were going to react to us, given the unpleasant story. The worst moment was the very first concert. I had been engaged to play at a Sunday concert in Worthing, something I'd done for years and the concerts were always sell-outs. But I had no idea how all the publicity about my divorce and then the business about my father could change my popularity. Worthing was and is known as a very respectable south-coast town, rather conservative and well mannered. Would they still come to hear me play? Even the car was nervous! For the first and only time in our association it let me down by having a puncture as we were driving south. But Jean was with me to give moral support; even though it must have been pretty ghastly for her, she was determined that we would share the bad with the good.

When we reached Worthing I drove straight to the Pier Pavilion

Theatre and anxiously went to the box office, where I was greeted warmly by the girl on duty. She knew me well and looked happy to see me. So off-handedly I asked: 'Anybody coming to the concert tonight?' And she told me the glorious news: 'I've got only one seat left.'

Well, that was marvellous; the sense of relief was enormous! 'You've just sold it,' I said and I bought it for Jean.

CHAPTER THIRTY

An American Adventure

The Trio's first overseas tour was fixed for 1961—and it came about through a series of coincidences. First of all, our twenty-six-part TV series was seen and liked by the American management Columbia Artists; secondly, Mantovani, who was very big in the States, had the same British agent as we did, George Elrick. So when various members of Columbia Artists came over to England to discuss the next Mantovani tour, George persuaded them to see us. They must have liked what they saw because soon they were enthusiastically booking concerts across the States and Canada.

Just as we were about to sign the contract, a personal hitch developed. It's always the way. But this time Jean's normally good musical timing let us down, as she discovered that she was pregnant, and calculated (in strict tempo) that the baby was due bang in the middle of our planned tour. It was impossible to leave England—never mind. When she was about seven months gone with Naomi, Jean was engaged to sing some arias with the Bournemouth Symphony Orchestra, conducted by Sir Charles Groves. Her first piece was from the *Messiah*, 'O thou that tellest good tidings to Zion' which is preceded by the recitative, 'Behold, a virgin shall conceive'! From my point of view, watching her sing this in her perfectly obvious condition was hilarious. But Jean was not amused: she'd been given a precarious place to balance right at the edge of the platform and she was bothered about falling off. Obviously, no one in the Bournemouth management had noticed anything.

Meanwhile, a year's postponement had given Columbia Artists plenty of time to plan an even more extensive tour and in 1962 we embarked on an eight-week epic which would take in forty concerts in twenty-eight states and cover seventeen thousand miles. It was

Packing for the trip

dreadfully hard to leave Naomi behind so soon, as she was only eight months old—but that's one of the hazards of a musician's life. Her grandparents and our Nanny were delighted to look after her and at least we knew she was in very good hands.

We somehow felt that as far as our style of music was concerned, we were pioneers, breaking into a new world, crossing virgin territory. We were very excited about the tour and were happy to go for what was really little more than expenses. We just hoped that American audiences would appreciate the kind of music we played as much as our British fans did. The tour didn't have an auspicious beginning, when we joined the liner *United States* to start what we thought would be a leisurely crossing to New York. The representative at US Lines had made a deal with us—in exchange for the use of our names in advertising, we would receive first-class cabins at the second-class rate. This was the sort of saving we needed to make since our fees would barely cover our expenses on the tour.

The send-off from London was spectacular. Aboard the boat train we were treated like royalty, with champagne, trays of canapés, flowers, the works—and the cameras clicked away. Once on the ship at Southampton, there was more of the same. We were shown to lovely cabins, with more champagne and flowers and we were really looking forward to a few days' break on the crossing.

But then, when the last call for visitors to leave the ship was being made, someone noticed a barrier going up along the corridor. They were closing off the ship into first- and second-class sections, preventing second-class passengers from wandering into the first-class areas. Nowadays, ships don't bother with separate classes—you have cabins according to what you pay, and the whole ship is open to you. In 1962 it was still very much a question of dividing the sheep from the goats. The trouble was that our cabins were definitely on the second-class side—our first-class travel had obviously ended in Southampton.

Given all the arrangements for the publicity deal, we thought there must have been some mistake, but no one was prepared to sort out the problem. It was quite clear to us that we'd been conned. So we picked up our bags and marched off the ship, creating more publicity as we told our tale. We would have paid to go first class (never mind the publicity)—but a deal is still a deal.

Another organisation saw the value in the story. We'd barely got back to London when the Israeli airline El Al were on the phone offering us return flights to New York—first class of course. We were delighted to let it be known that we were patronising their service! And it all turned out for the best in the end. The ship had the most terrible time crossing the Atlantic with storms every day and was so delayed by the weather that it arrived in New York three days late. If we'd stayed on board, we would have missed the opening concerts of the tour.

With Jean and Gladys Kilbey as well as the three of us, the fiddle, the cello and luggage for eight weeks, we were quite a crowd. Columbia Artists provided us with a large Ranch Wagon in which we drove ourselves for the seventeen thousand miles of the tour. Or at least, Jean and I drove, as Gladys didn't take to the American roads, and we wouldn't let Jack drive—it was too nerve-racking to have him wrestling with his cigarettes as well as a car that size. Furthermore, Reg coped with driving on the 'wrong' side of the road by insisting on straddling the white line in the middle! It's what you might call sitting on the fence. After three or four days, Gladys suddenly shrieked: 'Reg, you're not to drive any more. Max and Jean, you're not to let him drive again.' So there we were, with seventeen thousand miles to share between us.

Right from the start, we had some hilarious times; I don't think any of us had ever imagined being in charge of a vehicle the size of the Ranch Wagon, even though we each drove a large car. When we collected it from the garage, everybody decided that I should be the first one to drive.

It was an immense beast, exactly like a small truck. However, whether I could see over the bonnet was immaterial when we drove off—or at least tried to drive off. I emerged from the parking lot in a series of jerks, bumps and squealing tyres, feeling that this was the Wild West and we were riding a bucking bronco, even though we were still in New York. I hadn't even reached the road.

Then there was this quiet drawl in my ear: 'You ever driven an automatic shift before?' (Shift being their word for a gearbox, I think . . .) 'Lemme give you some good advice: throw away the left leg!' I was guilty of every beginner's habit of treating the brake as the clutch—using the left foot. Never mind; once that was overcome, it was a marvellously relaxing way to drive. I don't think we could have done the tour otherwise, and I never went back to manual gears again.

The tour proved beyond any doubt that we truly did get on with each other as friends—unlike some musicians. Our schedule was really punishing; in fact it was madness. We had concerts more or less every night, every one of them in a different town and sometimes a different state. Reg Kilbey worked out that on one occasion when we had three days off between concert dates, there was a small matter of nine hundred miles to be driven to the next venue.

Our average drive was about two hundred miles a day. We started in Connecticut and travelled round the country via New Jersey, Pennsylvania, the Carolinas, Georgia, Alabama, Texas, Indiana, Illinois, Michigan and Ohio. Then we crossed into Canada for ten concerts before ending back in the States.

In fact our worst journey happened to be the shortest. We were going only twenty-three miles to the next venue—so we had planned a morning off, with a lie-in and the drive after lunch. We reckoned that twenty-three miles shouldn't take longer than half an hour. But we were in Canada, and overnight there was the most prodigious snowfall; of course, we got stuck in it. And not only did we get stuck, but the tractor-cum-snowplough sent to dig us out also got stuck and blocked us further. Eventually both we and the snowplough were dug out and we arrived at the concert with about twenty minutes to spare, frozen stiff from the experience.

We all felt we deserved a rest by the end of the tour—but Jean, although she hadn't been singing, had taken the brunt of things. Her role was to act as our manager and 'roadie' (if roadies were around in 1962). When we reached a town our routine was to go straight to the hotel, unload all our suitcases and instruments, unpack and sort out the daily details (such as organising the laundry). Then we'd go off to the 'Hall of the Night' for the concert.

In the morning this whole business was reversed, with Jean sorting out the hotel bills, everyone's luggage and the major task of packing it all back into the wagon again. This was a work of art in itself, and woe betide any of us if we spoke to Jean while she fitted all the suitcases, fiddle and cello (especially the cello) back into the wagon.

In her 'spare' time, Jean's job was also to contact the concert organisers, write the thank-you letters as we went along and cope with any disasters. She certainly saved me one evening. My fiddle started to make the most dreadful buzzing sound when I put the bow to it. There was a fearful rattling which I knew would drown out the music, especially anything quiet. I saw to my horror that a large part of the side piece had come unstuck. There was a huge crack between the two pieces of wood, and when I played the fiddle, the vibration caused the pieces to jangle against each other. This is in fact quite a common problem for fiddle players, and not the end of the world, provided you're near a violin craftsman or 'luthier'. On this particular evening, however, there was no time to look for help. Jean came to the rescue with the perfect solution. She produced a bottle of clear nail varnish, which apparently she used for emergency repairs to her stockings. I think we must have put on about five hundred coats of varnish all through the night, holding it together by hand. Eventually the two halves of the fiddle stuck together, and all was well, if a little unsightly!

On another occasion, we found that the locking system on the Ranch Wagon's tailgate had broken—and that certainly was a disaster. We couldn't leave the car unlocked since it held all the worldly goods we had in the States. Once again Jean came to the rescue and drove over a hundred miles to collect an essential spare from the nearest Chevrolet dealer.

It's wonderful to know you have some kind of back-up when on the road. But we were left absolutely to our own devices when playing a concert in French-speaking Canada. In Quebec there was no one to show us around and as we couldn't understand their

French, this made life very difficult.

Like most events this had its funny side too. We arrived in the town, found the hotel, found the theatre where we were playing and the dressing rooms and made ourselves at home. There was no sign of anyone from the concert society or the theatre management. Obviously, they were going to leave the whole show to us—even to the extent of working out our own lighting and seating arrangements for the stage.

However, ten minutes or so before the concert was due to start, we became aware that there were people in the hall, so at least it seemed as though we were going to have an audience—remember, we still hadn't seen a soul. Re-reading the contract we checked that the concert should start at seven thirty, so at the appointed time we walked out on to the stage and started. I suppose we must have played for about forty-five minutes when we decided that there ought to be an interval.

It appeared to be going well. I had tried to talk to the audience in my limited French—I'd given it about three goes and they didn't seem to mind. But suddenly the door to the dressing room burst open, and there was this man shaking with so much emotion that he was almost incoherent. Eventually in his strangled English accent he managed to say: 'Your music . . . aah . . . make me . . . sick!'

Luckily we knew what he meant. He was quite overcome with how wonderful it all was, though his choice of words could have been more tasteful. We never found out where he came from, or whether he was the elusive organiser from the concert society— whom we never otherwise met!

Mostly, however, Columbia Artists had thought of everything in the arrangements for all this travelling and playing. They gave us marvellous sets of maps with all our routes clearly marked. We had contracts for every concert with phone numbers to contact in each town, confirmed bookings for all the hotels/motels, and a full set of directions to get to the halls.

Most of the venues were fantastic, usually on a university or college campus and beautifully equipped with comfortable dressing rooms and modern washing facilities. Nearly every evening, there was some kind of party or reception after the concert. It was always the same; there would be crowds of people to meet, and we'd be offered coffee and cakes. But as we never ate before a performance, what we really wanted was a solid meal. It did our systems no good waiting until well after 10 p.m. each night to have dinner. Luckily most motels had late night 'diners' serving food after midnight, so we found ourselves eating ham and eggs with French fries right across America. Our average bedtime was around one or two in the morning, and most days we would be up again at seven in order to leave in good time to drive to the next concert.

When we arrived in Texas we had three days off (the first free days since the start of the tour). We decided to split up before the next leg of the journey; Jack and the Kilbeys took the car to San Antonio where Jean and I would join them three days later.

I wanted to meet up with an old American friend from the war days, a pilot called Meyer Minchin who'd gone home to the States saying that I should look him up if I ever got to Houston, Texas. We'd kept in touch—mainly at Christmas—and here we were at last, about two hundred miles away from Houston. When I telephoned him he didn't believe it: 'Where are you? Nacodoches? I've never heard of it—are you sure you're in Texas?' I said he should be ashamed of himself: and that Nacodoches was the oldest town in the state.

Of course, we were immediately invited to stay and he organised a plane for us, which was waiting at the airstrip after the concert. In no time we were in Houston and being driven to his home. Meyer gave us a wonderful time with real Texan hospitality. It was so good to see him again. He told me that his work was something to do with 'holes in the ground', but I didn't know what he was talking about (of course he meant oil). Like the backdrop to a certain soap opera, his house was enormous, his car was enormous and his generosity was enormous.

The following morning Jean wanted to go shopping and Meyer took me to meet some of his friends. The most extraordinary part of that day provided the third in a series of strange encounters which had begun just before Jean and I were married. We were dining at the Caprice in London, one of our favourite restaurants, where we were very friendly with the owner Mario, a wonderful restaurateur.

On this occasion, Jean overheard an American couple sitting next to us discussing antiques with the waiter. The wife wanted to buy some antique china dogs—and the waiter was advising them to go to Selfridges. Well, Jean was beside herself, and when the waiter had gone, she interrupted the couple's conversation. 'Selfridges,' she said, 'may be a department store that prides itself on having almost everything—but it doesn't have antique china dogs. However, I know a shop that does.' She just happened to know the ideal place, just around the corner from her flat.

A few days after our dinner at the Caprice, we were honeymooning in Venice and were out in the Piazza San Marco having some drinks at Florian's and listening to their musicians playing, when Jean said: 'Don't look now, but there are two of your fans behind you trying to attract your attention.' In fact they weren't fans, they were the china dog couple.

Then all those years later in Houston, Meyer Minchin took me into a jeweller's shop which was run by a friend of his. I wanted to buy Jean a present. Who should be the owner of the shop, but the china dog man again. It was the most extraordinary set of coincidences!

We had three memorable days, rounded off by Meyer giving the most magnificent party. It's difficult to beat the Texan hospitality. To cap it all, Meyer personally drove us the two hundred miles or so to San Antonio where we met up with Jack and the Kilbeys to continue the next leg of the tour.

All in all our concerts were tremendously successful and we had rave reviews: 'An evening of rare musical charm' . . . 'pure, unalloyed pleasure, long to be remembered' . . . 'ever successful combination of informality, mirth and fine musicianship.' Those kinds of comment can do serious harm to your ego if you believe in them too much.

But good reviews do count for a great deal when agents are booking for the next season. We knew, even as we were leaving for London, that Columbia Artists were interested in bringing us back for another tour, the following year. Having travelled up and down the east coast, it now looked as though we would be welcome throughout California and other western states. All we had to do was to sign the contract. The trouble was that having once agreed to do so many concerts for such a low fee, we were expected to agree with the same terms again—which must have been giving Columbia Artists a magnificent return on their investment. However, for our next visit we felt the terms would have to be quite different. We knew we were wanted by concert promoters and we had several television shows lined up. The least we expected was to be offered fees in line with what we could command at home.

But somehow or other, our agent in Britain lost the battle with the mighty Columbia, which in those days had a virtual stranglehold

PROGRAM

1. Slavonic Fantasy — *Traditional (Arr. Byfield)*
Beginning with the great romanticist composers and continued to the contemporary Bartók, slavic folksongs have played no small part in musical literature. Many of these slavic tunes are as familiar to us as our own American folksongs. Composers have been intrigued by the strong rhythmic patterns, melodic content and general reflection of nationalistic traits—perhaps more vividly evident in folk music than in any other aspect of a nation's culture.

Largo — *G. F. Handel*
Of the opera "Xerxes," little more than a name in musical history, the Aria, *Ombra mai fu*, has survived the centuries and in various instrumental arrangements is known to us as Handel's "Largo."

The Great Waltz — *Johann Strauss*
MAX JAFFA TRIO
"The Great Waltz" remains one of the most popular of the five hundred or more dance pieces penned by the mighty "Viennese Waltz King" who conquered all Europe and finally America with his captivating melodies.

2. Après un Rêve — *Gabriel Fauré*
Gabriel Fauré holds a unique place among musicians. He is the best example of the refined aristocracy which is so peculiar to the French. His art is exceedingly subtle. Although a contemporary of Debussy, his music has little relation to that of the latter. He is more reflected by Ravel, who was his pupil. His genius expressed itself best in smaller forms, particularly in his art songs. Written for voice, *Après un Rêve* has been adapted for 'cello and is accorded to be this instrument's 'private domain.'

Harlequin — *David Popper*
Mr. KILBEY, 'Cello
David Popper was a Bohemian cellist, born in Prague in 1843. He was considered one of the greatest cellists of his day. He toured extensively, later becoming first cellist of the Vienna Court Opera and a member of the Hubay Quartet; after 1896 he taught at the National Academy of Music in Budapest. He wrote four concertos, a suite for cello and orchestra, many studies and short pieces for the instrument. He also composed a string quartet in C minor, Op. 74, and songs.

3. Hejre Kati — *Jenö Hubay*
Jenö Hubay was a Hungarian violinist, conductor and composer. He was a pupil of the great Joachim at the Berlin Hochschule, later becoming principal professor of violin at the Brussels Conservatoire. He formed a celebrated String Quartet which included Popper, as mentioned above. Although he wrote eight operas, four symphonies, and numerous works for the violin, plus many miscellaneous works, perhaps the first work which comes to mind when Hubay's name is mentioned is the *Hejre Kati*.

Romance — *Anton Rubinstein*
As a pianist Anton Rubinstein was second only to Liszt, but he wished chiefly to be remembered as a composer. His compositions may be considered as the legitimate successors of Mendelssohn's. They contain a fine broad vein of melody supported by true and natural harmony and thorough technical skill.

Largo al factotum — *Gioacchino Rossini*
MAX JAFFA TRIO
This is the famous aria sung by Figaro in "The Barber of Seville" where he gaily acquaints all who will listen with his many accomplishments—"beards must be shorn—yearning hearts must be joined together, by intrigue or entreat." In short, here is the factotum of the town—of all towns, delightfully arranged for Trio.

INTERMISSION

4. Pas des Fleurs ("Naila") — *Léo Delibes*
Léo Delibes composed almost exclusively for the theatre. His best known ballets are "Sylvia" and "Coppélia." His only opera which has remained in the repertory is Lakme.

Traumerei — *Robert Schumann*
MAX JAFFA TRIO
From the *Kinderscenen* (Scenes from Childhood), Robert Schumann, the foremost composer in promoting the romantic movement in music, has given us a veritable gem of melody, familiar to all.

5. Claire de lune — *Claude Debussy*
No program would be complete without some representation by that master of impressionism, Claude Debussy. Oscar Thompson has said: "Debussy was the poet of the nuances of Nature, not as the eye mirrors them, but as they are transmitted to the feelings." Debussy titled several works, *Clair de lune*, one for piano, one for voice, another attributed to him.

Fantasie Impromptu — *Frédéric Chopin*
Mr. BYFIELD, Piano
Chopin's *Impromptus* fulfil the implications of their title of being distinctly improvisational in quality. Although they have the air of being carefree, there is still a coherent and carefully worked-out structure.

6. Roumanian Songs and Dances 18th Century Drawing Room — *Traditional (Arr. Byfield)*
MAX JAFFA TRIO

7. Si mes vers avaient des ailes — *Reynaldo Hahn*
If my verses had the wings of a bird, they would fly into your chamber. This is a love song by Reynaldo Hahn whose songs have enjoyed wide popularity.

Sicilienne et Rigaudon — *Fritz Kreisler (after Francœur)*
Mr. JAFFA, Violin

8. Schön Rosmarin — *Fritz Kreisler*
Music by Request — *(Arr. by the Trio)*
MAX JAFFA TRIO
The noble and beloved Fritz Kreisler has composed many works, almost all for the violin, and has made scores of violin transcriptions, thus making a lasting contribution to the violin literature. Many of the popular Kreislerian pieces are original compositions although Kreisler, himself attributed them to ancient unknowns.

RAVES ON THEIR FIRST AMERICAN TOUR!

"The music lovers who expected to hear a run-of-the-mill concert by just another musical trio were happily surprised when **THEY EXPERIENCED ONE OF THE OUTSTANDING MUSICAL EVENTS OF THIS OR ANY OTHER SEASON . . . AN EVENING OF PURE, UNALLOYED PLEASURE, LONG TO BE REMEMBERED."**

Bristol, Connecticut Press 1/30/62

"A HAPPY OCCASION FOR ALL CONCERNED . . . The audience was familiar with most of the numbers and it probably NEVER HEARD THEM MORE EXPERTLY AND BEAUTIFULLY PRESENTED . . . It was a light, entertaining program in which the performers' sense of comedy and ability to communicate with their audience were given full play."

Clearfield, Pennsylvania Progress 2/1/62

"The Max Jaffa Trio . . . employing the **EVER SUCCESSFUL COMBINATION OF INFORMALITY, MYTH AND FINE MUSICIANSHIP** . . . The audience quickly sensed the **ARTISTRY AND SPIRIT OF THE PERFORMERS AND RELAXED TO ENJOY EVERY MOMENT OF THE MUSIC."**

Shelby, North Carolina Star, 2/7/62

"AN EVENING OF RARE MUSICAL CHARM . . . Music such as these expert players presented in a live concert in our city, FAR SURPASSED ANY TELEVISION PROGRAM."

Anderson, South Carolina Daily Mail 2/8/62

"IT WAS A RARE MUSICAL TREAT . . . The **EXQUISITE BALANCE** of the program, the **BLENDED BRILLIANCE** of the three artists, cemented by their GIFTED SHOWMANSHIP, enabled them to ESTABLISH A 'RAPPORT' with the audience too sadly lacking in many concert artists . . . Their own **DEDICATED DEVOTION AND AFFECTION FOR MUSIC IS POSITIVELY INFECTIOUS AND THE AUDIENCE CATCHES IT."**

Griffin Georgia 2/9/62

"'DELIGHTFUL ENTERTAINMENT' . . . The Max Jaffa Trio proved that MUSIC, even the more classical type, **CAN REALLY BE FUN!"**

La Porte, Indiana Herald Argus 2/21/62

"I have never seen a concert more enthusiastically received in a community. Since the concert, during the campaign here, I have heard nothing but 'RAVES' from the members and **they are hoping for a return engagement."** Jan Miller, reporting from Colby Kansas

"I heard the Max Jaffa Trio in La Porte, Indiana last week. They were terrific! For the committee that wishes to present a highly entertaining attraction, a group that plays familiar numbers — the kind the average concert goer loves — THIS TRIO IS THE ANSWER. Am sure they helped me in re-organizing this town."

Pauline Walston, Community Concerts

An American concert programme and some American reviews

over all the concert promotions in America. It was pretty much a David and Goliath fight and it seems Goliath won. We were never offered reasonable terms which we could have accepted, and so we never went back to consolidate our success.

297

CHAPTER THIRTY-ONE

Summers by the Sea

In 1960 I went to Scarborough for one season. As is fairly well known, I ended up staying there for twenty-seven years! Furthermore, when first invited to take on the job of conducting music on the Spa I apparently said: 'Don't be ridiculous—it's all bloody mills and flat 'ats up there.'

Of course, I was being stupid and I should have known better. That remark was particularly silly because I had been to Scarborough before—but only to play and with no time to look at the beautiful countryside. Indeed, it was the first place the Trio visited for our new TV series *Look Here* in 1958 and we were invited back in October that same year, to end the summer season with a special extra concert. Eugene Pini had been in charge of the orchestra for the whole season and did his final concert with a great flourish in the afternoon; we were the gala attraction that evening. If I'd stopped to think, I might well have remembered that as a seaside resort, Scarborough had a long and distinguished history and, as far as their music went, over a hundred years of tradition.

However, much of our lives were spent constantly on the road travelling to different towns two or three nights a week. We hardly ever saw anything of the places where we played; they all passed by in a blur.

But Jean had no problems with Scarborough. She knew it well, having been for three years a guest artist on the Spa, singing with my predecessors Eugene Pini and Charlie Shadwell. She'd also done a complete season in 1955, singing in the big summer show *King's Rhapsody*, and could see that it would be wonderful to stay in one place for a whole summer. She promised me beautiful countryside and scenery, historic houses, old ruins, fresh air; and the best fish and

298

Jean as Countess Vera in King's Rhapsody

chips! What choice did I have? I agreed to do one season.

In October 1959 the Corporation announced, with an enormous fanfare, that I would be taking over the music at the Spa from Whit Saturday until the last weekend in September. I was to have a sixteen-piece orchestra and we would be 'the biggest ever attraction at the Spa'.

Well, I took that with a pinch of salt. I sensed that Scarborough was pushing the boat out to attract a bigger public for the summer; the Spa ballroom had been completely redecorated, Dickie Valentine would be leading the stars with a show called *Make it Tonight*, the Black and White Minstrels were booked into the Futurist Theatre and at the Open Air Theatre, Ralph Reader (of *The Gang Show*) had written a new entertainment called *Summer Holiday* —starring Jean!

There was also great excitement about plans to record and broadcast my regular radio and television programmes from Scarborough. During that season *Music from Scarborough* was transmitted on the Home Service, and the BBC put out four television programmes called *Music with Max*.

299

A wonderful surprise was a late evening broadcast from the Candlelight Club, where everyone who was doing a show in the season gathered to let their hair down. I leapt at the chance to do something completely different—and there was astonished comment in the press the next day, saying that I'd 'led a jazz session with a verve that must have made the matrons gasp'.

I'm sure that was the start of programmes for ITV. I wonder now whether it gave the BBC the excuse to drop the Trio from their schedules as we only ever did one more TV show from Scarborough for them. From October we joined ITV with a series called *At Home with Max Jaffa*, and continued guest appearances on all kinds of other programmes.

My first Scarborough season was without Reg and Jack. Reg definitely didn't want to come as he was busy doing a lot of conducting in his own right, and Jack seemed busy with his arrangements and composing. So I left them to their own devices until the Trio concert season restarted in the autumn. Meanwhile I went about the business of finding an orchestra and soloists, and getting the music together for a long summer season.

We were to play a two-hour concert every night, including Sundays, and a short concert every morning. I wanted to have completely different programmes for at least three weeks, to ensure that holiday-makers who might stay longer than the average of a

The Spa at Scarborough

fortnight would always hear something new. That meant we had to plan forty-two complete changes of programme in one go. After three weeks we would start all over again, but with variations and elaborations. After all, and very importantly, we also had to think of the people living in Scarborough who were regular concert-goers, some of whom bought season tickets and came to the Spa every night during the season. The Borough also dreamt up another scheme whereby holiday-makers could buy a weekly ticket very much more cheaply than buying tickets separately every night.

The one really sensible stipulation I made was not to appear at the morning concerts; instead these were directed by the leader of the orchestra. Obviously I kept an eye on the proceedings, and used to sneak in and listen every now and then to make sure they were playing and behaving properly.

That first year, we also featured Ena Baga on the Extra Voice Hammond Organ, the only one of its kind in the country. This was more than a novelty attraction for the audience—it was an extraordinary instrument which could add all the rich sounds of a full brass section and the depth of a string section, yet also give us that well-loved 'Palm Court Orchestra' sound of a harmonium and a piano accordion.

Getting the band together proved to be remarkably easy. The first thing was to find a leader who could be my right hand—and that first year Sam Spurgin was just the person to give me rock solid support. Then we collected together the players from his circle of contacts in the north. Many of them came from the Royal Manchester College of Music (which later became the Royal Northern College), while another group came down from Scotland. This was a connection which continued through the years and made me particularly happy because of my experiences with the Scottish Orchestra in the thirties.

As a result, I hardly ever auditioned players but accepted recommendations from friends or colleagues in the profession. This worked very well indeed. Anyone who came to Scarborough knew that I expected them to be able to play their instruments and to sight-read well, but perhaps more important was their ability to get on with everyone else in the orchestra. We were such a small group that there was no room for feuds.

It turned out that it wasn't feuds that I needed to worry about but romance—and lasting romance, which happened practically every year. We had a lot of marriages which owed their start to the Spa orchestra—right from the very first season, when young Barry Griffiths, who was then on the back desk of the fiddles, met Angela Caldwell and pursued her till she married him. (They now have six children.) Then there was Harry Cawood, another of our leaders, who also met his wife in the orchestra—Mary Wilcock, who played the cello beautifully; and Joyce Mills (who frequently deputised for absent players) became the wife of our last leader, Eric Mills. Eric played with me in Scarborough for seventeen out of my twenty-seven years, thirteen of them as leader and librarian. He is a kindly and much admired man, and was a tremendous help to me.

Barry Griffiths was promoted to lead the orchestra in the second year and eventually went on to become the leader of several orchestras, including the BBC's Northern Symphony Orchestra in Manchester. For many years now he has led the Royal Philharmonic Orchestra in London. Apart from Barry, most of my leaders went on to good careers. Harry Cawood was joint leader of the Northern Sinfonia. Other members of the Spa orchestra who have gone on to great things include Pat Morris who became principal flautist with the Liverpool Philharmonic, and then the BBC Symphony Orchestra; Martin Robinson, principal cellist with the English National Opera; and Jimmy Archer, one of our finest players, who also led for me. He is still a successful freelance musician, and added to this he and his wife Jane have become excellent cheesemakers in the West Country.

With Eric Mills on the final last night

I introduced Jimmy to the freelance recording world, knowing full well that the session world's gain would inevitably be my loss. But Jimmy did come back to visit us with his caravan and his family.

Very soon I was inundated with applications from musicians wanting to join the orchestra. Word had spread that the experience gained from playing our seventeen-week season couldn't be matched elsewhere. It certainly did wonders for the nerves of young players, performing live in a concert hall every day with an ever changing repertoire of music.

As it turned out, and I must stress this, most of our players were very, very young; some were still students. Having grown up in a totally different world from mine, none of them had ever played the light classical repertoire before. They had to keep on their toes and learn quickly. The first shock always came when they discovered that I didn't rehearse all the programmes for the season. We would go over some of the music for the first two weeks, but after that we'd gather for a quick talk-through in the band room fifteen minutes before the performance, where everybody had their music ready for the concert, when I would go over the programme. The exception to the rule was for broadcasts, when we had full rehearsals.

We showed how this worked on the television show *Farewell to Scarborough* made by Yorkshire Television during my last season. They filmed us gathered together in the band room with the music, as I went through a piece we hadn't played before. All I ever needed to say was: 'This passage gets a bit quicker, then we slow up four bars later. At letter "E" we'll make a cut, we'll leave out this repeat or we'll put in that repeat.' By the way, I feel I must tell you of one incident that gave us a big laugh during the filming of that TV programme. David Lowe, the producer, suggested that Geoff Druett (the presenter) and I should walk along the Scarborough foreshore, and Geoff would stop various people at random and ask them what the name Max Jaffa meant to them. The reply that came from one young man was: 'Max Jaffa—doesn't he sing with the Culture Club?' I had no idea that I looked like Boy George!

Now let's get back to the orchestra. I feel that my approach, although nerve-racking, was good for the players, the music and the audience. Everyone was very keen since they naturally didn't want to play badly, even though they may have been sight-reading; so they sat on the edge of their chairs, concentrating like mad and playing for all they were worth. So often you see players leaning back with their legs crossed, looking bored and just scratching away at the music. As we were such a small group, we all depended on each other and helped and supported each other. When we were playing together, I would always play with them, facing them, and turn to the audience only when I played a solo. I'm told that the orchestra always looked as though they were listening during the solos, and were generous enough to join in the applause afterwards.

Some people might have thought that I was taking a considerable risk using such young players. Perhaps some were not as good as others, but I'm thrilled that so many of the players who were with me at Scarborough have gone on to hold very responsible positions. What's more—and this was very gratifying—some time or other, most of them came back to Scarborough to say hello and spend a couple of days there. They've also paid me the great compliment of saying publicly how invaluable their experience of playing in Scarborough had been.

For a small orchestra, fifteen all told, we developed a large repertoire with strings, woodwinds, piano and, most important of all, the percussionist. He played everything—timpani, drums, xylophones, vibraphones, glockenspiels, the lot. In the end we turned him into a soloist and gave him a spot every Saturday night. On other nights of the week the flautist, oboist, clarinettist, viola, cello and even double bass were given solo spots. I was absolutely adamant that these young and talented musicians should get the recognition they were due. With a band that size, there isn't much for a conductor to do, so most of the time I stood up in front of them playing along and keeping a fatherly eye open for the difficult bits.

Perhaps the greatest difference between us and most other orchestras of the time was my engaging a few lady players. They not only looked good, but were fine musicians. Have I said that I've always liked women?

Strangely enough, somehow it had never occurred to me that Jack Byfield might enjoy coming up to Scarborough for the summer—I'd just taken it for granted that, like Reg, he was too busy with his own kind of music. So I was absolutely horrified to discover that this wasn't the case. In the world of music most of the work was going to younger people closer to the changing music styles, so when I asked him to come up and join me for the summer in 1961, he leapt at the chance. I think the Spa music only really settled down properly when he arrived.

The Spa Orchestra, with Jack Byfield at the piano

Jack took charge of the morning concerts and with his vast experience devised programmes that gave tremendous pleasure to his audiences. His only problem was having to arrange these in advance, completely unlike the planning approach of the Trio. There was a printed programme of items every day for both the morning and the evening concerts, so we had to plan carefully.

Jack did his programmes before me, and I would cross-check his music with my ideas for the evening concerts. By and large, the same people came to hear us daily, so we ensured that there was plenty of variety within each day's programmes, as well as from one day to the next.

The music library grew at a rate of knots, and by the end of my twenty-seven years I had amassed some two thousand pieces with scores and all the parts. This collection came from publishers, with many new arrangements from Jack and various other sources. It all had to be gathered together, catalogued and filed under groupings like overtures, Viennese waltzes, show selections, operettas, entr'actes, movements from symphonies by Mozart and Haydn and so on. We couldn't possibly have done it without the help of Eric Mills. Jean is the librarian now and the collection is based in London.

I planned the week's programmes with two simple criteria in mind: they had to be as varied as possible and they had to give everyone a chance to shine with solos. Jack played more than anyone else since he always had to accompany the guests and soloists as well as do his own spot; he played piano solos on Sunday, Monday, Wednesday and Friday nights. Every Tuesday and Thursday, we would feature one of the orchestra as a soloist—and of course on Saturdays we let the percussionist have his head. Each week we also had a guest singer, alternating a man and a woman through the season. They had a lot to do, because we wanted a different group of songs from them in the mornings, and in each half of every evening.

I developed a format for building each programme. We had to start with a curtain raiser, an overture of some kind, and follow it immediately with a piece in a completely contrasting mood. As most overtures wind up to a blaze of glory and noise, you could almost guarantee to follow it with a quiet, romantic, sentimental piece. The singer followed that very well, and we'd probably go on with some kind of dance movement, such as a Viennese waltz, followed by a short selection of something from a show to take us to the interval.

Part two always started with a 'bang bang' piece with lots of joyous noise, followed by a solo from somebody in the orchestra. We would then go back to the orchestra before the singer's second group of songs. It was always tricky to decide what this particular piece should be, since we never really knew what music the singers would feel like on the day. We just had to chance it.

My guess was that the singer would most likely end with something sentimental which would give us the chance to follow with some bright music. Then it was time for my solo spot—I played every evening—and on to the finale, either a large selection or a suite of ballet music. It was always something very popular. I felt that no matter what was in the programme before it, whatever we ended with had to move the audience to rapturous applause; if they went out feeling: 'Oh gosh I did like that, that was good!' then the whole concert was a success. They might even come back for more!

CHAPTER THIRTY-TWO

Family Man

For our first season in Scarborough we rented a farmhouse called Holly Tree Farm from John and Mahlo Hollywood, who over the years became good friends. It was during this time that Jean, as promised, showed me all the beautiful country that abounds around Scarborough; and my interest in horse-racing was kept very much alive by discovering the lovely courses of Thirsk, Ripon, Beverley and York. We had a wonderful time and enjoyed ourselves very much indeed.

Scarborough is a highly sociable place and over the years most of the top entertainers—such as Harry Worth, Frankie Vaughan, Dickie Henderson, Jimmy Wheeler, Ken Dodd and Danny La Rue— came to the town to do summer shows. We occasionally went to Sunday evening parties given by one or other of the entertainers on their night off, although of course I worked every Sunday evening. During our many years we also met a large number of Scarborians, and have some very good friends in the area.

I was of course busy with the orchestra and the nightly concerts; and Jean had a good part in the Ralph Reader show *Summer Holiday*, an epic musical extravaganza at the Open Air Theatre. This is a natural amphitheatre and faces the 'stage', which is in fact a big island set in the middle of a large lake. It was for many years the venue for large-scale productions of famous operas and operettas such as *Merrie England*, *Hiawatha* and *The Merry Widow*. All the shows were put on by the Scarborough Operatic Society, composed of enthusiastic and talented amateurs, and they engaged professional singers for the leading parts.

Jean sang in four musicals with the Operatic Society, and she had some hilarious experiences at the Open Air Theatre. One of the

The audience at the Open Air Theatre, Scarborough, facing the island stage

funniest of these was in *King's Rhapsody* in which she played Countess Vera, lady-in-waiting to the Princess Cristiane. Their first entrance—and the opening to the show—was on a magnificent barge, actually a large rowing boat with a rather unwieldy superstructure. It was rowed by a stalwart member of the Scarborough Rowing Club dressed as a royal courtier.

On the island stage, set allegedly in the country of Murania, were all the numerous members of the Operatic Society, waiting to greet Princess Cristiane and Countess Vera. As the orchestra played the overture the royal barge moved out ponderously from behind the island, into the view of the audience of about five thousand people. The boat was difficult to manoeuvre, and one night it unfortunately got caught on an underwater tow-rope stretched across its path. (This rope was attached to a glass raft used for a ballet later in the show.) The royal barge became totally ensnared by the rope, and the audience was treated to the spectacle of a man rowing furiously—but getting nowhere! The entire stage cast kept coming forward to greet the ladies, then retreating because of their non-arrival. Eventually, after the orchestra had played the overture three times, someone managed to disentangle the rope and the Princess and her companion arrived—at last—in Murania. They were greeted by the Prince's mother, with the immortal lines: 'Welcome to Murania. I expect you are a little weary after your journey!'

Several seasons later, when Jean was back at the Open Air Theatre singing Bloody Mary in *South Pacific*, a second amusing incident occurred. Tudor Evans, another of the leads in the show, had a dreadful time with the island stage. After one of his songs he had to exit out of the back of the stage and into the pitch black night (extra black after the bright stage lighting)—and he fell straight into the lake! During this debacle, the famous glass raft (beautifully lit from underneath) moved to the middle of the lake in front of the audience, and on it were the two lovers miming to 'Happy Talk'. Alone on the stage Jean had to try to sing this song—all too aware of a very damp singer behind her in the darkness, violently splashing around in the water, accompanied by a rich stream of Anglo-Saxon expletives! She had great difficulty in stifling her laughter.

The greatest joy of Scarborough was getting our family started. Naomi and the twins, Jenny and Lisa, were all conceived up there. Could it have been the sea air . . .? Later the three girls really grew up with two homes. London was for school-time but Scarborough meant holidays and fun.

After five years of renting houses each summer, it seemed that as our annual pilgrimage north was likely to continue for some time, we ought to think of organising our own place. We were lucky to find exactly the right kind of house in Scalby, a small village just outside the town. It was absolutely ideal for peace and quiet, away from the holidaying crowds, with enough space for the five of us, plus Bernie McCarthy (for nine years), then Jo Mahon, a great lover of the concerts (for the next five years)—both our invaluable nannies. The house was soon filled with all the considerable accoutrements that three little girls collect. One room became my office and practice study, and the whole house was a hive of activity in every way.

The twins were born on February 4th 1965, nearly four years after Naomi. They came as a tremendous surprise. No one knew that two were on the way, not even the obstetrician who was most upset at having failed to spot them before the delivery! In those days, scans weren't invented and it was thought X-rays were most inadvisable. It seems that they were so close together that their heartbeats sounded as one! When I rang Luigi and Doreen to tell them that they were the proud grandparents of not one but two more granddaughters, Luigi made the perfect remark: 'Dear Jean, she always did over-cater!'

To this day, Jean and I always have an argument about the very first dinner party we gave after we were married, when Arthur Askey came round after a TV show I was doing with him, and Jean's favourite uncle, Roy Klean, was another guest. I swear that Jean provided ten pheasants for ten guests. She says that she cooked five! But to be fair, I think Jean's style was bred into her. I soon found out that marrying into the Gluckstein family was somewhat more complicated than I'd bargained for. When all the dust of the divorce had settled and we'd built ourselves an elegant new home, I wanted to give a small party to say thank-you to the nearest members of the family, for all their support, advice and moral encouragement.

Now I'd never given a party like this before, and naturally went to take advice from the expert in the family business—who was well used to catering for the 'gathering of the clan'. 'Close family?' he said. 'Well. You'll be catering for a hundred and three for a start...' It was a memorable housewarming party, due mainly to the special welcome given me by Jean's 'small' family and, particularly, by her parents, Luigi and Doreen. (Everyone called Sir Louis 'Luigi', not because he was Italian but simply because his name was Louis G.) They became such good friends that we really loved spending a great deal of time with them—and we made a point of choosing to live just around the corner from them in London.

We found a house for sale in exactly the place we wanted. Even though it was too small (and had a very little garden) we bought it and rebuilt it to our own specific designs. It was a very ingenious rearrangement of space, which has made a classically elegant three-storeyed house, but supported by all the latest technical wizardry.

The children had their own floor, right at the top of the house, where they could express themselves to the full. They could have friends round and enjoy themselves giving parties while the rest of the house continued in its calm routine; the top floor was, and remains, self-contained, with even a little kitchen! Luckily Jean's parents had a large garden so the girls had plenty of space to play outside.

The demands of the music profession had always ordered my life. But now, with three young daughters, I wanted to spend as much time with them as possible—when I wasn't touring. When I was at home I would try to help them with their homework, and particularly enjoyed the mathematical problems. On Sundays we'd all troop next door to Luigi and Doreen for a huge family lunch. Luigi and I would have tremendous conversations after those Sunday lunches, putting the world to rights in a cloud of cigar smoke while

Jean, Doreen and the girls gathered at the other end of the lovely panelled drawing room, playing games such as mah-jong, six-pack bezique, gin rummy and (very noisily) racing demon until a walk in Regent's Park seemed a better idea.

Luigi was one of what we would call today 'the great and the good'; his work brought him into contact with the most fascinating people in government and in business. I could listen to him for hours, he was such a compelling talker. He was also a tireless organiser and when President of the Royal Albert Hall (a job which lasted for fifteen years) he set about raising an absolutely astronomical sum of money to get the place completely refurbished and cleaned up for the centenary. Goodness knows how many millions it eventually cost.

When the Albert Hall was done up, we were all invited to the great centenary celebrations and our eldest daughter, Naomi, was asked to present the bouquet to Her Majesty. It was a wonderful surprise for her—because when she came forward with her flowers and did her little curtsey, the Queen thanked her and said: 'I understand we share the same birthday.' Naomi was taken aback! It was obviously Luigi's doing; he knew the royals quite well, having had a lot to do with them over the years. What's more, some years later on another Royal Albert Hall occasion, Naomi again presented flowers to the Queen, who shook her hand and said: 'I remember you, we have the same birthday don't we?' Naomi couldn't believe it, and neither could we.

Naomi presents a bouquet to the Queen at the Albert Hall, with her grandfather behind her

Luigi was probably more of a father figure to the children than I was, especially when I was away playing so much of the time. It must have been awful for them to see both their parents packing to go, as we did every winter when we were invited to play on the *QE2*.

That brief but eventful journey on the *Avelona Star* to Buenos Aires and back in the twenties was the only time that I'd ever considered joining a ship's company to make music. However, many musicians would sign on to work their passage or to have a working 'holiday'; it was part of the honourable traditions of 'music while they eat'. By the early sixties, shipping companies found increasing competition from air travel and had to think quickly about changing their plans—which is when the idea of the cruise holiday became fashionable. Our kind of music became exactly right for some of the entertainments they put on on board as part of the holiday attractions. Our first experience came with a Christmas and New Year outing on the *Queen Mary* in 1965; Jack and I did two seven-day cruises on her, in an event organised by the *News of the World* which made it a real knees-up of a voyage. Jessie Matthews was there too, and Max Wall, Ivor Emanuel, Patricia Bredin, some very flamboyant flamenco dancers and a teenage rock-and-roll group, the Applejacks, hot from the Top Ten. It was certainly fun for all!

Unfortunately it was a very rough voyage, and the passengers had to be helped to enjoy themselves. Poor Jean was egged on by the purser to do her bit too! I was very worried for her since she was seven months' pregnant, but she bravely joined in for the Fancy Dress

Jean on the Queen Mary *cruise*

Parade when it looked as though there might be a serious lack of initiative from most of the voyagers. This was round about the time when Cunard was building a new ship and there was much discussion about what she should be named. Jean made herself a funnel for a hat, draped herself with a sheet and hung a notice on her rather prominent front with the question 'Q4?' on it. A pair of watching ladies were overheard getting quite the wrong end of the stick: 'She's having quads then, is she?' They obviously knew more than everyone else (including the obstetrician). Only a few weeks later, the twins were born.

We also worked for P&O on the *Canberra*—but I think our real favourite had to be the *QE2* cruises. They couldn't possibly be described as anything else but a relaxing holiday with a little playing once a week. It was minimal indeed: a fifty-minute concert and no more, once a week for six weeks, between nine thirty and ten thirty in the evening. There were solos from me and solos from Jean, all heroically stitched together by our new pianist Vincent Billington who came to join us when Jack became too frail to go on playing. Our concerts on board were always followed by a film, and (depending on the film) a change of audience.

We were very lucky to find Vincent. He'd been to Scarborough, where we'd met him and liked him, and he joined us from doing the music on the *Canberra*, so he knew almost more about cruise music than we did. He was also marvellous in Scarborough during the season, and we had a very happy concert life together.

Cunard were lavish with their entertainers—and one of the first and most wonderful surprises was to discover that dear old Joe Loss was a permanent fixture on board the *QE2*, running the band in the ballroom. It's extraordinary how often his career has touched on mine, yet we inhabited such different worlds. I only ever worked with him once, when he asked for me specially to lead his string section on a recording session.

New entertainments were laid on each week as guest artists came and went at every port of call. Among them were Dickie Henderson and Max Bygraves, Bill Cosby and a young James Galway. I was delighted to help this marvellous Irish flautist by lending him several encore pieces. The rapport was instant and further enhanced by our mutual admiration for Heifetz. I know we are all living in a very small world, but events a few years later were still extraordinary. Having moved from music to music management, my daughter Naomi found herself looking after the career of none other than James Galway. Moreover she decided that after a gap of twenty-five years it was time for me to have a manager again. On my sixtieth anniversary concert (organised entirely by Naomi), Jimmy sent a lovely telegram saying how much pleasure my playing had always given him.

But back on the QE2, Victor Borge arrived, probably the most brilliant and versatile entertainer of them all, and a man who obviously spent his time jetting around the world between one hall, theatre or liner and another. In keeping with his marvellously deadpan humour he opened his evening by glancing round the impressive ballroom with a rather jaded eye and shrugging: 'So this is Barbados!'

For six weeks we idled away our days on the very topmost deck, which most of the passengers failed to find. We would soak up the sun there, well looked after by three stewards who made us their personal concern and kept us supplied with a constant stream of food and drink. We gossiped and joked about music and musicians— nothing ever gets in the way of talking shop when musicians or entertainers meet.

But in the evening we were on duty for idle chatter of another kind. The captain and other officers organised a cocktail party almost every day, with yet another batch of new people to be entertained. We felt it was our job to help them cope with this endless stream—and I found it rather useful to act as Scarborough's unofficial ambassador. It was easy to fill the gaps in conversation by extolling the joys of the place and tempting Americans to come to try the bracing East Yorkshire air. And, I might say, quite a few took up the invitation.

The most extraordinary part of this shipboard gathering was people's strange behaviour when removed from their usual habitat. While some kept themselves to themselves, others dropped all their inhibitions and either had a constant party and were very friendly indeed—or became totally obnoxious, their manners obviously left on shore. Anxiety was another shipboard phenomenon and the purser would daily regale us with yet another idiocy. One lady asked if the crew slept on board, and there was a difficult moment when a passenger demanded to reserve a seat in a non-smoking lifeboat!

In many ways, it was a sad parade of rich, unhappy and insecure people, who had no idea what to do with their time, no idea how to enjoy themselves. The ship was a time capsule, a cosy escape, where they looked after your every whim in the most magnificent style. And if you still needed further comforting, there was always the constant theme of eating. If you were so minded, you could eat all day long and half the night too; in between the official meals, there was always a burger and hot dog stand near one of the swimming pools, with a constant stream of customers—all free, of course. One woman was even seen going into the dining room to have lunch while chewing on a hamburger. 'I can never eat on an empty stomach,' they overheard her saying.

Luigi and Doreen really stepped in as the most wonderful surrogate parents to our daughters when we were away. Luigi would take them off to school and help them with their homework. In fact, Naomi got special coaching from him on her Classics for the Oxbridge Entrance exams—and no one was more pleased than he that she got a place at his old college, Lincoln.

The twins chose very different paths: Jenny went to the University of East Anglia to read History of Art and French, while Lisa did Business Studies in Cambridge. All three of them were awarded very good degrees. It was so far removed from my start in life. They were always very intelligent and well educated, asking questions, probing and exploring ideas for themselves. Education

Making music with the girls: left to right, Lisa, Jenny, Naomi

was certainly in the Glucksteins' family traditions—but it was an absolute thrill to me that my daughters should have turned out so bright.

Although music was very important to the girls, neither Jean nor I forced them to go on with their music lessons, because we both knew that you have to want to practise before you can enjoy it and make satisfying progress. To be a professional musician is to dedicate one's life to that art, excluding most other studies. Jenny learned the piano and the recorder; and Lisa played the recorder, the violin and then the clarinet. (She's also a very good and keen tap dancer!) Naomi played the piano and (briefly) the violin.

When Naomi had been studying the violin for about two months, she was managing to produce an excruciating sound out of the instrument. One day when Jean and I were out of the house, Naomi (on the top floor) decided to practise. We had two invaluable daily helps: Margaret who came in every morning, and endured us for twenty-two years; and Kay, who came in the afternoons. Jean returned home and found Kay working in the kitchen. She was greeted by Kay who put her finger to her lips and said very quietly: 'SSSHH . . . sh. Mr Jaffa is practising!'

Naomi's violin playing was very short-lived, but once she saw Marisa Robles performing on one of my shows, she took to playing the harp. We never found out whether she was attracted by the actual sound of the harp or the magnificent sight of all that gold on the instrument—or Marisa's wonderful, effervescent personality. But she was adamant that she wanted to play the harp. Marisa wanted to take Naomi on as a pupil. From the start she made marvellous progress until, after about four years, she decided not to continue. Marisa was tremendously patient, saying that Naomi could certainly go far as a harpist if she wanted to—because she was one of her most talented pupils.

I invited Naomi to play a couple of solos at the Spa: Brahms's 'Cradle Song', and that famous harpist's party piece, the 'March of Brian Boru'. I couldn't have guessed that the worst would happen; a string broke during her performance, and she had to put on another one during the interval and start all over again. Of course the audience cheered her—but the broken string could have been the last straw. Actually I suspect that horses had become more attractive—besides which, she was beginning to think about her looming A levels.

Jenny with Bluey

The girls have had a dreadful time as 'Max Jaffa's daughters' — and there were several occasions when other people spoilt their fun, simply because of that. There were some unpleasant incidents, especially when they began to ride seriously, when their success was publicly questioned by what one can only describe as jealous mothers who thought they were getting special treatment from the judges. They were even accused of cheating to win. It used to make me white with rage — but of course, none of us could possibly show such feelings. We all had to bear it with dignity and brush the hurt aside. I think it was one of the hardest lessons the girls had to learn.

The first pony was definitely part of a conspiracy which I learnt about only when we were thousands of miles away in Africa, on tour with Kenneth McKellar. We were all sitting by the pool — McKellar, Billy Dainty, Elizabeth Larner, Jack Byfield, Jean and I — chatting about pets. While people talked about their Great Danes or their goldfish, Jean just casually mentioned that we'd got a pony. I was so surprised that I nearly fell into the pool.

'Oh! Didn't I mention it to you before?' she said, all innocently. 'We've had him for some weeks now. He's grazing on York race-course until we get back and take him to the field I've organised in Scalby.' I was appalled. I knew that horses were dangerous, that

317

people fell off them, that you could break your neck on them and that I had no desire to get on one. But it was a *fait accompli*; Bluey was soon to be followed by Seamus, April Glory and Razzmatazz, and the girls went horse mad. Naomi has even taken exams which have made her a fully qualified riding instructor. Jean was soon spending much of her time driving the horsebox over half the country, as they went from one show to another.

I preferred racehorses to show horses. I was very keen on racing, studied the form and followed the horses either on TV or, better still, at somewhere like Beverley—an absolute gem of a country course. Incidentally I have my very own race there, the Max Jaffa Sprint Stakes, first sponsored in 1985 for three years by David Bott, a very dear friend whom Jean had known since childhood, and racing mad. He insisted on only one condition—that it be known as the Max Jaffa Sprint. After the first three years the directors of Beverley did me the great and unusual honour of saying that my race would be run annually 'in perpetuity'.

The very first season we were in Scarborough an invitation was sent to all the stars appearing in the town to come racing in Beverley; Jean and I were the only people to take up the offer and in fact we have gone every single season since. Curiously, when we went on our annual winter holiday to St Moritz, we met and consequently became close friends of Dadie and Brian Oughtred—who, it turned out, were directors of Beverley race-course.

Funnily enough, I rarely bet, even though I became part owner of a fairly successful racehorse. He was called Schumann; his father's name was Hotfoot, a very prolific sire. I half-owned him with Clare and Tony Villar, whom we'd also met winter holidaying in St Moritz. They too are great racing enthusiasts. We bought him when he was a two-year-old, and were thrilled to bits when he came fifth in his first race at Newmarket. His next outing was in quite an important race at Doncaster, and he won, just! Naturally there was jubilation all round, and also on subsequent occasions when he did well.

A much more momentous occasion for jubilation in the family occurred for all of us when Jenny (the older twin by fourteen minutes) was married in September 1988. She and her husband, Barry (Isaacson), who is in the movie business, now live in Hollywood—although they met and married in London, both being Londoners. Our number one daughter, Naomi, and younger twin, Lisa, have long since fled the nest. They've grown to be very attractive young ladies, living independently and happily in flats of their own, no longer under any sort of Aged Parent restraints. We are very proud of our three daughters.

With the whole summer taken up at Scarborough, and with the autumn and spring booked for concert tours and part of the winter for cruises, we could only ever take time for a proper holiday in the depths of winter. For years we went to St Moritz. Luigi and Doreen and their children had long been regulars at the Kulm Hotel, and it seemed absolutely natural that we should continue the tradition.

I wasn't allowed to ski, in case I broke something like a finger which would have been an expensive disaster for me and the insurance company. For some reason they allowed me to take up curling. (Obviously, no one in the business had ever been near a curling stone in full progress.) My curling tuition started in the most unorthodox manner possible. Jean decided to give a beginner's lesson on the shiny kitchen floor of our London flat. She instructed me about 'in' and 'out' handles—and how to 'lay the stone'—using the handle of our kitchen kettle in lieu of a forty-pound curling stone.

On that first holiday in the winter of 1960–61, Jean was heavily pregnant with Naomi, and obviously couldn't ski or curl. That season she took to walking. But all the Glucksteins, who had curled for many years, were keen that I should join in the games, so I had some 'proper' lessons on the ice—given to me by wonderful Billy

With Jean and Luigi at St Moritz

Luigi and Sir Gordon Richards standing side by side on the same piece of ice

Griggs, a top jockey in his day. I immediately became a most enthusiastic player, and fairly good at the game.

In fact curling was the perfect sport, played outdoors in the wonderful mountain air. It provided good exercise; and often the sun would shine brilliantly hot, and our faces and hands became marvellously tanned. At lunchtime food was brought out to us on the curling rink from the hotel. The St Moritz Curling Club, of which we were all members, was extremely sociable. (It is the oldest curling club in Switzerland.) Among the members were many top jockeys and trainers—Doug and Pat Smith, Eddie and Susan Hide, Tony Hide, Gordon and Marjorie Richards—and the world's greatest billiards and snooker player, Joe Davis, for whom a winter holiday in St Moritz became a tradition as it was for us. One of my most treasured photographs is of the giant Luigi standing side by side with the extra diminutive Sir Gordon Richards. We all spent our holidays joining various teams and entering many curling competitions.

In Scarborough we took our exercise on the golf course, which was about five minutes away from our house in Scalby. We'd try to go at least twice a week, getting there around eleven in the morning, when no one was about—and there was hardly any possibility of hitting a human being with a badly directed golf ball!

I hadn't played since my Scottish Orchestra days, when I'd left Glasgow with a full set of clubs and a handicap of twelve, which I thought wasn't at all bad for just a few months of playing the game. Goodness knows what happened to my clubs and handicap during the years in London when I played no more. Then Jean gave me a new set of clubs and a bag—and suggested that we should take it up again. We were regular players during the summer, though I'm not sure that I ever got back to that early Glasgow success. I'm happy to recall that my return to the fiddle was far more successful than my return to golf.

The twins loved caddying for us—or rather, they spent hours rummaging about in the rough searching for lost golf balls, which, if in good condition, they sold to us. They would then happily spend their ill-gotten gains on the fruit machines at the nineteenth hole, usually with little success! Occasionally, after watching a long losing sequence, I would claim 'my turn', and once in a while hit the jackpot—much to their annoyance!

Another pleasure that Jean and I shared was in collecting furniture. When we married, my wedding present to her was a dressing table which I'd spotted in the window of Partridge Brothers in Clarges Street. I've always loved spending any free time I have just walking around town, window shopping and watching the passers-by. That's how I happened upon this splendid piece of furniture, which opens up to reveal all kinds of intricate nooks and crannies and special compartments in which to hide away the powders, perfumes and pomades. It's the most marvellous piece of cabinet-making.

Jean was absolutely thrilled when it was delivered and threw her arms around me when I got back to the flat that evening. But a little later on I understood that she had been thinking of getting me a bedside refrigerator as a present, because I was so devoted to the idea of nocturnal feasts. I don't think she was really serious. Instead she gave me a most beautiful pocket watch, which of course I still have and treasure.

Perhaps my love of antique furniture was due to my possessing and playing on an antique fiddle. As a youngster I visited and enjoyed looking at the treasures in the Wallace Collection which was a few minutes away from where I lived. Later, when playing at deb dances in beautiful houses, I would take in and admire the many lovely pieces of furniture.

We spent a good deal of time going round antique shops and salerooms to see if there was anything worth buying. It was a wonderful way to pass the time before a concert when we were on the road, and in Scarborough we permanently kept an eye out for notices of auctions. It was very sad, for example, when the Caley family decided to sell up after the death of Sir Kenelm and his wife. We'd once been invited to tea by Lady Caley with Luigi and Doreen—an occasion made absolutely unforgettable by the whisky cake which was so strong that I remember asking Lady Caley if she would 'pour me another slice'. Among many pieces of furniture in that house Jean and I both loved in particular a sideboard. So when the sale of the contents of the house was announced, we determined to attend the auction—and if at all possible, we would acquire the sideboard. Jean and I stood inconspicuously at the back of the crowd attending the sale. Eventually the sideboard came up, and the bidding started. With every bid that was made Jean kicked me and stage-whispered: 'Bid,' and I said: 'Not yet.' Soon my shins were very sore! As the bids became fewer and far between I made my move. Two more bids from me secured the beautiful sideboard—which stands proudly and much admired in our dining room.

Jean would go down Portobello Road, a famous London market, most Saturday mornings — and occasionally bought something that took her fancy. She had a good eye and her fancies were very sensible — take me, for example! (Another antique . . .) Many years ago Jean had bought a gilded antique landscape mirror which hangs in our hall. It's lovely, and I thought how nice it would be if we could have a similar one over the fireplace in our sitting room. One day walking down Marylebone High Street, I passed an antique shop that specialised in crystal chandeliers, antique drinking glasses, decanters, etc. I could see through the window on to the floor — and there, leaning against a showcase, was a slightly larger version of Jean's landscape mirror. The owner of this shop was an eccentric woman, well known in the neighbourhood. I enquired the price of the mirror but she wasn't sure, as this was not her usual line of country. She had just bought it 'on spec'. She then asked me what I was prepared to pay for it. I said: 'Five pounds'; she said: 'Sold.' As I write this in 1990, I am talking about thirty years ago.

Jean always maintains that I only married her because I found that she could write decent letters, type, answer the phone, cook beautifully and — apart from her own two-week engagement — stand in at short notice for any of the singers who were indisposed during the Scarborough season. She was, and is, much more social than I've ever been. I enjoyed chatting to people after the concerts, and certainly when I was invited to open charity fêtes or bazaars. Otherwise I kept myself to myself. I rarely went into a shop in Scarborough during the whole time I was there. But then, what could I do when my every need was looked after by a 'superwife' who really kept the whole operation going?

My daily routine was pretty regular. Breakfast was a cup of tea and a slice of toast, followed by a bath, a shave and dressing. Then, at eleven, there was the ritual of coffee with Kitty who looked after the house for us. Every Monday, and for twenty years, we were joined by our irreplaceable and excellent gardener Alf Ridgeway. As far as I can remember the only disagreement we had with Alf was over our love — and his loathing — of the daisies in the lawn.

Kitty became an essential, and much-loved, part of the family. After she'd been with us for some time she asked me: 'How long is a fortnight?' — and I said: 'If you're not pulling my leg, it's two weeks.' To which she replied: 'No, it's fifteen years. Because fifteen years ago I came to you for a fortnight.' She ended up by staying with us for twenty-eight years—and that almost caps my having gone to Scarborough for one season and staying for twenty-seven!

CHAPTER THIRTY-THREE

The Scarborough Years

I don't believe any other musician has had the good fortune to play to an audience as wonderful as ours at Scarborough. We made personal contact with so many of them and they really became good friends. Night after night, year after year, people would come back and you would see the same faces in the audience. We used to look out for them specially.

When I think of names, I'm amazed at how many people became part of our lives: Lilian and Alan Barritt, Kitty Potter, Barbara Christy, Norman and Joyce Forrester, Jack and Marion Appleby, Stan and Agnes Hodgson, Iona Hood, Diane Tasker, Margaret Dowell, Barbara and Frank Green, Louise Jones, Iain and Marion Macleod, Dadie Oughtred, Duncan McLellan and his parents, Jeannette Purkiss, Maria Shaw and Christina Poole, Irene and Bert Seymour, Maurice and Peggy Gayler, Winnie Huck and Irene Appleby, Dorothy Salmon, Irene and Alan Scott, Nan Kidd, Cynthia Dacre, all the Robertsons, Marie Horner, Charlie and Iris Davidson, and Joyce and Arthur Mollon (Jean's oldest friends in Scarborough). But it's impossible to list everybody. Their loyalty was tremendous; for example Norman and Muriel Rayner came across from Wakefield to spend every weekend in Scarborough and Aidan and Bridie Harlow, who had moved to Australia, came all the way back—twice—just for old times' sake. There was a family who brought their caravan down from Scotland every year; and Iain and Marion, the couple who met at the Spa, married at the Spa and even called their house The Spa!

Others came to hear us play out of season; Gladys and Barbara Jones (whom we visited at their home in Eastbourne) were fans who travelled to many of our concerts all around the country, as did Betty

Blair and her Grimsby Silver Blues Association. This is a ladies' club, which came by private coach to a number of concerts during the Scarborough season and always turned up for the last night. They were regulars for about ten seasons—and we'd developed such a friendship that Jean and I have even stayed in Grimsby with Betty and her husband Robbie. When the BBC gave me a concert recording at the Queen Elizabeth Hall to celebrate my sixty years in music, I was very touched to discover that also present were the Silver Blues.

Betty Blair has a wonderful talent for creating spectacular cakes; they're beautifully made and decorated to celebrate special occasions. She is a pâtissière extraordinaire—and her work is really in the realms of high art! Never mind the delicious baking, these cakes with their breathtaking icing are sculptures in their own right. It's very humbling to know that she's prepared to take such trouble over us. On one of the Last Nights, she made individual cakes for each person in the orchestra, with their names iced on top.

We were given so many lovely presents over the years, some 'official', some unexpected. At the end of my twentieth season, in 1979, Cynthia Dacre's unofficial Max Jaffa fan club had the most wonderful surprise—they presented me with a glorious silver coffee pot. And of all the times my name has been taken in vain, as it were, I think I get the greatest pleasure from my fuchsia, which was created specially for me by David Burns to celebrate the centenary of the Scarborough Horticultural Society in 1985. I think Max Jaffa (now grown for me by Bill Poyner of Scalby) looks pretty handsome standing up straight and proud in our London garden.

There are quite a few Max Jaffas about. Two Scarborough children won a competition when they came up with 'Max' and 'Jaffa' as the appropriate names for the new baby chimps in the zoo; a lively pair, though I'm not sure how musical they are. Then I read somewhere that a Yorkshire lady had named her dogs after me: Max was a Dobermann and Jaffa a lady lurcher.

Of course, there were what you might call enjoyable penalties to all this. I found myself becoming almost an expert at opening garden fêtes, appearing at various annual fairs, judging beauty competitions and talent contests, but that was all part of the season. We felt (and feel) far more than visitors—much more like true natives of the area. After every performance there would be quite a number of people waiting for us, and we'd join them for a chat and occasionally for a drink in the bar. People who had to leave the concert early would

With Betty Blair and her Grimsby Silver Blues Association

Playing to Max and Jaffa

always wave goodbye to us and I'd wave back. Every year, all the players in the orchestra would find themselves 'adopted' by various members of the audience, who were extraordinarily kind to them.

Year after year we were told we'd broken the box-office attendance records, and of course the box office take. (It's astonishing how our kind of music filled a need.) What's more, with our concerts at the Spa we not only paid for our keep, in terms of the fees for me and the orchestra, the soloists, the music hire and all the other bits and pieces—but Scarborough also made a profit which helped towards some of the other entertainments. The hundreds of letters and requests we received every week showed that our music was very popular, old-fashioned or otherwise.

I remember one night Jean asked me to play an arrangement for the orchestra of the song 'Ma Curly Headed Babby'. As a rule she never asked for any programme changes, but on this occasion she was most insistent and said that this was an urgent request. So I agreed to alter the programme and include the piece. When I turned to the audience in order to announce the requested item, I was even more mystified because—for some unknown reason—they were all laughing. I discovered the cause of this hilarity only when I turned back to the orchestra. They were all, including Jack, wearing wigs of the most extraordinary shapes and colours! It was a very funny sight, made even funnier when I too was handed a wig, and obviously expected to wear it—which I did! This little joke was engineered by Jean and Cynthia Dacre, a good friend of ours, who regularly came to the concerts.

We rarely played to an audience of fewer than a thousand people. Most of the time, despite rival attractions, it was nearer to two thousand people who came to hear us and the queue for the last night's concert seemed to start earlier and earlier in the day each year. It was always a sell-out. Not only did people turn out to see us night after night when we played, but you could hear a pin drop among the audience. In fact, I used to get quite annoyed with Jean who would often pass the time at the back of the hall by doing the crossword, reading the evening newspaper or getting on with her tapestry. I thought she was really letting the side down—and I was very worried that she might drop something and make a noise. My concerns grew when the girls joined her at the concerts and followed her example.

On the other hand, the odd mishaps we had on stage were all

Two new Freemen of Scarborough: with Alan Ayckbourn and the Mayor, George Tuby

part of the fun. Starting off on the wrong piece was probably the favourite. We played so much that inevitably some of the music would get muddled up in the folders—with the magnificent result of the orchestra attempting two tunes at once! There was nothing for it but to stop and say: 'Well, I'm not sure that I like that sound very much, I think we'll start again . . .' always to a round of applause.

Twenty-seven years is a long time to spend making music in one place—and it was heartening to see the different generations attending the concerts. Those who had once brought their children now had their grandchildren coming to enjoy the music. By the end of my time on the Spa, there was a fair sprinkling of young heads among the grey in the Grand Hall.

Given my tremendous love of Scarborough, and, as I've mentioned, my feelings of belonging there, it was a very great honour when in 1987 I was officially given the Freedom of the Borough of Scarborough, along with Alan Ayckbourn, the town's famous international playwright and director. Following the ceremony in the Town Hall the council gave us both a wonderful party in the Royal Hotel. It was a great privilege and one that makes me feel that I truly belong to Scarborough. After twenty-seven years the love affair is still going on, even though I'm only an occasional visitor now.

In return for this loyalty, I've always felt a strong sense of responsibility; I couldn't let anyone down by missing a concert. Maybe this was silly, or perhaps it was pride, but I felt that if people bothered to come to hear me play, I should always be there. Whatever my reasoning, it certainly led to some extraordinary endurance tests.

There was the time I did my leg in playing in a charity cricket match at Scalby. The local team took on a showbiz team which had Dickie Henderson as captain and included Vince Hill, Nicholas Parsons and such genuine cricket stars as Colin Milburn, Ray Illingworth and Freddy Trueman. I had an ignominious innings: just as I was about to take off on a run, my leg felt as though I'd been hit by a very fast-moving cricket ball. I really thought the wicket-keeper had thrown one at me. However, it turned out to be a nasty set of torn ligaments which meant that my leg had to be in plaster—and I had to play the fiddle sitting down. There was the most astonishing stream of gifts and letters of sympathy from all kinds of people, and we all had great fun laughing at my new concert style.

When I was injured again a few years later, I thought of my father's dire warnings not to play any games because they would interfere with my career. Injuring myself playing cricket was one thing, but slipping a disc in the most ridiculous of circumstances was another. I did it at a charity event where I was selling autographed cartons of oranges—or rather 'the original Jaffa juice', as comedian

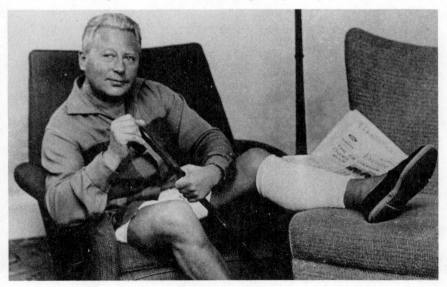

After the cricket match!

Eddie Molloy once said. I felt very foolish indeed as once again I had to do the concerts sitting down.

Although I was in absolute agony, it also had its funny side because I was 'stuck' from the waist down. Although I could play all right, I really couldn't manage to do much else. Dressing myself was out of the question—I simply could not step in and out of trousers, or pull them up properly. Poor Jean suddenly found herself with a fourth child on her hands; Naomi was eight and the twins four, and that year we had no nanny. Every evening she had to drive me down to the Spa, help me in and out of my trousers, lace my shoes—and do nearly everything else! It took a whole month of traction every day at the local hospital to get better.

Slipping a disc is frightful for anyone, but it's a nightmare for a fiddle player because it's important to have a free-feeling back—it mustn't be tense or tight, because then the arms seize up. Actually string players are rather prone to back trouble; if you think about it, violinists do hold the instrument in an unnatural way. When there is any tension, trouble soon follows.

I feel very lucky in having had so few problems throughout my career. The worst injury of all happened fairly recently. A nerve became trapped in my neck and back—and there seemed to be absolutely nothing anyone could do to stop it locking further and further into spasm. Thank goodness this happened in Scarborough when I was amongst friends.

I'd returned to the Spa Grand Hall to conduct an evening with the Northern Sinfonia very shortly after celebrating my sixty years in music at an enormous BBC concert at the Queen Elizabeth Hall in London. This had been a marathon evening of talking, playing solos and conducting all kinds of music, from which I never really had time to recover before travelling up to the next event in Scarborough.

I don't remember when the nerve became trapped, but it got worse and worse in the few days before the Northern Sinfonia concert. The pain was excruciating and there was no comfortable position for resting, let alone playing the fiddle. But I was sure that my lifelong luck would hold and everything would be all right on the night. So we drove up to Scarborough.

As the concert progressed I became more and more of a hunchback, stooping ever lower to play my solos, which must have looked very strange to the audience. But it was the 'Gipsy Carnival' which finished me off—I was forced, for the very first time in my long years of giving concerts, to apologise to the audience and ask to be helped from the stage. It was terrible, and quite the worst ordeal of my musical career. The only light relief came when Jean heard that some people were wondering if I was drunk.

Fortunately there was a doctor in the house. But it was inevitably rest that I needed—and back in London with this nightmare behind me, my neck began to mend slowly. Two kinds of nerves had caused this problem, the trapped nerve in my neck and also my inevitable anxieties about the concert, and whether I'd be able to make it through the evening.

I can only thank my lucky stars that this sort of thing didn't happen forty years earlier, because my career would have been dogged constantly by the worry that it might happen again. I now have a series of exercises which I do religiously every day—back exercises which were prescribed me by the marvellous physiotherapy department at Scarborough Hospital and some neck exercises to keep the muscles supple.

Of course, life in Scalby village was quite different from the holiday scenes in Scarborough. Scalby has its own character and purpose even though it is only minutes away—and we all enjoyed being part of the village, joining in the various events such as the Easter walk and the village fair. We played cricket and the twins, having been wonderfully coached by Arthur Collins, took up residence on the local tennis courts. They have become very good players. It was calm and peaceful, and I could retreat to the back garden to work or read, without any danger of being disturbed . . . Privacy could be quite a problem otherwise because we often found curious holiday-makers walking up the garden path to peer into our front windows. The ultimate accolade came when we found the house had been advertised as a special attraction on the itinerary of a holiday tour bus. They didn't annoy us because the house is set back from the road, but we could hear the guide's commentary: 'Now on your left is Max Jaffa's house . . .'

Afternoons were the time to sort out the programmes for the coming weeks. With all Jack's morning concert ideas spread out before me, I'd cross-check the music for any possible clashes between morning and evening. It was a fiddly task, but always made much easier if the sun was shining. I think I was the best walking advertisement Scarborough could have had for holidaying in

England—I would come back to London at the end of the season with a tan that was the envy of many friends who'd spent thousands of pounds going abroad to get something not nearly so rich and deep. 'Where did you get that tan?' they'd say—and I loved saying it was courtesy of Scarborough! However, I only once went into the sea; my loyalty to Scarborough ended at the water's edge.

From a very early age the girls came to the concerts, but they would leave early. I would wave them goodnight with my bow, from the stage—which I later discovered embarrassed them all dreadfully. The twins were supposed to be asleep by the time I returned home, but they invented an extraordinary game of 'Last one to turn the light out wins'. They each had an overhead light operated by a string pull above their beds. I could see their lights continually going on and off as I drove back at about ten thirty—but suddenly darkness would descend as they heard the car. It was only when writing this book that I discovered the final part of the game. Jenny and Lisa would continue holding the light strings—until they knew that I was downstairs having supper in front of the TV, out of sight and earshot. Their game would then continue.

Some weeks before the end of our final season there was a phenomenal thunderstorm. Not only did it black out the hall so that we had to play in the dim emergency lighting, but the rain also

My loyalty to Scarborough took me to the water's edge

flooded through the roof of the building at the exact spot where Kevin Barrand, Scarborough's excellent catering manager, was constructing a vast cake in the shape of the Spa for presentation to me on the Final Night. After weeks of work this was almost finished, but it was ruined by the deluge. There was not enough time to make another cake, so I never saw that thoughtful and lovely tribute.

On the very last night of each season Jean and I always gave a party for absolutely everyone who had been involved with the Spa concerts. They included two men in particular: Ken Warwick, Manager of the Spa for eighteen years, who was so helpful to me at all times; and Don Waterman, Director of Tourism and Amenities for sixteen years, a great friend who gave me unfailing support. Of course all the members of the orchestra and their respective partners came, together with the Mayor and Mayoress, many councillors and other personal friends. One year the usherettes arrived with a glorious painting of the Spa as seen from the ballroom entrance, inscribed 'from your many friends in the Roof Garden'. We all celebrated together in the Music Room above the Grand Hall, and each year was always a wonderful occasion—part sad, to say goodbye, and part huge relief that it was all over. It meant also the end of another summer in Scarborough, and another drive back to London.

But Jean and I only truly felt that it was the end of the summer when we had our own private celebration on the Monday, the night after the last concert. It was a ritual we always observed; the first proper evening meal we had together after seventeen weeks deserved to be something special. We would go to the Pavilion Hotel to have lobster, grouse and the pudding of the day, washed down by a bottle of Krug champagne. The cigar at the end was always perfect. After the Pavilion was pulled down, our ritual dinner continued at the wonderful Forge restaurant in Brompton. The owner, Ken Matthews, must be one of the finest chefs in the country.

CHAPTER THIRTY-FOUR

Endings

The only time I ever missed a complete concert was in June 1977, the day of Jack's funeral. It was a desperately sad occasion; I'd met him way back in 1929 and we'd had a lasting friendship, working together from the end of the war right up until his death. The management of the Spa were adamant that I couldn't possibly play that day and I should be at the funeral, to say goodbye to an old friend and someone who was well loved by so many people in Scarborough and so many regular visitors.

He'd had a 'warning' heart attack in 1965, but was very happily back at work on the Spa two years later, apparently fully recovered. But in 1975, it happened again, and this time it was much more serious. We sadly sent him back home to Eastbourne in an ambulance, while someone else drove his car back—with the enormous old ashtray still clamped to the dashboard. He'd given up smoking after the first attack, until we did a concert at Elstree some years later when he said the temptation was just too much.

Jack was far too sunny a character to be at all concerned about little matters of health or creature comforts. All the time he worked with us in Scarborough, he spent those seventeen weeks of the season in one room in a boarding house, living on pork pies, fish and chips and whisky—practically nothing else. His wife Jill not surprisingly preferred to stay back home in Eastbourne, though she always came up to Scarborough for the final week of the season.

Jack enjoyed himself making music and being sociable. After every performance he'd be first at the bar to set up the drinks that we often had before going home. Jack could change out of his evening clothes faster than anyone I've ever known; he was always waiting for me with a whisky already poured but he would have had a head

334

start in the drinking, downing at least four before I turned up. And after we'd gone our separate ways, goodness knows how many more doubles he'd have before the night was over.

The extraordinary thing was that I don't ever remember Jack with a hangover. He was always back on the Spa at nine thirty every morning, getting in considerable practice on the piano before going on to direct the morning concert. And of course, he never drank before a performance.

Everyone who worked with him at Scarborough would agree, I'm sure, that Jack was the life-blood of the orchestra. He may have played the piano but he was much, much more than just a pianist; he was the rock on which the whole orchestra was built. Musically, he added exactly what was necessary to make a piece work properly — given our limited forces, soloists received just the right kind of support whatever music they decided to perform, and young players learnt from his enormous experience.

Yet he was very modest about everything he did. I think of him often; he's still making music with us even now, because he left us so many of his wonderful arrangements. When he was recovering in hospital and itching for something to occupy his mind, I commissioned him to do a lot more for me as well as to write out all those piano parts which he kept in his head. They're his legacy — and they're a treasure trove.

Those summer days at Scarborough had to come to an end. The times changed, people changed — and for many the idea of taking time off in England lost its appeal when the package tours swept through the holiday business. Towards the end of my time, Scarborough, like so many resorts, had to face up to dwindling numbers and a decline in its summer income. By the mid-eighties every holiday town in the country was changing its image, dropping the idea of traditional entertainments and attractions and promoting conferences, exhibitions and other year-round facilities to back them up.

The management in Scarborough saw it coming in the late seventies, and a plan was drawn up to build a new complex in the place of the Grand Hall. But the opposition to it was so vociferous that a public enquiry was forced. A Government Inspector came up from London to chair the enquiry in January 1979. This was open to the public. The public's case was pleaded by Maurice Gayler, Diana

Tasker, Iona Hood, Robert Luff and Tom Laughton (brother of the actor Charles)—all Scarborians, with the exception of Robert Luff. The Inspector found in favour of restoring and refurbishing and in no other way altering the beautiful hall, which still stands as an enduring memorial to Scarborough's important part in English entertainment—and indeed in musical history. These days the Grand Hall really lives up to its name. A glorious example of Victorian elegance, it has been beautifully restored with improved acoustics and facilities, and new chairs which I was happy to see were in a good shade of Jaffa orange. It's a truly splendid concert hall for the north of Yorkshire and compares favourably with any in the country.

Of course, I was sorry to leave—but enough was enough. As Jean pointed out, at age seventy-five it was time to retire gracefully, and I have to admit that seventeen weeks of concerts every night was becoming something of a marathon. The physical strain of playing and planning and talking and socialising is difficult enough even for a younger man.

But I'd found the last few years a torment in another way. It started when we moved to the Ocean Room while the Grand Hall was having her face lifted. I suddenly became aware of a tremendous rushing noise in my ears. It was like the sound of the sea breaking, except it was continuous—and it couldn't have been the sea as we were playing indoors.

It has never gone away. Some days are better than others, but at times this rushing noise blanks out everything else that is going on. It is a dreadful, endless nightmare which dogs me day and night. Sometimes it becomes so loud that I can't hear myself play the fiddle, even with the instrument held right underneath my ear. On these really bad days it's the most extraordinary sensation to know I'm playing my violin, putting the fingers down on the strings in the right places, changing the bow as I ought to and feeling a sound coming out. But I can't hear it. I can only hope to God that I'm hitting the right notes and that they're in tune.

Strangely, no one seemed to notice there was anything wrong at all. The noise sounds so loud to me that I was sure everyone ought to be able to hear it too. The doctors diagnosed it instantly: I had tinnitus, a puzzling ear condition suffered by many thousands of people, for which there is no known cause or cure. I went to specialist after specialist to hear the same news. There is nothing to be done except to grin and bear it.

It must have been ghastly for Jean and the family, since I decided that I wouldn't burden them with the knowledge. I kept it to myself for years and all they noticed was that the television sound was turned up louder and louder, and that I seemed more and more absent-minded and aloof, often ignoring their conversation. Worst of all, I became very irritable—so much so that Jean finally asked me what on earth was wrong, and then the whole sorry story came out.

It's interesting that talking about my condition helped a good deal. Playing has become very much easier and the really bad days are less frequent. You see, I still do love playing and I couldn't possibly give it up. Perhaps it takes a little longer every morning to get round to opening the violin case and practising—but once I have that marvellous instrument tucked under my chin, there's still that wonderful joy from making music. That never changes. I've always said that first and foremost I am a musician; notwithstanding all the TV programmes and variety evenings I've taken part in, I've never been a showbiz person. While the others have done their 'act', I've only ever played music. I may have joked and chatted to the audience—but the important part of the evening was always the music.

However, there's still a showbiz connection in my life—The Celebrities' Guild of Great Britain. This is a fund-raising charity to help handicapped people get what they need in every possible way, and I love working for it. People come to us for simple and practical things which can vastly improve the quality of their lives. The real satisfaction from the work we do is that there is no great media hype about it. The money we raise goes straight out to the people for whom it was collected. The Celebrities' Guild committee is composed of dedicated men and women, mainly writers, actors,

With Ella Glazer of The Celebrities' Guild, presenting a dialysis machine to the hospital at Peterborough

actresses and musicians—hence the name. Ella Glazer is its founder, leading light and unsung heroine. At our annual award ceremony in November we are joined by a veritable galaxy of celebrities—Janet Suzman, Pete Murray, Maureen Lipman, Raymond Baxter, Lord Tonypandy, Jill Gascoigne, Leslie Crowther and Brian Johnston, to name but a few. The support they lend is incredible.

But my most important friends still come to me through music. When the BBC brought back *Grand Hotel* in 1984 the Concert Hall at Broadcasting House was packed, with more queuing outside. Our producer Monica Cockburn was absolutely delighted that her hunch to revive the show had been right, and I was thrilled to be leading the Palm Court Orchestra once more.

In my long musical marriage to the BBC, I've enjoyed largely faithful relationships with Radio 2 and the World Service. I must, however, confess to the occasional flirtation with Radio 4, but *never*, it should be said, with Radio 1. Popular music can sometimes not be *pop*ular enough! But I was absolutely thrilled to find myself, at the mature age of seventy-eight, having my first fling with Radio 3 — thanks to overtures made by one of my oldest friends, that great broadcaster Brian Johnston. Vocal rather than violin chords were requested for this particular engagement. Radio 3 invited me to talk to Brian during the team's lunch break at the Cornhill Test Match, Australia versus England at the Oval in 1989. 'It might have been more convenient for you had it been at Lord's,' remarked Brian. He claimed he could probably throw a cricket ball from there into my garden!

Throughout my career I have been extremely fortunate to work with a large number of charming and highly professional producers, amongst whom were Barry Knight, Jimmy Dufour, Natalie Wheen, Monica Cockburn, Bill Relton and Alan Boyd—all of whom I think of with gratitude and great affection.

These days there's a new Max Jaffa Trio, with Gordon Langford and Alan Dalziel. We're busy recording new collections of old favourites for the current market—everything on CD, of course! Our concerts too seem full of younger people. Could it be that the current trend for nostalgia has caught up with me yet again? Life begins at eighty?

Music always makes the connection. In 1982 I was awarded the OBE 'for services to music'. It was marvellous to be honoured alongside such figures as Elisabeth Frink, Bob Willis, Arnold Ridley,

With the family outside Buckingham Palace, after my investiture with the OBE

Ken Dodd and Ninette de Valois. There were a great number of us at Buckingham Palace waiting for our names to be called to go up for the investiture. Jean and the twins were with me, while Naomi waited outside as our chauffeur—since she'd met the Queen before! To keep us all happy as we queued up for our turn, there was a string orchestra from the Scots Guards regiment playing a selection of light music. When it was my turn to approach Her Majesty, there was barely a pause in the music (probably a beat) as they changed their tune to the Strauss waltz 'Roses from the South', the *Grand Hotel* signature tune. 'They are clever,' said the Queen with a twinkle in her eye, 'the way they choose the music for these occasions!'

I was deeply touched since it was such a nice salute from a group of fellow musicians.

And even though it should have been Schubert's 'Serenade', my personal signature tune, if it's *Grand Hotel* they remember me for—I'm well pleased.

It's a funny feeling, getting to the point where all these reminiscences reach the present and there's no more to tell. 'What's left for him to do?' you may be asking. Well, only a couple of years ago I had the dubious privilege of reading about my premature demise—while in a state, I should add, of perfect health! Truly a case of 'reports of my death being greatly exaggerated'.

One morning, while we were both enjoying our usual early cup of tea, Jean began to receive telephone calls of shocked condolence. 'How long had Max been ill?' 'When did it happen?' 'We're so sad for you,' etc., etc. It's one thing to be married to an old fiddler, but quite another hearing him referred to as a 'Lost Chord'! With

"Now to brainwash them back, we give them three months solid of Max Jaffa and the Palm Court!"

"Where did we go wrong, Moira?"

customary efficiency, Jean soon got to the bottom of this little mystery. Running a story on new music at the Spa in Scarborough, the *Daily Telegraph* had referred to me that morning as 'the late Max

Jaffa'. (Had my father-in-law been alive, I'm sure he would have pressed me to sue for defamation of character—after all, I'm a most punctilious sort of man!) As it was, Jean rang the editor, Max Hastings, and firmly insisted that I was still very much in the land of the living. Within the hour, a limo arrived bearing champagne, flowers and the following letter:

> *The Daily Telegraph*
> 181 Marsh Wall,
> London E14 9SR
> 27th May 1988

From the Editor

Dear Mrs Jaffa,

I can't tell you how appalled I am by the disgraceful error in the paper this morning. We are still investigating the exact cause. Our Picture Desk supplied an entirely accurate caption for the printers which spoke of 'the legendary Max Jaffa'. For reasons that are beyond me, a sub-editor changed this to 'the late Max Jaffa'. We will publish a picture and a correction tomorrow morning. Meanwhile, I wanted to make a tangible gesture of apology to you and your husband for the embarrassment we have caused. I do hope friends will treat it as a joke at our expense.

Yours sincerely,
Max Hastings

I was duly resurrected in the *Telegraph* the very next day.

Perhaps I shouldn't be surprised any more when people do a double-take and stop me in the street to exclaim: 'Good Heavens! Didn't you used to be Max Jaffa?'

Index

Page numbers in *italic* refer to illustrations

351